The Global Economy as Political Space

Critical Perspectives
on World Politics

◇

R. B. J. Walker, Series Editor

The Global Economy as Political Space

edited by

Stephen J. Rosow
Naeem Inayatullah
Mark Rupert

LYNNE
RIENNER
PUBLISHERS

BOULDER
LONDON

Published in the United States of America in 1994 by
Lynne Rienner Publishers, Inc.
1800 30th Street, Boulder, Colorado 80301

and in the United Kingdom by
Lynne Rienner Publishers, Inc.
3 Henrietta Street, Covent Garden, London WC2E 8LU

Library of Congress Cataloging-in-Publication Data
The Global economy as political space / edited by Stephen J. Rosow,
    Naeem Inayatullah, and Mark Rupert.
    (Critical perspectives on world politics)
    Includes bibliographical references and index.
    ISBN 1-55587-462-2
    1. International economic relations. 2. International relations.
I. Rosow, Stephen J. II. Inayatullah, Naeem. III. Rupert, Mark.
IV. Series.
HF1359.G57 1994
337—dc20   93-33348
                                                               CIP

British Cataloguing in Publication Data
A Cataloguing in Publication record for this book
is available from the British Library.

Printed and bound in the United States of America

        The paper used in this publication meets the requirements
 ∞   of the American National Standard for Permanence of
        Paper for Printed Library Materials Z39.48-1984.

Contents

Acknowledgments   vii

Introduction:
Boundaries Crossing—Critical Theories of Global Economy
Stephen J. Rosow   1

Part 1   Questioning International Theory

1   Nature, Need, and the Human World: "Commercial Society"
    and the Construction of the World Economy
    Stephen J. Rosow   17
2   The "Properties" of the State System and Global Capitalism
    Kurt Burch   37
3   Hobbes, Smith, and the Problem of Mixed Ontologies in
    Neorealist IPE
    Naeem Inayatullah & Mark Rupert   61
4   Timeless Space and State-Centrism: The Geographical
    Assumptions of International Relations Theory
    John A. Agnew   87

Part 2   The Construction of Identities:
Feminist Rewritings

5   Reginas in International Relations: Occlusions, Cooperations,
    and Zimbabwean Cooperatives
    Christine Sylvester   109
6   Latin American Voices of Resistance:
    Women's Movements and Development Debates
    Marianne H. Marchand   127

**Part 3   The Construction of Identities:
Advanced Capitalism**

7 Foreign Policy and Identity:
Japanese "Other"/American "Self"
David Campbell   147
8 Between Globalism and Nationalism in Post–Cold War
German Political Economy
Frank Unger & Bradley S. Klein   171

**Part 4   The Construction of Identities:
Peripheral Capitalism**

9 Inscribing the Nation: Nehru and the Politics of Identity
in India
Sankaran Krishna   189
10 Development as a Civilizing Process:
State Formation in Mexico
Richard W. Coughlin   203

References   225
The Contributors   243
Index   245
About the Book   253

Acknowledgments

This book developed out of our collaboration in putting together a panel at the 1990 International Studies Association (ISA) meeting in Washington, D.C. We are grateful to the International Political Economy Section of ISA for sponsoring that panel. We also owe thanks to all those who attended, including our discussants, Rob Walker and James Der Derian, and especially those who engaged in the lively (and in at least one case rather heated!) dialogue that led us to believe that a book of this sort would continue to engage critical scholars of international political economy and international studies.

We began our collaboration believing that our varied backgrounds and perspectives on critical international theory could produce a volume from which we, as well as others, might learn to think differently about international politics and international political economy. The project initially included four of us. Although Ahmed Samatar had to drop out due to other pressing demands and commitments, the volume reflects some of what we learned from his participation in the early stages.

Several people have been supportive throughout various stages of this project. The early encouragement of Craig Murphy, Stephen Gill, and Roger Tooze helped to convince us that the work was important. We owe special thanks to Rob Walker, who supported this book from the beginning, and Steve Smith, who offered encouragement and assistance at a crucial stage. The staff at Lynne Rienner Publishers were accommodating and helpful, especially Steve Barr. Finally, we thank Margo Clark for the index, and those—who know who they are—without whose personal support this book never could have happened.

Stephen J. Rosow
Naeem Inayatullah
Mark Rupert

Introduction:
Boundaries Crossing—
Critical Theories of Global Economy

Stephen J. Rosow

What happens when boundaries are crossed? New things come into focus; horizons are displaced; limits are extended; identities are transformed. Experience takes on new textures as common ground is forged where it never before was expected; diversity takes on new perspectives. Crossing boundaries engenders new ways of seeing.

Perhaps boundary crossing leads to spiritual renewal—to a revival of the sense of excitement that has been lost amid the routinization of everyday activity. Often, the crossing of one boundary leads to the crossing of another: we get the bug for travel and come to depend upon it, even crave it. Some never return home. Boundary crossing—the traversing of territories, scientific disciplines, gender, race, and class lines—heightens the ambiguity of our positions, as nationals, as scientists, as women, as men, as workers. What once seemed clear, even certain, clouds, at a minimum taking on new hues and tints; at worst, appearing in the new light as opaque and sterile.

To remain suspended in this liminal space is difficult. Yet this threshold—though its light may be barely perceptible—is an essential moment of contemporary scientific inquiry. In this space the spirit of inquiry rejuvenates. This is the space the chapters in this book inhabit.

The effect of crossing a boundary may be to experience the embrace of the new (by the adoption of a new home); or it may be to undertake the strengthening of borders in defense of some solid ground. Borders are often guarded. As a boundary becomes porous, an identity may become rigid and turn back into itself, overwhelmed. This seems to have happened to international relations theory. During the past ten years, a version of realism has reasserted a claim of identity with the discipline of international relations. It has done this with a vengeance, rallying historical troops within the Western fort—Thucydides, Hobbes, Weber—to defend the idea of the identity of international relations. Pressed by the emergence of "nonstate actors" and subaltern classes and social groups in world politics, current neorealist theories in international political economy thrive on excluding them from the realm of serious international practice. Various strategies of inquiry serve to maintain the privilege of *state* boundaries, the division of political economy into discrete "issue areas," for example, which accommodates global economic crisis tendencies to the politics of state management.

An example can be found in the "discovery" of the relevance of economics to international relations theory by neorealists in the 1970s and 1980s. International political economy gained relative autonomy as a field of study, and as a set of pressures, in world politics in the early 1970s, becoming a popular subdivision of the academic discipline of international politics. But rather than leading to a questioning of basic assumptions, the aforementioned discovery has led most often to the importation of new techniques from economic analysis in order to undergird traditional realist intellectual structures. Defining the problem of economic world order as one of "interdependence," mainstream theory constructs international political economy as a relation between states (as opposed, for example, to concepts such as *internationalization* that explain political economy as itself a political and global practice). Significant differences emerge between neorealists, but all confirm rather than challenge the privileging of secure state boundaries in the analysis of global political economy.

Some, like Kenneth Waltz (1979), persist in excluding economic interdependence almost completely from "high" politics, importing microeconomic theory into the explanation of "high" politics, but without recognizing any fundamental change in the identity of the field under study. Waltz's strict application of discrete "levels of analysis," seemingly giving it ontological status, offers theoretical insurance against the overwhelming of boundaries. Robert Gilpin (1981, 1987) is more interesting, importing new materials to strengthen the traditional architecture. Economic analysis, especially in his *War and Change in World Politics,* provides a new, stronger mortar to secure the traditional concrete realist structure. Theorists of transnational cooperation and "regimes" have added a new wing to the realist building, drawing on a variety of techniques from ancillary social sciences (economics, organization theory, rational choice theory) to explain, as one popular text puts it, "The Politics of International Economic Relations" (Spero 1977). The conceptual boundaries between "political" and "economic" continue to reinforce the geopolitical and geoeconomic boundaries between states, even as neorealist theories recognize more frequent boundary crossings.

Another group in this debate, world-systems theorists, have made a home within *alternative* fortifications, identifying the field of international relations more broadly. Drawing together Marxian theory with new developments in historical sociology and economic history, they have constructed an alternative foundation of international studies, redrawing boundaries and marking off new territories. Eschewing neorealism's preoccupation with techniques of inquiry, world-systems theorists have attempted to see the world-economy/world order as a whole. They have done so from an alternative, but no less foundational, intellectual apparatus. Their strength is the recognition that crossing intellectual boundaries involves not merely importing new techniques to strengthen given assumptions, but redefining the very field under study.

But, boundary crossing may also enhance tolerance for ambiguity and respect for difference: it need not lead to the rerigidifying of boundaries (old or new). What appears to mainstream theorists as an overwhelming of boundaries (requiring containment) appears to others as a fluid conveyer of new ideas and new possibilities for global change. We cannot be sure, ahead of time, what the effect of boundary crossing will be; what sort of strategy of inquiry will prevail. This effect is part of the struggle—intellectual, political, professional—over the definition of the inquiry itself.

Some critical theorists are beginning to follow this *critical* strategy, reacting differently to boundary crossing from both neorealist and world-system theorists. They celebrate the transformation of borders into open spaces in which identities are not secure but form and reform as a matter of course (e.g., George and Campbell 1990). They are content to speak "the language of exile" (Ashley and Walker 1990a). The essays in this volume are more comfortable with this critical attitude (some more so than others), exploring how it might be possible to resist permanent exile without capitulating to any strategy of sovereign bricklaying. The task is to vitalize inquiry into global political economy without revitalizing (and resurrecting) disciplinary walls.

These essays cross boundaries in several senses: territorial, disciplinary, social (gender and class), and historical. They bring together scholars both from different disciplines (geography, political theory, political economy, feminist theory, international politics, foreign policy, security studies, comparative history, and African studies) and from different countries (Pakistan, India, United States, Australia, the Netherlands, Germany, and Great Britain). All exhibit a willingness to cross boundaries in their own work, to draw from disciplines not their own. Amid our differences, a common attitude toward inquiry emerges, as do common themes.

In this introduction, I first rehearse several common themes in general terms. Then, I offer a more historical background to why the broader, critical approach suggested here is important. Finally, I introduce the organization and specific contributions of this volume.

FOUR COMMON THEMES

This standpoint of boundary crossing reveals assumptions and commitments that are lodged, often inconspicuously, within mainstream theories. Viewed from within, these assumptions seem to be settled: they are taken for granted. All the contributors to this book, notwithstanding the significant differences between them, insist on critiquing implicit assumptions and philosophical commitments. The essays in Part 1 focus explicitly on ontological assumptions and commitments. In their own ways, each of the chapters in subsequent parts of the book carries through a critique of these ontological assumptions of international relations theory. These critiques reveal a plurality of strategies of inquiry open to contemporary international political economy scholars, denying the liberal and modernist ontologies of international theory.

A second common theme of these essays deals with the traditional, truncated vision of who is able to participate, and how, in international relations. These essays cry out against the emptiness of realism's and neo-realism's walled city. Realist theories are empty in a double sense: in the sense that they are empty of people—people with their self-understandings, hopes, fears, projects, learning capacities, histories, and social institutions; and in the sense that these works purify the philosophical ambiguities of their traditions and thereby leave their texts empty of nuance, context, and sensibility. This emptiness commits violence against the rich, textured, colorful experience of world politics, illuminated by boundary crossing. The chapters in this volume seek to reflect this rich tapestry, not so that it can be hung in a museum as a new icon of intellectual completeness (a new paradigm to be admired and copied), but so that it can be undone in the evening and rewoven, in new ways, each day.[1]

This critical theme gives the later sections of the volume their organizing principle: the construction of identities within the practices and structures of the world economy. The liminal space constituted by the practice of boundary crossing is a space in which many can speak without either losing their identity (and hence becoming the universal citizen who recognizes no boundaries at all) or subordinating themselves to the sovereign voice of a "paradigm." Voices located here are sites of ambiguity, of identities being formed, challenged, and reformed. These essays are all well aware that to adopt a "paradigm" is to adopt a territorial position. Holsti (1985) and Hoffmann (1977) have shown that in the postwar world, as before, intellectual paradigms in international relations have been tied to the national experiences of the dominant. These essays try to allow participants to speak as they are caught in wider discourses, not reducible to one or another. The co-op that Sylvester studies, for example (see Chapter 5), is neither exclusively "a nonstate economic actor," a women's enterprise, nor a socialist experiment but all of these, depending on who is addressing it, from what angle, and for what purpose.

The later sections of this book map political spaces in the global economy in new ways: They are mapped not as sovereign spaces but in relation to others, for it is through such relationships and interconnections, not through assertions of sovereignty, that identities emerge in the global economy. Perceptions of sovereignty certainly play a role, but not as a given; not as foundations of policy or identity but as institutional and ideological features to be explained as cultural and discursive achievements.

Boundaries are historical and mutable, dependent upon historical practices for their construction and reproduction over time. This suggests a third common theme of these essays: the historically produced and contestable character of international practices. Representations of the world economy are themselves historically contingent, constructed in theories that themselves constitute the reality they explain. The essays in this volume bring a historical sensibility to the study of global political-economic practices. We see international political economy as "identity-inducing," a matrix of institutions, forces, and practices within which people struggle against identities foisted on them; within which women, men, technocrats, multinational executives and their corporations, diplomats, politicians, peasants, workers, and academics inter alia struggle both to create identities that can be effective in their everyday lives and to sort through the conflicting identities presented to them by the complexities of the global political economy. The contributors differ on their specific accounts of agency, autonomy, and structure in global politics, but all recognize identities as ambiguous; all recognize all agency as structured agency.

A fourth common theme, which follows from the third, is that these essays approach international politics as broadly cultural, not confined within narrow, Western definitions of "economic" and "political" experience. Social experiences are multiple and engaging of plural selves. As literary critic and theorist Raymond Williams says, culture is an expression of people's ongoing engagement and struggle within and with their way of life (Williams 1981). Culture is simultaneously reproductive, interpretive, and critical of a way of life.

Why would epistemologies consistent with boundary crossing, the nomadic scholarship advocated here, interpret the world economy more presciently than those resident within the normal science of international political economy? Why such an open-ended inquiry into the world economy? Especially, why one focused on the contestability of ontological explanations and the constitution of identities? Why embed history deep within "social science" explanations of the world economy rather than note them as background or foundational conditions? Finally, why focus inquiry so broadly on culture, rather than on the more commonly studied "politics," "economics," or renewal of "political economy"?

PREFACES—UNWRITTEN AND WRITTEN

As the world economy moves through the cyclical downturn of the 1990s, certain structural changes persist. Many of these changes, having to do with the globalization and internationalization of finance, and the remarkably rapid shifts in the international division of labor, are not in themselves new: they have been part of the Western capitalist economy for several centuries. But new technologies, competitive pressures, and historical contingencies have intensified and altered the forms of internationalizing practices (for example, transnational money markets and foreign direct investment).

To cite one example, speculation has always involved transnational dimensions. Yet only recently has it become possible, and hence necessary, for speculation to be a nonstop, twenty-four-hour affair. Specific historical circumstances have made this possible: the growth of and increasing prominence of international money markets: and the all-important changes in communications and computerization. During the 1980s, this created a novel climate for investment, first by making speculative investments far more profitable than investment in production; second by making larger and more diversified corporations more manageable (aided by tax laws and deregulation in advanced states); and third by making possible the accumulation of vast amounts of debt. In turn, this has established a new role for knowledge as an "input" in the production of wealth. And again in turn, this has encouraged in the society at large transformation in educational demands and practices: the better-paying, prestige jobs in advanced capitalist states now demand new forms of knowledge.

At stake here are not simply questions of efficiency and effectiveness of economic processes, or only the traditional, political-theory questions of inducements to peace and war that are lodged within political economy. Recent developments raise philosophical and political questions about the extent to which it is possible to alter and reconstitute forms of subjectivity and social organization in a world driven by the logic and imperatives of increasingly global (rather than national) economic practices. What strategies of political and social action are likely to encourage democratic change and renewal? This volume insists that studies of the world economy be able to address these questions. The burden of Part 1 is to demonstrate the inadequacy of prevailing work in international political economy (IPE) by demonstrating the discipline's "unwritten preface" (Tooze 1988)—that is, one of positivist epistemology and national/essentialist ontology.

The seriousness of recent changes—involving dislocation in the world economy, the dramatically altering division of labor, and the "stagflation" and financial instability after Bretton Woods—created problems for the major disciplines of political economy, both mainstream and Marxist. But, in this changed context, new theoretical explorations invigorated study of the world economy. The recession that persisted throughout much of the 1970s encouraged a boom in the academic field of international political economy.

The growth of mainstream international political economy took off with perceptions of declining U.S. hegemony. Noting that international economic coordination had not disappeared with the U.S. economic decline—though it had become more tenuous—a new set of theorists suggested that a political dynamic of transnational cooperation had arisen in postwar capitalism; and, they further suggested, it could be nurtured by the right kinds of studies. Politics and economics seemed to move closer together: political coordination seemed to be as important to international stability as were the self-regulating mechanisms of the liberal market. Viewing continued stability in the world economy as of increasing importance to peace and prosperity, the field of international political economy prospered, drawing closer together, but not overturning, the traditional divisions of liberal theory: between politics and economics, high-politics and low-politics, diplomacy and international (civil) society.

Spurred by a broadening of the study of international organization to focus less on "international governance" and more on the rules and principles of cooperation (often informal) within "regimes" (Kratochwil and Ruggie 1986), international political economy developed as an explanation of the institutional and organizational capacity of international capitalism. Secure that it had discovered an important anomaly in the "normal science" of international relations, the new institutionalism conceived IPE as a "research program" in which hypotheses about cooperation and transnational economic management could be tested empirically. Theoretically, the new field of IPE—whose coming of age was signalled by the publication of two extremely influential texts, Keohane and Nye (1977) and Spero (1977)—sought a middle ground between the traditional polarities of international theory: realism and idealism. They understood themselves as asking idealist questions within a framework of realist assumptions.

This new field sparked interest in scholars dissatisfied with traditional studies of international relations as well as those theorists on the left who were dissatisfied with Marxist theories of imperialism (often seeing these as too economistic) or with dependency theory. Importantly, many of these theorists did not share the liberal-political or the positivist-epistemological commitments of the new institutionalists or neorealists. This diversity, while generating considerable richness and excitement in the field of international political economy, also led to animosity and a hierarchical organization of the scholarly community, marginalizing those scholars who did not fit easily into the mainstream research program.

As the field of IPE has drawn in a diversity of scholarly perspectives, the limits of the mainstream research program have become more apparent. Its limited view of politics as technocratic management and its view of economics as a depoliticized system of private relations have been exposed. Its strength was to problematize the current developments of capitalism; to suggest that the "age of interdependence" could not be understood by means of received ideological and academic categories. Its weakness was to use traditional epistemological and ontological tools to apprehend the change. The result was that mainstream IPE generated an impression that, while much had changed in the world order, the fundamentals of capitalism had not.

Various theoretical strategies in neorealism, through which it constructs its concept of interdependence, create this impression. Most notable is what Roger Tooze (1988) calls its "unwritten preface"—its assumed positivism. One consequence of this is to reify as "units" the subjects of interdependence. This reification has a double weakness. On the one hand, it hides the fact that in neorealist theory the "units" (the subjects of interdependence) do have a specific content; that is, that they are states. To recognize this fact it is necessary, at a minimum, to have a theory of the state. Neorealism does not see a need to supply such a theory. On the other hand, the roles of other historically specific institutions—most significantly, multinational corporations—are rendered invisible. Their role in structuring the environment of interdependence is obscured. In general, to neorealism, interdependence appears as a timeless practice subject to nomological laws rather than as an environment embedded in historical structures and context. The changed structural context of global political economy is never assessed. The fact that interdependence is now effected through global structures of communications (which usually bypass state regulation and control) and hence through more hidden and routinized modes of power seems to have no relevance in neorealist analyses. One other consequence of the positivism of IPE ought to be noted. Not only does it consider it to be unnecessary to investigate many of the subjects of interdependence (e.g., why must they be states?), it also finds it unnecessary to investigate those "subjected to" interdependence—those whose identities emerge for them out of the everyday struggles to survive. (An example of this is the increasing number of so-called economic refugees—new nomadic bands now roaming the world economy for economic survival and livelihood (Attali 1991). An adequate concept of interdependence must address these questions and issues.

We can cite here one example of the effects of the changing international division of labor as it is manifested in the rethinking of gender relations and relations of public and private life within capitalist states. Women are playing new roles and are under new pressures in the global economy. In advanced states (and in advanced sectors of less advanced states) women are occupying increasing numbers of professional positions. The current global economy demands intensity and time from these positions—positions in law, finance, policy, and business. In less advanced sectors, multinational corporations often prefer women for relatively low-skilled, low-paid factory work; women are also preferred in outsourced sweatshops. In both cases, the domestic demands of household work and childrearing remain disproportionately intense for women. As a result, as women's voices are empowered in public discourses in many societies worldwide, they are subjected to numerous disciplinary pressures of private life as well as those demanded in their new economic roles. Their position as subjects within the interdependent global economy is ambiguous and multiple. In complex and multifarious ways, women are struggling to renegotiate fundamental structures and understandings of social life. As women renegotiate this terrain, changing received understandings of gender and of the definitions and relations of public and private life, it is not clear how the world economy will be affected, but it is surely important to an understanding of the global economy on various levels. These renegotiations will surely have significant effect on the efficiency and success of development strategies, for example.

A new preface—a *written* preface—to the study of the world economy seems to be in order to address these questions. It might begin, as critics of mainstream theory such as Tooze (1988) and Gill and Law (1988) suggest, with a change in terminology. Gill and Law suggest replacing *international* political economy with *global* political economy. Tooze suggests *world* political economy. Both works point to the internationalization of capitalism, the increasing importance of transnational money markets, a global division of labor able to keep ahead of and supersede national regulations, and the internationalization, or what might be called the denationalization, of consumption.

The usual tack in political economy has been to postulate some essential qualities and characteristics of human nature and analyze economic practices, structures, and institutions in terms of them. It should be clear that such a tack is inadequate, given that theories of human nature actually constitute those practices, structures, and institutions. It is possible to move alternatively. One might work interpretively, seeing what characteristics of "human nature" are required by historically specific economic systems, as Hirschman (1977) and Sahlins (1972) do. Kratochwil and Ruggie (1986), in fact, argue from a different perspective: that "regime" theory is inconsistent unless it incorporates a more interpretive epistemology. This demands that students write the history of the global economy, and be open to the many ways in which it might change.

One might go further, investigating discontinuities between the beliefs, aspirations, and consciousnesses of the participants and the demands of the economic structures, practices, and institutions, as do theorists of the "regulation school" and analysts who follow it, such as geographer David Harvey (1989). This would lead to an attempt to see how, in practice, an economy works to shape human beings as certain kinds of subjects. Sometimes it does this successfully, sometimes not. To the sense of an economy as a cultural achievement that emerges from interpretive studies, we can add the sense of an economy as a political achievement that emerges from dialectical, critical studies. Economies can be analyzed as effects of political struggles to constitute the identities, consciousnesses, institutions, and practices in which people live and experience their social world.

We are now prepared to address the question, why write about boundary-crossing as part of a preface to the study of the global economy? International political economy (IPE) presumes that identities are essentially fixed: Social identity follows the postulate of human nature as self-interested and acquisitive—the "rational man" of civil society; political identity is deemed fixed by the nation-state. However, if we recognize these identities as historically and politically produced rather than simply as given and essential, we must also recognize their mutability and contestability.

As capitalism becomes more global (even if, as Marxists and liberals such as Schumpeter would suggest, this is an inevitable result of the internal logic and dynamic of capitalism), the forms of subjectivity appropriate to it and produced by it change. These changes, in turn, may have significant effect on the structures, practices, and institutions of capitalism. This shift has been addressed in numerous ways by contemporary analysts of the global economy. Stephen Gill (1990) and Augelli and Murphy (1988) extend Gramscian theory to suggest a crisis and supersession of Fordism, the regulatory system of capitalism associated with standardized mass production, mass consumption, unionized industrial labor, and the welfare state. Even more explicitly, David Harvey (1989) addresses this change as a change in the experience of space and time in modern states.

Harvey's analysis is suggestive. Non-Marxist analysts such as Alvin Toffler (1990) have diagnosed similar changes. The experience of space and time assumed by "international" (in contrast to "global") political economy, and constitutive of the assumed concepts of social identity (civil society) and political identity (the nation-state) depended upon certain limits imposed by spatiality on temporality; limits that seem to be eroding. Put simply, we are suggesting in this volume that as the world economy has developed global networks of communications, and as the speed of transactions in the world economy displaces the significance of physical presence, the nature of political space radically alters. This can be understood in part (as in Attali) in terms of the shifting centers of economic power and the technologies that undergird them. Explanations of the global economy must map the changes in identity and the fields within which these changes are taking place. In the global economy, what it is, for example, to be a worker, an American, a woman, a consumer, a refugee, one of the unemployed, a husband, or a lover is changing.

From a perspective that studies the construction of identities, these developments are of crucial importance. The shifting relations of speed and space unhinge the traditional bearings of people who are bound up with place; with any fixed character of nation or self. Identity becomes a problem in the global economy—and this seems to be one of the primary cultural effects of the global economy—because the global economy's logic of spontaneity eclipses all sense of stable space. But then, in what does identity inhere, given that, at least in Western societies and in the global order that it has spawned, identity is spatially oriented? For example, does "Buy American" make sense when automobiles are composed of a multinational array of parts? When the marketing of such vehicles is determined as part of global strategies by companies producing cars in many different countries (including territories that have, in effect, themselves been internationalized—such as free trade zones or industrial zones such as that between Texas and Mexico) with increasingly multinational workforces?

The changes this may portend in the global economy are fundamental and powerful. The *global* economy (as opposed, in fundamental ways—although not all ways—to an *international* economy) suggests a social experience of time and space that contradicts the role that has been played by identity in the modern world. Both in contemporary-traditional and contemporary-modern societies, this role of identity has been an anchor of consciousness; a foundation of secure beliefs and social practices. As time accelerates in the global economy it does not simply challenge *particular* identities, but the very practice of identity.

BACKGROUND TO THIS BOOK

The idea for this volume emerged from a panel at a 1990 International Studies Association meeting in Washington, D.C. This panel explored the ontological commitments implicit within liberal, realist, and neorealist representations of the world economy. The essays by Rosow and Burch and the one jointly authored by Inayatullah and Rupert are drawn from this panel. Burch reveals a driving commitment to competing ontologies of property rights, one fixed, one mobile, within mainstream theories of international political economy, but hidden by the false dichotomy between the states-system and the world economy. He uses recent theories of structuration and conceptual analysis to argue (in a more open-ended way than do world-systems theorists) that the world capitalist economy and the states-system are structurally interdependent. Inayatullah and Rupert draw out an unacknowledged social ontology in liberal political economy that puts pressure on the individualist ontologies that inform theories of IPE. They reinterpret the theories of Thomas Hobbes and Adam Smith, demonstrating the interpretive prejudices in neorealist interpretations of Hobbes/Smith, and refashioning these theories into a critique of the disguised ontologies of contemporary neorealist international political economy. Rosow studies the genealogy of the Enlightenment idea of the European economy as leader of a single world economy, identifying the importance of two traditions of early modern political theory to IPE: the early modern scientific account of history and nature often labeled Universal

History; and the utilitarian and rationalist theory of need associated with social contract theory. These bequeath to modern IPE ontological assumptions still prevalent within much of current IPE. Geographer John Agnew adds to Part 1 an interrogation of geographical assumptions in international relations theory. Agnew demonstrates how international theory generates a closed system of unacknowledged spatial assumptions that sets the analysis of geographical realities beyond the critical gaze of mainstream theories.

The organization of the three other parts of this volume reflects the themes of historicity, ambiguity, and culture to be found within global political economy. Six chapters are devoted to three sites of cultural expression and struggle: feminist rewritings, advanced capitalism, and peripheral capitalism.

The first of these three divisions requires some explanation. Feminist theory is not usually understood to be a site of international political economy, but it has done more than any other theoretical disposition in contemporary social theory to open up global political economy to inquiry as a cultural and identity-inducing matrix of practices and institutions. More clearly than other theoretical dispositions, the variety of feminist approaches recently applied to international relations reveals the arbitrariness of state-centered constructions of the world economy. Since women have rarely been regarded as participants within states, the recognition that women play significant, and distinctive, roles in global politics most easily dispenses with the traditional vocabulary and preoccupations of foundationalist theories in international political economy.

The contributions by both Sylvester and Marchand show women as sites of boundary crossing, their identities woven in complex, overlapping, and crosscutting ways. Sylvester studies a women's silkmaking cooperative in Zimbabwe, writing women into the international political economy and showing how neorealist theories of cooperation in regimes have systematically written women out. Sylvester shows these women as struggling to survive and make their own way within competing theoretical paradigms and identities with which the world economy seeks to imprint its power on the co-op. Marchand seeks space in the theory of international political economy within which Latin American women can be seen to rewrite theories of development. To do this she studies the testimonies of poor women in Latin America, weaving their insights into a critique and new vision of the meaning of "development"—a meaning at odds with that supplied by traditional liberal and statist international political economy.

In Part 3, advanced capitalism is viewed as a cultural site of struggles over identity in the global economy. It takes on hues very different from the usual in the essay by Campbell and another jointly authored by Klein and Unger. Campbell studies the discursive economy in U.S. foreign policy toward Japan, showing how the United States constructs itself as it seeks to imprint its identity on the contemporary global economy. American subjectivity, he argues, is bound to the characterization of Japan as *other*. Japan is depicted as dangerous and threatening. By laying out an alternative account (of foreign policy as a discursive economy of identity/difference) and a detailed critique of revisionist literature on Japan as an economic security threat to the United States, Campbell seeks to "bring the 'subjectivity debt' to the political agenda" in U.S. political economy. Klein and Unger also address foreign policy as a discursive economy of identity/difference, offering a reappraisal of the power and place of Germany in the emerging European and global capitalist economy. Together, these essays suggest an alternative approach to the study of advanced capitalism in the contemporary world economy.

In Part 4, Krishna, writing about India, and Coughlin, on Mexico, historicize the national and state identities of these two countries. Both see these peripheral capitalist entities as having been written at the intersection of dominant, colonizing cultural practices and indigenous struggles. In their readings, these regions, and cultures, of India and Mexico become identifiable entities—become intelligible as "nations"—only within the context of global capitalist economy. Krishna studies how Nehru's political writings imagined "India" as a "national" entity by situating it within Western socialist discourse in order to enable the effective development of India into a major player in the world economy. Coughlin returns to the emergence of modern Mexico in the confrontation of colonizer and colonized. Both read so-called developing states as forms of "peripheral modernism."[2] Each questions the success of these historically bounded identities in the emerging global economy.

Increasingly, academic studies of global political economy are recognizing the multiplicity of participants, the multiplicity of ways in which they participate, the disparate social and political positions from which people become enmeshed in the global economy, and the dizzying complexity of the forces at work. The essays in this volume study this diversity, not from the standpoint of a new orthodoxy but from that of the need for a more open, scholarly conversation about the identity of participants and forces. The goal is not a blueprint for a new academic enclosure. Rather, it is to inspire openness and movement.

NOTES

This chapter owes much to the collaboration with my coeditors, Naeem Inayatullah and Mark Rupert. I also thank Ahmed Samatar, whose early participation in this project helped to shape its final formulation.

1. I am indebted to Naeem Inayatullah for the wording of much of this paragraph.
2. I credit this term to Ahmed Samatar.

PART 1
QUESTIONING
INTERNATIONAL THEORY

1

Nature, Need, and the Human World: "Commercial Society" and the Construction of the World Economy

Stephen J. Rosow

In his third volume of *Civilization and Capitalism, 15th–18th Century*, Fernand Braudel distinguishes the phrases *the world economy* and *a world-economy*. The former "corresponds, as Sismondi puts it, to 'the market of the universe,' to 'the human race, or that part of the human race which is engaged in trade, and which today in a sense makes up a single market.'" The latter "only concerns a fragment of the world, an economically autonomous section of the planet able to provide for most of its own needs, a section to which its internal links and exchanges give a certain organic unity" (Braudel 1984: 21–22). During the eighteenth century, a particular representation of the modern world emerges in which these two concepts are merged, combining the representation of the economy as organic with the universality of the market. This representation has great political significance, for it endows the European experience of capitalism with universal significance.

This chapter asks how this conflation came about in modern political thought. I look first at the genesis of these problems in the material and ideational dislocations of Renaissance Europe, discontinuities in social experiences brought on by the discovery of the New World, the expansion of trade, the rise of a public sphere (especially in book publishing and the circulation of accounts of "strange" peoples and lands), and state-building. I then turn to two philosophical problems that, I argue, converge in the representation of the global economy in the eighteenth century: the articulation of a historical order of nature to replace the theological conception of global order inherited from medieval thought; and the rationalist account of human needs as socially constructed rather than naturally given. I then read the eighteenth-century philosophy of commerce, particularly the economic writings of David Hume, as an intervention in the philosophical discourses of universal human history and the social construction of human needs. Hume's philosophy of luxury and trade generates the possibility of a science of international political economy by rearticulating the ontological problems of need and history as epistemological problems; that is, they become problems of how subjects can know the effective actions that will maximize their positions within an assumed global order.

THE NEED FOR NEW ONTOLOGIES

Many factors unsettled the understandings and practices of Western life between the sixteenth and eighteenth centuries. State development, the expansion of trade, the discovery of unknown peoples, the invention of printing, and the mass-marketing of books, journals, and newspapers—all contributed to the unsettling of the largely local and natural horizons of feudal social life.

That such horizons were broadening is clear in the cultural reception accorded in Europe to the discovery of new lands and peoples. Early in the sixteenth century, the tradition of modern utopian literature portrayed the newly discovered lands as ideal—critical contrasts to European normality. Throughout the seventeenth century travel literature was extraordinarily popular. Tzvetan Todorov tells us that Columbus sailed with many motives and alternative discursive frameworks for understanding the New World and its peoples (1984). Some who sailed with him sought commercial gain, some religious conversion, some the glory of queens and kings, some to satisfy their curiosity and to accumulate new knowledge of nature. The practice of discovery brought all these motivations and the alternative social practices, beliefs, and ways of life they implied, together, without unifying them under a wider master scheme or purpose. The plurality of the possible terms of involvement with discovery signaled the unhinging of the universalistic account of global order inherited from medieval Christianity and natural law.

The inherited, unitary vision of a divine order of nature gave way to numerous possibilities. Nature was viewed by Columbus, apparently without any attempt at a unified vision, in a number of ways: either as an aesthetic object of contemplation (in which the natives, lacking signs of Western civilization such as clothing and money, appeared as merely part of the landscape); or as a hierarchical system of beings integrated vertically by God's will and providence (in which the Indians appeared either as innocents who could be converted or as heretics who could not); or as a virgin field given by God to man (which meant that the New World was ripe for economic exploitation by those who would use it best to meet human needs as God intended) (Todorov: Chapter 1).

Social contract theory, with its reliance on the literary representation of a "state of nature" (whose image was often drawn from accounts of the newly discovered), reflected the ambiguity that attended discovery. The medieval sense of the unity of nature had been sufficiently undermined by the midseventeenth century as to allow for the reconstruction of the unity of nature in new, imaginary forms. But these new forms lacked the sense of truth and givenness that informed medieval thought. In social contract theory, *nature* has an ambiguous status as an imaginative representation of otherness and as a determining set of given but unformed capacities of beings and the world.

The social transformations associated with the development of states during this period contributed to the unsettling of ideas of nature. The rise of powerful, central monarchies and states intruded on local structures and identities. These new political formations came to depend economically and culturally on a public sphere in which social and political identities expanded into the wider networks of interconnections that are characteristic of capitalism and modern territorial states.

Feudal social relations did not give way to capitalist and statist relations all at once, as Anderson (1974) shows. Rather, the transformation was marked by subtle and ambiguous penetrations of the base of feudal power in the countryside, and by social practices emanating from manufacturing and market practices on the one hand, and centralizing, bureaucratic state practices on the other. States had to struggle to enlist the people in them, both materially and ideologically. Local traditions and economic practices resisted incorporation into the larger networks of social and political power. Yet, through numerous penetrations into local life—the most notorious being taxation and the recruitment, often forced, of soldiers, seamen, and public workers (in the corvée, for example)—the state constituted new senses of community and political authority. These were reinforced and encouraged by fundamental social realignments, such as the intermarriage of merchant families with the nobility (in England, for example) which Eric Wolf (1982: 268–269) cites as a factor in England's early manufacturing success.

The development of the modern state was predicated more on intensified horizontal linkages across family and corporate groups than on the vertical linkages of feudal societies. This horizontal spreading resituated inequalities in more wide-reaching and abstract relations, especially class. The new sense of community that attended this change was reflected in the expansion of the market society (both within and across traditional feudal boundaries) and in the development of new forms of communication, which could draw those who were formerly strangers into a common perception of the purposes and destinies of their lives. This new public sphere required coordination by centralized states, for it could no longer rely on feudal modes of social coordination, which privileged local relations, family ties, and "natural" authorities.

As political space expanded, it became more territorially grounded (rather than grounded in family or corporate function). Relations of trade became more common and more central to the expectations of people for a good life (Strayer: 5–7, 17–19; Poggi: 19–26). States had to secure and coordinate larger territories, as well as coordinate relations among social equals. The nascent capitalism of medieval towns, as its scope expanded, created more and more settled patterns of life in which political identity, and the circle of relations in which needs and wants were satisfied, became more varied and complex. Social relations came to be concentrated under the purview of rulers of broader and more functionally differentiated territories, a change reflected both in the intensifying interdependence between town and country and in the growth of estates (Poggi: 46–48, Chapter 3). In this emerging form of life, nature no longer seemed so closely bound up with everyday human life and human needs came to be seen as socially constructed rather than naturally determined.

The tensions between the natural determinism of the feudal order and the will to power of new rulers—the former legitimated by God's plan, the latter by the effective administration of power—took on new prominence in political theory. The tension is most evident in Machiavelli's rewriting of the civic humanist tradition, especially in the tension between *fortuna* and *virtú* that runs through his work. Machiavelli's bold view of how the political man could impose his own order on circumstances using his own skills and resources proved to be an immensely appealing language to statesmen seeking to negotiate between the new forms of bureaucratic and military power, and between traditional allegiance (to a given, natural hierarchy of social rank) and privilege (Machiavelli 1961; Meinecke 1962; Pocock 1975: 156–160).

The new public sphere also owed much to the intensification of long-distance trade, which generated significant effects on the local orientation of communities. Trade, of course, had been instrumental in challenging and changing received understandings of the world, most significantly in its effect of introducing lost or new texts, such as those of Aristotle and, later, influential works such as Ptolemy's *Geography* and Lucretius' *De Rerum Natura*. The great expansion of long-distance trade had further effects throughout the early modern period. Not only did this trade expand the scope and importance of commercial centers, but "foreign" goods, and with them more cosmopolitan cultures, penetrated local identities. The presence of strangers and commodities from strange lands, representing cultures unlike the local and Christian ones, increased. By the seventeenth and eighteenth centuries, luxury goods (mostly foreign commodities) spread from limited circulation among the nobility and court to a wider social network, inspiring imitations and "fashion."[1] Increasing numbers of people sought wealth from the New World as a way of participating in the glory and adventure of discovery and exploration. As more people left local settings, they left behind holes and fissures in received understandings of the world. These gaps would be filled by travelers, reporting back, often in wildly entertaining and frightening texts (which proliferated through the book trade), as the erstwhile local person's fate was pondered and imagined by those at home. In short, both materially and ideologically, the expansion of trade unsettled structures and identities that were primarily local in focus. Of course, this occurred over a long period of time and was never complete. Yet it certainly problematized the models of the world, both in the Christian natural law tradition and in the local imaginings of nature in which a given hierarchy of beings and authority gave local and particular identities a secure place in the world (even if a subordinate one).

Gender relations, too, changed in the emergence of the new public sphere. Within medieval traditions, especially in rural communities, women participated in production along with men. I do not want to overstate the public status of women in medieval Europe, but it seems clear that their relegation to a private sphere was nowhere near as thorough, and certainly did not take place on the same terms, as in modernity. The new public sphere grew out of those practices that men could more easily participate in than women, given their gender positions within feudal societies. Women's roles in feudal communities were closely tied to the land. The new social roles within the public sphere—long-distance trade, banking, soldiering, law, entrepreneurialism—reinforced even as they transformed feudal conceptions of masculinity. Among the emerging wage-labor working class, the position of women was more complex. The role of women in production persisted out of necessity in the poorer classes (as it has always persisted in the industrial working class). But one consequence of the shift to a horizontal axis of public relations (relations of individuals across family and local boundaries) was the breakdown of the extended family. This doubled the burden on women, especially poor women who could not afford servants to take care of domestic work.

All of these changes unsettled the sense in which nature determined human life. Formerly a real, immediate presence, nature became more abstract, associated with some given order that could hold together the strange, multiplying forces at work in the practices of trade, state building, and discovery. Rather than cyclical recurrences of natural time, as in the seasons or days, nature became a more vast and abstract presence. As the horizons of social, economic, and political institutions expanded, *nature* took on a more abstract connotation, as it came to denote a primary-object domain of Renaissance science. Feudal conceptions came increasingly to be replaced by more universalistic notions of nature: to cite two of the most well-known and significant—"human nature" and a natural law considered less as a set of innate moral principles and more as systematic physical regularities reflecting God's will. The alliance of mysticism and science that informed the new science of alchemy, and then chemistry, in the Renaissance began a tradition of looking at nature as a discrete object of human cognition and investigation, linked to God not through direct providence, as linked in a chain of being, but as a representation of God with its own discrete logic of movement (Debus).

The abstract conception of nature was most apparent in the way that *nature,* still considered a site of God's will, became an independent object of reflection and study in the Renaissance. Nature was increasingly viewed as a representation of the divine plan (and less a direct consequence of God's will) to be described and investigated as an interlocked system of causes. Viewing the world as such a system of regularities, historians could see nature as articulating the global society of men and communities. Nature assigned to mankind and man a place in the interlocked system of causes. Man became a genus, a general category within nature. But he also became the cognizer, the knower of nature. To figure nature as a representation was to assign mankind a dual position: as created (and hence an object subject to natural determinations) and as a knower (who constructed nature through reason). Hume's theory of commerce, I suggest below, can be read as a philosophical intervention into this ontological duality.

As representation and organic system, nature could be studied in its own right, as having its own logic, reflective of the will of God but independent of it.[2] The Paracelsians, for example, pioneers of modern chemistry, considered nature as a book on a par with scriptures, to be read in order to divine the will of God. Moreover, the discovery of nature in modern science is bound up with the discovery of nature in a geographical and social sense. Studying nature for Renaissance scientists meant traveling in order to observe the world. The Paracelsian Peter Severinus (1540–1602) told his readers "they must sell their possessions, burn their books, and begin to travel so that they might make and collect observations on plants, animals, and minerals" (Debus: 21). The discovery of the New World, it would seem, was important not only to specific sciences during the Renaissance but to the very idea and general practice of scientific investigation. The novelty and strangeness of the objects of discovery (people and nations included) encouraged careful, accurate descriptions that effectively broke down the received understandings of how the world worked (Debus: 52). The Renaissance representation of nature suggests that the discovery of new peoples is no different from the discovery of the rest of physical nature—as is the case for Columbus, who at one point describes the natives in tone and language no different from his descriptions of the flora and fauna of the New World (Todorov: 14–33).

UNIVERSAL HISTORY

New conceptions of history emerged that sought to negotiate this dual sense of nature as determining presence and as rational, human construction. Jean Bodin's innovative understanding of history, which he terms

"Universal History," links the natural (in the sense of immediate, particu-lar/local effects and context—climate, geography, typography) with nature (in the more abstract sense of a universal world order as a representation of God's will, but one constructed in human reason). He begins to elaborate history as an epistemological project (governed by scientific methods) but remains primarily concerned with the ontological question of mankind's being and place in nature considered as a given universal order. For him, epistemology remains an integral part of ontology (Bodin/trans. Reynolds 1969).

Like the Paracelsians, Bodin reads nature as a representational text: "In history," Bodin asserts, "the best part of universal law lies hidden" (Bodin: 8). Historical science is a hermeneutic, an interpretative science that, when guided by proper method, yields knowledge of universal order. Bodin's faith that the proper application of reason will confirm a truth we already know is faithful to medieval scholarship. History in the sense of man's writing of nature must integrate knowledge of natural, human, and divine developments; general, universal principles are to be read in the chronology of events, because the goal of chronology is to confirm the di-vinely given order.

First one constructs a chronicle of all known peoples: "I call that his-tory universal which embraces the affairs of all, or of the most famous people, or of those deeds in war and in peace [which] have been handed down to us from an early stage of their national growth."[3] In this chroni-cle, some can stand for all: the most famous represent the universal traits of the species. Next, one studies natural developments, placing human so-cieties into the schema of natural determinations (climate, geography, etc.).[4] The final step is the study of world religions; their origins and teachings. The end result is a general science of politics and history that articulates the general principles governing political phenomena.

Bodin says his general vision takes its bearings from cosmography: "Like a man who wishes to understand cosmography, the historian must devote some study to a representation of the whole universe included in a small map" (Bodin/trans. Reynolds: 25).[5] This representation entails a unity of knowledge, in the two interconnected senses of Renaissance sci-ence, one vertical, one horizontal: the three different fields of knowl-edge—human, natural, divine—must be integrated; and the expanse of human differences must be catalogued and hence ordered: "So it will come about that nothing in the reading of history may occur, whether worthy of praise or blame, which cannot be listed suitably in its proper place (Bodin: 39). Only in terms of a whole of universal history in these two interrelated senses (the integration of all knowledge, and the knowledge of all peoples) can any particular history be known.[6] General principles can then be read in the particular situation of peoples, and particular nations represent gen-eral meanings: "We must make some generalizations as to the nature of all peoples or at least of the better known, so that we can test the truth of histories by just standards and make correct decisions about individual instances" (Bodin: 85).

Here, in new ways, in spite of Bodin's participation within the traditional ontological problematic of Christian understandings of history, knowledge is power. Knowledge is power not through the mysteries of the Word, but through the power of representation. To represent the world in the correct way (which is the task of reason and science) is to reveal the secrets of universal order and truth. Representation is both secular and divine because of this: it is both revelation and human creation. Method is crucial, because what is at stake is access to the power of order and truth. Here, Francis Bacon's philosophical and scientific utopia, *The New Atlantis,* makes a parallel point, establishing the scientific ruling caste as, simultaneously, the high priests of society: the society knows order because it constructs the truth in science. The divine authority of the high priests of Solomon's House derives from their scientific wisdom; simultaneously, it legitimates their political rule. Indeed, their political power is indistinguishable from their scientific powers.

Bodin's intervention in the discourse of history assigns new importance to a schema of global order. It also generates new ways to articulate this schema. To do so is to harness the power of truth and right that God has put in the world. Bodin may not yet be concerned with the comparative advantage between nations, or with articulating an international division of labor in which different, naturally determined peoples and regions play a distinct functional role, but he is concerned, for ontological and ultimately theological reasons, to articulate human societies as linked in an organic system of relations. A scientific understanding of such linkages and the ordering of differences unlocks power, telling men how rightly to order their actions and institutions. Indeed, much of *Methodus* is concerned with such an ordering, expressed in those attributes of peoples and their circumstances that differentiate them from others and that link them in a global, human community.[7] Although done in a secular fashion, the idea of an economy as a structure will serve a similar function—and does so in much contemporary international political economy. To know the laws of the market is to unleash its power to order human societies, telling people (and thereby constituting them) what will work and what will not.

History is an amalgam of particular and general causes, as Montesquieu (1951) would put it in the early eighteenth century, explicitly following Bodin's ideas about the natural determinations of social character and esprit. Different peoples in different regions possess different characteristics: "characteristics . . . which are stable and are never changed unless by great force or long training" (Bodin: 85).[8] As peoples exist in history, they are particular entities subject to change over time through events and human will. Yet in the course of change and particular development they generate relatively fixed structures, determined by parameters set in natural determinations ("the situation and character of the region") that establish general causes. This is true, most significantly, for language:

> Finally, the cause of the change of language depends on the very nature of the area. For it is characteristic of all peoples who live in a northerly region to make words with consonants striking sharply without vowels from the inner chest, and with frequent aspirations. This happens on account of the great strength of their breath and the inner heat rushing out (Bodin: 343).

These general causes enlist societies in a common world with others: a world in which they are linked, as a people or nation, with the rest of humankind. To represent those linkages is to unlock the power of divine truth and secular (including political) order.

INTERLUDE:
SOVEREIGNTY AND COMPETING ONTOLOGIES

In Bodin, sovereignty is the great effect of the power of representation. His new use of the term is rightly seen as a significant innovation in Western political thought. Sovereignty mediates the particular and general causes, and hence locates the power unlocked by the representation of universal history. The sovereign orders the nation according to its natural circumstances (including its customs and "fundamental laws"): climate, topography, language. As such, the sovereign inscribes the power of the nation.

From at least the fourteenth century, *sovereignty* referred to the presence of a supreme ruler and power, and was used in at least three spheres: for political rulers; for males in the context of family; and for divinity.[9] One new use that arose in the sixteenth century sorted out the difference between these realms, and sovereignty came increasingly to be restricted in modern political thought to the political realm. Bodin uses sovereignty in this way when, in both *Methodus* and his *Six Books of the Commonwealth,* he insists that any state have a single decision-center with the absolute authority to assign administrative functions to magistrates, and to make decisions when factions break down the effective exercise of central power. By limiting sovereignty to the political sphere, and identifying it with the allocation of administrative functions, theorists like Bodin transformed the concept *sovereignty* into a new and active discourse of legitimation in modern states. To use Max Weber's terminology, this new use of *sovereignty* made possible the modern state: it constituted legitimacy as legal-rational authority, severing it from traditional authority (the fundamental laws of the kingdom which, Bodin argues, the king should but cannot be compelled to uphold) and charismatic authority (the association of the king, and the king's body, with God, or in Germanic custom the king as symbolic identity of the community).

But, the new restricted use of sovereignty was not exclusive of other uses in Bodin's theory. The distinctiveness of political sovereignty did not rule out Bodin's more traditional use of it in references to male authority in the family, suggesting that sovereignty remains lodged within an ontological vision of a transcendental concept of authority. In fact, in Bodin's theory, the independence of the political sovereign depends upon the older understanding of sovereignty to apply to fathers in households. Bodin also uses the word *sovereignty* in a different, older sense when he discusses the father as sovereign over the family in order to demarcate sharply public and private spheres of sovereign authority. Here sovereignty entails the natural authority of the superior being. The link between patriarchal authority in the family as an entry point into political sovereignty is also clearly made in Bacon's *New Atlantis,* in the feast in honor of the father.

Sovereignty unleashes a power that Bodin's schema of universal history implies but does not sufficiently account for: the sovereignty of individual will. It is no wonder that others would draw out this aspect of sovereignty in ways that contradict Bodin's assumed ontology of divine representation. In both the new political order of territorial states and in the developing capitalist market economy of sixteenth and seventeenth century Europe, the individual was more or less thrown out on his own devices and desires. The limited effectiveness of local associations (extended families and villages) in securing status and basic needs left individuals more or less on their own to negotiate their survival and fortunes. Systems of social discipline came to act more directly on individuals rather than being mediated through local associations. Limits were removed; but so were bridges to reservoirs of secure human relationships. These developments generated further uses of the term *sovereignty,* which connected to Bodin's reinterpretation of political sovereignty but undermined the ontological framework within which Bodin nested it.

During the sixteenth and seventeenth centuries, *sovereignty* came to refer to a final authority in the sense of a final act of human will rather than the hierarchical power to allocate resources and authority. This act creates a unity out of diversity, order out of anarchy. *Sovereignty* as act of will suggests an alternative ontology to that found in Bodin's universal history. It suggests one in which God recedes much further from the world so that nature cannot be taken as a secure representation of God. Nature is no longer to be read as a book but as an ambiguous text constantly being rewritten by human desires and will. Nature becomes the "state of nature" of social contract theory, an ambiguous site in which human beings are simultaneously free to constitute their own world according to their passions and reason, and are constrained by natural laws and physical necessity. As the idea of a "state of nature" implies, *sovereignty* is in this use linked to fixed territorial boundaries (of a self and state) rather than to the more fluid sense of nation as linked to the sovereign being of the king under fundamental laws (as in Bodin).

This use of *sovereignty* gave rise to new visions of the self, generating what might be termed a political theory of privacy. In different ways, Montaigne and Hobbes are important pioneers in what will become a crucial component of liberal political theory. The Hobbesian account of the will as "the last appetite in deliberating" constitutes the human being as an active agent, a "final authority," a will (Hobbes/ed. Macpherson 1981: 126–127). Earlier, Miguel de Montaigne had investigated the mind as sovereign over itself. As such he initiates the French tradition of the sovereign individual (different in important respects from Hobbes), wherein *sovereignty* is linked to *self-love*. The picture of the individual that emerges from Montaigne's *Essays*, especially "Of Solitude," is one of self-chosen, worldly resignation. Happiness is a matter of being content with oneself. What one needs to live a good life is not determined by nature but by the self and society, and in determining "need" the self distances itself from others: it constitutes itself as sovereign over its own terrain. In Montaigne, sovereignty of the will resolves itself into privacy. The end of the sovereign self is solitude (Montaigne/trans. Frame 1958).

Sovereignty, for both Montaigne and Hobbes, was generated by a lack. Montaigne's view is nostalgic for a world of secure connections to others, whereas Hobbes's view seeks out new forms of artificial "interdependence" to replace a world of natural interconnections. Society replaces nature in social contract theory because nature lacks the requisites to secure human needs. God provides man with capacities and resources to meet his needs, especially the capacities of reason and labor. By utilizing those capacities, man can achieve the moral ends and the political security that are worthy of God's creation. The faith in God secures that, by developing his reason and labor, man will achieve a higher, moral life.[10] *Sovereignty,* in this second new use, fills the void left by nature's inadequacy. It provided terms on which commercial society (in which man seemed to create his own world) and natural order (in which man seemed to be determined by natural forces) could be resolved into a new unity of global order to replace the medieval Christian ontology.

THE CHALLENGE TO
TRADITIONAL ONTOLOGIES OF NEED

Commercial society linked the circulation of human needs to a concept of nature that encompassed the entire world. The Renaissance science of nature, reflected in Bodin's theory of universal history, supplied the latter but offered little analysis of the dynamic of commercial society. In social contract theory, the second new use of *sovereignty* (which continued to coexist, often in tension, with the first, as well as with older conceptions) informed a theory of the circulation of human needs that was universalizable. The universalizability of human needs, even as they are socially constructed, is one of the central assumptions of international political economy.

A language of human needs must negotiate the treacherous waters between the natural and the social. In Western political thought, this negotiation takes place within boundaries set by the concepts of *need* and *desire.* Classical and Christian societies in the West built upon an opposition between these, sharply distinguishing a condition of life in which people pursued what they needed as human beings, on the one hand, and a condition of luxury (in which they pursued desires) on the other. The former referred to an essential human condition, whereas luxury designated wealth beyond what was needed to live an essential, human life. These two conditions of life coexisted, uneasily and in tension, in both Greek and Christian conceptions of social and political life.

We can take Plato and Augustine as representative. In different ways, they set patterns of meaning in which luxury signified a movement from nature to a social world, and from simplicity and order to complexity and disorder. Augustine associated luxury with the needs of the flesh, opposing it sharply to the needs of the spirit (the famous distinction between the "City of Man" and the "City of God"; Augustine/ed. Knowles 1972). Earlier, in the *Republic,* Plato had described the transition from the simple city of basic needs and harmony to the luxurious city in which luxury entailed, first and foremost, the need for expansion and war (Plato/trans. Grube 1974: II: 369d–375). Although different in important ways, these two conceptions involve the claim that, from a moral point of view, luxury represents a proliferation of desire that harbors detrimental consequences for justice and for the moral disposition of the person; from a political point of view, luxury implicates societies in expansion, violence, and war. Liberal international political economy would reverse this relation—trade and exchange of luxuries generate peace as the proliferation of desire draws people into necessary social relations based on their pursuit of self-interest. In this sense, luxury consumption can be seen as setting the terms for moral action and a distinctive form of moral life in which need and desire are one. The science of political economy develops in the eighteenth century in part as an epistemological code in service to this conception of the moral life.

A sense persisted throughout the Middle Ages that the closer to nature needs remained, the more sharply they could be opposed to "desires," and the more they could restrain the unsavory consequences of luxury. In Greek philosophy, and then in medieval Christianity and feudalism, what one was entitled to depended upon what one needed to maintain one's naturally given station in life. This natural hierarchy depended upon luxury as a sign of status and power. The irony of this language of need and desire was powerful, expressing itself as trade and commerce expanded. The association of wealth and luxury with natural hierarchy and status generated a need for commercial and productive activities that could not be validated. Throughout the Middle Ages, those practices that mixed need and desire (i.e., those practices in which people made their living by providing luxuries to satisfy the desires of the wealthy—trade, banking, credit/usury) remained suspect even as they were essential. In order to reproduce itself, feudal society furthered a system of needs and powers that undermined it. In short, a conceptual language in which the oppositions between need/desire and natural/social were viewed as synchronous developments had limited capacity to support the commercial society. Whereas needs retained traces of the opposition of need (as natural) and desire (as social), increasingly a way of life took hold in which the oppositions of need/desire and natural/social no longer ran parallel.

The natural limitedness of human needs in classical and feudal societies is, of course, itself a social construction; the limits that mark off need and desire, poverty and wealth, luxury and necessity, are set in frames of social meaning. The medieval scheme depended on the ability to reference need to some ultimate ground and end of human life. Greek metaphysics and Christian faith gave men reason to believe that they needed only certain things, and that the needs of the spirit were more significant than the needs of the body. But this grounding of needs was not part of commercial practice. In commercial practice needs appeared as progressive, open-ended, and multifarious, changing as men and societies developed, rather than being fixed in nature. In commerce, needs seemed to proliferate and to have value independently of any ultimate ground. Even *use* did not provide a ground to determine need in the market (as Locke's discussion of the invention of money makes most clear): because the market rendered need and desire indistinguishable. The logics of risk, exchange, and profit worked according to different constitutive rules. It did not matter why someone needed something, or in what sense they "needed" it. All that mattered was that the purchaser felt a need, a lack of something. In the marketplace, the ultimate ground of need in a natural hierarchy gave way to the ambiguous and relative ground of personal desire and social fashion. Needs represented an inner lack, not unlike—if not identical with—desire, that could be satisfied by getting hold of the corresponding object. Enlightenment political economy emptied *need* of the rich ontological meanings it had in Greek and Christian societies, where it was associated with a given order of nature.

Social contract theory renegotiates the relation between need and desire. The identity of need and desire in the commercial circulation of commodities is situated anew within an opposition of the natural and the social. Social contract theory recognized that need had a social history and that therefore the relation between nature and society became more complex. Nature became a situation *out of which* and *in which* man developed. This ambiguity was lodged in the ontology of the "state of nature" as a set of God-given resources and capacities *for man*, i.e., that he could use to supply what nature lacked. Rather than being positively *given* in nature, need was set *in opposition* to nature. In social contract theory, need then becomes associated with the social, the necessary world of interdependence through which individuals supply what is lacking in nature. Among social contract theorists, Rousseau is perhaps the most perceptive analyst and critic of this relation (Rousseau/ed. Masters 1978).

Social contract theory can never decide finally whether society perfects nature or overturns it. Hobbes's leviathan is a "Mortall God"; Locke's constitution is both natural law and social construction; Rousseau's political freedom is a recapturing of "natural" freedom. In this context, "development" becomes a universal human project, always seeking both to conform to nature's dictates and to create and recreate the human world. This formulation of the ambiguity of the early modern conception of nature allowed a new formulation of the universality of human experience that avoided the traditional theology of Renaissance universal history. All men were the same everywhere and hence could be linked in a single system of economy. Yet they were different because they utilized nature differently. What differentiated peoples was social and economic development; it was not referenced to any substantive account of natural human needs. The latter were replaced by social criteria of political order and sociability: the ability of the people to maintain peaceful, cordial, and comfortable relations—*felicity*, in Hobbes's term. This required a focus on the increasing of the general wealth of the society. In the world order, need develops according to a single, prototypical history of man: the economic anthropology suggested by Rousseau and written by the Scottish historians of civil society. Different peoples at different times express different stages in this history. Here, universal history incorporates the dynamic of commercial society.

HUME'S THEORY OF A WORLD ECONOMY

David Hume is the first theorist to apply the discourse of universal history and the modern discourse of need to explanations of commercial society. He draws the two together, despite their origins in different theoretical problems and realms, in order to explain the continuing spread of commercial practice to all peoples as a force for modernization and development.

Hume, philosopher and historian, explicitly draws a linkage between the world economy and the self: "Everything in the world is purchased by labour; and our passions are the only causes of labour" (Hume: 11). As quoted here, Hume draws out the Lockean theory of labor, although in a way that replaces Locke's ontology of nature as a reservoir of God-given capacities and resources, with the assumption that the world is a singular unity constituted by consumption. This shift in focus to consumption is central to Hume, for it allows him both to avoid any linkages of need to nature and to associate luxury with the morally beneficial sociality of civil society. Hence, he is able to evoke the discourse of need and universality of history, situating the moral problem of human societies into the context of a single, global market.

In "Of Refinements in the Arts," Hume insists that luxury makes possible "industry, knowledge and humanity" (Hume: 22–23). Consumption, and the social forms that accompany it in market societies (fashion, for example) drive the development of the rational self. Hume takes Rousseau's critique of self-love and turns it into a positive development, linking it to the Hobbesian idea that social stability and security over time derive from the transformation of the self from passion-driven to interest-driven (Hirschman 1977). Here, Hume defines luxury in a distinctive way, as those commodities that refine life: luxury makes life more civil and makes persons generous toward others. Luxury, in this sense, is the basis of virtue. Luxury, for Hume, is both a spur to accumulation and a moral discourse that civilizes men. (By *men* Hume means those predisposed by nature to seek a public life of honor and recognition.) Hume shifts the discourse of economy away from the opposition of need and luxury (that is, needs constituted as natural) to a discourse of different kinds of luxury. The moral opposition remains, although in a new form: it is now internal to the relations of a market society. Moral lines are drawn by means of a distinction between kinds of luxury: "innocent" (those that encourage sociality and what he calls "higher" pleasures and culture); and "vicious" (those that encourage self-aggrandizement).[11]

This concept of luxury shifts the focus of economic analysis away from the theology that underlies Lockean theory. It exercises the mysterious power of transfiguring man's egoistic self into the virtuous social self by providing a civil means of comparing oneself to, and competing with, others. Luxury provides a framework that can solve the Hobbesian dilemma of countering the passions that lead to war with passions that lead to peace and cooperation without the intervention of the state. Likewise, Hume's concept of luxury universalizes man's condition without recourse to religious conceptions of the world. Human needs are deeply social, bound to a politics and psychology of emulation, conspicuous consumption, and status; characteristics that can themselves be universalized.

The centrality and positive function of luxuries in creating civil order leads Hume to recognize the importance of expanding international trade.

Much of the late seventeenth and eighteenth century debate about luxuries was about the value of expensive imported goods that constituted the social status of their consumers. To endorse the positive value of luxury consumption, and the conspicuous consumption of homegrown imitations that it spawned in fashion, was simultaneously to recognize the possibility, and to endorse the value, of an ever-expanding and more integrated world market. This increasingly integrated world market, when linked to the concept of luxury as encouraging self-refinement, moral behavior, and social order (i.e., civil society), encouraged action to spread commercial society to all parts of the globe in the search for luxuries that would further induce the refinement, and hence rationality, of social life.

On what basis could such a theory justify this expansion of commercial society that was consistent with the values of social refinement and "modernization"—values that grounded the theory of luxury? Imperial and colonial conquest seemed inappropriate. Violent conquest of resisting peoples vitiated the claim that modernity represented development and moral progress. The balance of power system could not supply this explanation either, for it assumed that human societies were already formed into states. Hume required a vision of human interconnectedness that explained the differential formation of human communities and that was nevertheless based in a singular system of human motivations. In its naturalistic conception of world order, the discourse of universal history provided Hume with a language, suitably revised to eschew any reference to need as natural, within which the necessary vision could be realized.

Hume used the language of universal history, especially its theory of geographical and natural determinism (the secularization of which had been pioneered by Montesquieu) to link his theory of luxury to the division of labor, generating a representation of the world as a single, global economy based upon European, commercial, capitalist practice (as understood by the discourse of need).[12] Different regions of the world have different characters and forms of production as a result of natural factors. Hume uses this discourse to explain, in part, why some regions remain agricultural and poor, and others (namely, the British) develop wealth and manufacturing. Here it seems best to let Hume speak for himself:

> It may seem an odd position, that the poverty of the common people in France, Italy and Spain, is, in some measure, owing to the superior riches of the soil and happiness of the climate; yet there want not reasons to justify this paradox. In such a fine mould or soil as that of those more southern regions, agriculture is an easy art; and one man, with a couple of horses, will be able, in a season, to cultivate as much land as will pay a pretty considerable rent to the proprietor. All the art, which the farmer knows, is to leave his ground fallow for a year, as soon as it is exhausted; and the warmth of the sun alone and temperature of the climate enrich it, and restore its fertility. Such poor peasants, therefore, require only a

simple maintenance for their labour. They have no stock or riches, which claim more; and at the same time they are for ever dependent on their landlord, who gives no leases, nor fears that his land will be spoiled by the ill methods of cultivation. In England, the land is rich, but coarse; must be cultivated at a great expense; and produces slender crops, when not carefully managed, and by a method which gives not the full profit but in a course of several years (Hume: 16–17).

Despite their differences, all material formations have roots in common practices: work, agriculture, manufacturing, property. These economic categories are presumed to be universal. Note how even the social distribution of property, the existence of landlord/peasant relations, is attributed to natural conditions, as the language of universal history would suggest. The presumption of the universality of the categories of economic experience and practice is also clear in Hume's essay, "Of Culture," which ends with:

> We may form a similar remark with regard to the general history of mankind. What is the reason, why no people, living between the tropics, could ever yet attain to any art or civility, or reach even any police in their government, and any military discipline; while few nations in the temperate climates have been altogether deprived of these advantages? It is probable that one cause of this phenomenon is the warmth and equality of weather in the torrid zone, which render cloths and houses less requisite for the inhabitants, and thereby remove, in part, that necessity, which is the great spur to industry and invention. *Curis acuens mortalia corda.* Not to mention, that the fewer goods or possessions of this kind any people enjoy, the fewer quarrels are likely to arise amongst them, and the less necessity will there be for a settled police or regular authority to protect and defend them from foreign enemies, or from each other (Hume: 17–18).

Differences between the customs and political organization of peoples are to be explained on the basis of how natural circumstances are socially developed, reproducing the ambiguity of social contract theory that humans live as a part of nature and live by developing out of nature. On the one hand, this allows the conclusion that nature has "deprived" some peoples of the "advantages" of modernity: there are natural limits to development. But unlike in Bodin and the traditional language of universal history, natural causation of this sort cannot be linked to any larger system of meaning (such as God's Great Chain of Being) and hence seems to have no moral significance. Therefore, on the other hand, peoples are responsible to order their own civil societies in order to maximize their social development. Political economic science describes the code of natural causation that enables the optimum development under the naturally given circumstances. The Humean theory of luxury consumption in civil society as the key to moral action, having severed any account of morality from a substantive account of natural needs, provides political economy with its own, distinctive, moral sanction. If political economy is to be part of a moral discourse at all, it can do so only within the global system of trade that makes the sociality of civil society possible by creating a never-ending stream of choices for individuals and thereby implicating them in inter-dependent relations with others.

This left a system of simple natural determinism, whose laws could be discovered by a science of political economy (laws such as "comparative advantage"). In Hume, the ontological ambiguity of social contact theory—that men live both *as a part of nature* and *by developing out of nature*—re-solves into the epistemological idea of a society as a system governed by natural laws animated by universal human drives and capacities. By follow-ing reason, one comes to know these laws and thereby to reinforce behavior that reinforces the happiness and prosperity of all peoples (of course, to the extent that nature makes this possible). The ontological dilemma (How can man be both a part of nature and develop according to his own wishes and designs?) becomes an epistemological dilemma (How can man know nature as a structural order?). The idea of the world economy as a single, rational mechanism knowable by reason (i.e., nature both *is* a system of natural laws and *appears* as such to men who develop their reason) provides comfort in the face of the philosophical problem that the world seems to create man, and is created by him. The power of representation merges with the power to represent (i.e., to construct). Hence, in the work of the Scottish social the-orists, the philosophical grounding is set for the idea of a world economy as a great economic machine (although Hume nowhere explicitly develops this idea) (Meek 1965). The new idea of universal history as man-made, and therefore knowable, as reason shifts the ontological problem of early mod-ern thought from its theological orientation to a secular, structural one, gives man, once again, a secure place in being. The growth of commerce and sta-tism had disrupted this security for three centuries.

CONCLUSION: THE LITTLE-QUESTIONED ONTOLOGY

The theory of commercial society was a crucial component of En-lightenment thought. In the eighteenth century, this theorization returned a sense of wholeness and security to the theory of human society. The mod-ern world seemed again to be whole; yet now it was integrated by univer-salistic economic laws rather than by God's providence. The particular discursive totality that underlies the invention of international political economy relinks a universalistic account of nature with a theory of human needs. Political economy, it must be remembered, arises as an intervention in philosophical, and especially ontological, debates.

This new sense of wholeness and totality, of "world order" through economic laws, formed the language within which the European commercial system projected itself onto the world stage in the nineteenth and twentieth centuries. Sismondi's division between the concepts *a world-economy* and *the world economy* makes sense only in the context of an assumed ontological unity of human societies in a single world economy in which the opposition of need and nature, and the moral virtue of luxury consumption, are inscribed. This assumed ontology remains largely unquestioned in international political economy. Few recognize how the universalistic theory of nature and the individualistic theory of human needs inform the basic conceptual framework of international political economy.

NOTES

The author thanks Naeem Inayatullah, Mark Rupert, Rob Walker, and James Der Derian for helpful comments on earlier versions of this chapter.

1. Luxuries marked the interpenetration of what had been previously two distinct trading networks. On this distinction, which gradually gives way through the seventeenth and eighteenth century, see Wolf (1982: 32, Chapter 11). For an important interpretation of this development see Xenos (1989).

2. Medieval nominalism had pioneered such a view in its characterization of God as an infinite being that could not be specified within language because such specification would limit him. The world of language and meaning then had independent signification.

3. Bodin's definition of universal history is stated on page 21 of the Reynolds translation of *Methodus*. However, the "comparative method" is cited often by Bodin. Most significant is the reference to Plato in the Dedication (page 2). We should note here the organic metaphor that grows in importance when Bodin discusses the state in Chapter VI of *Methodus*. See page 153:

> Other things, indeed, seem very valuable for a knowledge of the nature of the soul and really admirable for shaping the morals of each man, but the things gathered from the reading of historians about the beginnings of cities, their growth, matured form, decline, and fall are so very necessary, not only to individuals but to everyone, that Aristotle thought nothing was more effective in establishing and maintaining societies of men than to be informed in the science of governing a state.

4. The Reynolds translation reads: "The second book will cover in a suitable division the history of natural things, which are encountered rather often in reading the works of historians; first it will treat the principles of nature, time and place, rise and fall, and generally motion and change; the elements and their nature; imperfect bodies; metals and stones" (Bodin/trans. Reynolds: 35).

5. It is also significant in this respect that Bodin ends the *Methodus* with a chapter on universal time.

6. Witness Bodin's critique of geographers: "As they err who study the maps of regions before they have learned accurately the relation of the whole universe and the separate parts to each other and to the whole, so they are not less mistaken who think they can understand particular histories before they have judged the order and the sequence of universal history and of all times, set forth as it were in a table" (Bodin/trans. Reynolds: 26). Note the similarity to Severinus's recommendation mentioned earlier in the chapter. Knowledge of general principles in

science is linked closely to travel, which was, of course, bound up with the plurality of practices of trade, commerce, and religious conversion.

7. Bodin expressly criticizes theological attempts to explain the differences between peoples. For example, he says, speaking of the Ethiopians: "I can hardly be persuaded that men are made black from the curse of Chus" (Bodin: 87).

8. Here we can see emerging the distinctly modern tension between the determination of human life by natural forces (conceived as abstract regularities) and human free will. Bodin goes on to say:

I have, however, a firm conviction that [astrological?] regions and celestial bodies do not have power to exercise ultimate control (a belief wrong even to entertain), yet men are so much influenced by them that they cannot overcome the law of nature except through divine aid or their own continued self-discipline (Bodin: 86).

Note the similarity to, yet important difference from, Machiavelli's description of the difference between *fortuna* and *virtú*. For Machiavelli, *fortuna* is formulated within an older language of fate, not natural determinism.

9. See the entries, *sovereign* and *sovereignty* in *The Oxford English Dictionary*.

10. Lucien Febvre describes how Renaissance life, at least in France, knew little of, and cared little for, privacy. How novel the idea of the modern self, of cordoning off a space of "mine" as different from and opposed to a space belonging to another! (1977: 8–11)

11. In Hume's words:

Where they entrench upon no virtue, but leave ample subject whence to provide for friends, family, and every proper object of generosity or compassion, they are entirely innocent, and have in every age been acknowledged such by almost all moralists. To be entirely occupied with the luxury of the table, for instance, without any relish for the pleasures of ambition, study, or conversation, is a mark of stupidity, and is incompatible with any vigor of temper or genius. To confine one's expense entirely to such a gratification, without regard to friends or family, is an indication of a heart destitute of humanity or benevolence. But if a man reserve time sufficient for all laudable pursuits, and money sufficient for all generous purposes, he is free from every shadow of blame or reproach (Hume: 20).

12. For an earlier, fascinating account of the regional division of the world, see Bodin/trans. Reynolds: Chapter 5.

2

The "Properties" of the State System and Global Capitalism

Kurt Burch

In this chapter I call into question the institutions of global capitalism and the state system and consider how these two entities are related. I consider how these fundamental social structures of the global order—indeed, of the modern world—were generated and joined, and I take advantage of social theory, some of it critical in perspective and prescription, to address the issue. I wed this epistemological stance to an ontological view that sees the state system and capitalism as an operative whole and, as a matter of theory, use constitutive principles and recursion to explain the coherence of the whole.

The chapter is in six sections. Section 2 deplores the fact that few scholars have paid attention to diachronic change of the global system *itself:* instead, the section notes, they deal with change arising *within* the system. I note that theorists usually render the competitive state system and global capitalism as givens, not as subjects. In Section 3, I introduce critical theory to address the ontological questions that arise when one questions these foci, as well as the epistemological issues that follow from inquiring into how the foci are related. Section 4 elaborates on critical theory as an epistemological view and modifies structuration theory by introducing what I call constitutive principles. I discuss such principles both generally and (as regards property) specifically. In Section 5 I render the competitive state system and global capitalism as a coherent, unified social system, focusing on how actors' understandings of "property" affect their behaviors.

I argue that prior to 1700, no distinction between the state system and global capitalism existed. Understandings of "property" and "property rights" unified them. Yet by 1700, approximately, the prevailing understandings of property and property rights bifurcated. Distinctly real and mobile forms emerged. Real property (rights) grounded the territorial state system and mobile property (rights) propelled the fluid, burgeoning capitalist system. What they held in common—as property—united them. Section 6 offers concluding remarks.

CHALLENGING A SO-CALLED NONISSUE

The competitive state system and global capitalism comprise two fundamental organizing structures of the international system. This claim is one of the great premises of international relations (IR) scholarship. Yet the premise is implicit, since most theorists—if they try at all—have great difficulty explaining how the twin realms of the state system and global capitalism are related in comprising the global order. For those working in the mainstream tradition of political realism, the international system comprises a prominent, privileged state system. Finance, production, and exchange serve as background conditions, or as specific forms of broader conflicts over power. Indeed, (neo)mercantilists argue that production, exchange, and wealth-generating activities are the objects of power over which nations struggle (Sylvan 1981). Since Morgenthau's time, a line of inquiry that questions fundamental propositions is absent from international relations' mainstream scholarship. Realists and neorealists typically do not question the origins and transformational possibilities of social institutions and practices. Ruggie (1983b) criticizes Waltz (1979) on just this point. Gilpin (1987) can be seen as an interesting exception in light of his realist roots and acknowledgement—albeit at arm's length—of the insights to be drawn from Marxian critique. By contrast, world systems theorists, such as Wallerstein and Chase-Dunn, although they draw from the critical Marxian tradition to demonstrate that the dynamics and structures of global capitalism profoundly affect state formation and sources of interstate conflict, they do so with a critical eye that is not so acute. They often devote considerable attention to the origins of capitalism and the state system in comprising the global order, but they take capitalism and the state system as givens and read the past in this light (Burch 1992).

This inattention to the specific question of how global capitalism and the competitive state system jointly comprise the modern world is not an oversight by IR theorists; nor is it even an identified yet unexplored gap in the literature. Rather, it is evidence of a specific worldview—one shared by most IR theorists; hence, the specific way in which the discipline is predisposed. Since the body of liberal theory and practice appears to provide the connective webbing, theorists have had little reason to examine the specific relationship between capitalism and the state system. Consequently, theorists offer few explanations of capitalism, the state system, or their connections; liberalism—the ideological foundation for IR as a discipline—reinforces implicit acceptance of these elements as the definitive elements of the global order. Further, few scholars—either from the realist IR field or from international political economy (IPE)—attempt explanations of the origins, evolution, and diachronic change of the international system itself. In the traditional research program, the proper subject of inquiry is not the international system but rather problems for state action and sources of change arising *within* the system as a given.[1] Consequently, global capitalism and the competitive state system are analytic givens, not subjects; in the traditional program, the relationship between capitalism and the state system remains a nonissue—a largely implicit, unexamined premise.[2]

Scholars working in other analytical frameworks make similar claims about this relationship that go similarly unexamined. Some theorists suggest that capitalism and the state system are related at their origins, thereby sharing a common ancestry (e.g., Schlumbohm 1981: 126–134; Kriedte 1983: 15–16). Others argue that the twin foci share an organizing logic (e.g., Mann 1988: 86 et pass.). Speculation about the system per se or on what happens to the system also arises outside of the self-established purview of mainstream IR work. One must look to world systems theory (e.g., Wallerstein 1974a, 1974b, 1980), long cycle theory (e.g., Modelski 1978, 1987; Thompson 1988), or in the debates on the transition from feudalism (e.g., Hilton, ed. 1976).

Chase-Dunn (1981) is an exception. He makes the issue explicit. He concisely asks whether capitalism and the state system comprise for the modern world "one logic or two?" He specifically asks in what ways the state system and global capitalism are related. Are they not a unity? He calls them a single "interactive socioeconomic system" (Chase-Dunn: 21), and says "the interstate system is the political side of capitalism, not an analytically autonomous system" (Chase-Dunn: 19), arguing that they "can be understood to have a single, integrated logic."

Chase-Dunn's view of the connections between capitalism and the state system, and his question as to how they are related, leaves us with the task of explaining the relationship.

RAISING ONTOLOGICAL AND EPISTEMOLOGICAL ISSUES

Such issues are troublesome and poorly appreciated by IR/IPE scholars, who do not rise to the simultaneous, but unavoidable, theoretical, ontological, and epistemological challenges. To question how capitalism and the state system are related is to question our ontological assumptions about the global order: to question it as either a largely economic structure maintained by fully or partially capitalist (mode of production) dynamics; or as a political structure of states competing for power. Possible relationships between capitalism and the state system are typically expressed loosely in terms of "structural articulation" or how one "affects" the other. The global order becomes a given if not a cipher. By posing the problem in this manner, one raises epistemological concerns about how to understand these circumstances.

These twin concerns arise immediately and inextricably. Yet when concerns about theory-construction arise, ontological issues are typically easier to grapple with than the concomitant epistemological ones. The former are clearly more tractable, and far more tractable than a confrontation with both at once. A critical perspective offers a means for effectively treating these issues.

INTRODUCING CRITICAL THEORY

Critical theory "stands apart from the prevailing order of the world and asks how that order came about." It focuses on "the social and political complex as a whole rather than [on] the separate parts" (Cox 1981, in Keohane 1986: 210, 209).[3] "Critical theory . . . does not take institutions and social and power relations for granted but calls them into question by concerning itself with their origins and how and whether they might be in the process of changing" (Keohane 1986: 208–209). The purpose of critical theory is to illuminate possible alternatives. It is an invitation to think creatively. It is an invitation to consider new practices from a speculative, comprehensive perspective.

Agreement with this comes, perhaps strangely, from Hans J. Morgenthau (1946: 9, 102), one of the foremost voices of political realism and the target of much critique. He argues that a superlative approach to political inquiry expands the realm of the political to encompass the totality of social relations. By rearranging our cognitive and conceptual orientation, by adopting new viewpoints and worldviews, by asking different questions, we can navigate the morass in which we find ourselves. Thus, both Cox and Morgenthau direct our attention, if not our energies, toward critique. In so doing, they return us to worldviews and attendant social practices. They (re)direct us toward critical concerns apparently lost in North Atlantic realist theorists' preoccupation with the Cold War.

In general, rather than offer any critical theory—indeed, rather than offer any *explanation*—IR and IPE "theorists" typically *describe* the world and apply their descriptions to particular problems arising in the world. The phenomena are related. IR and IPE theory are descriptive in the sense that problem-solving work begins from a set of unexplored premises, amply described. Such descriptions confirm and inform worldviews that are ideologically and paradigmatically driven, thereby establishing the world "as it is," in a manner of speaking. IR and IPE theorists ably depict aspects of global relations, often in structural terms, but appear unable to transcend the conservative limitations of description to address issues concerning the generation and transformation of the global order. Those that directly address such concerns—such as world order theorists—are routinely marginalized and demeaned.

The consequence of privileging the competitive state system and global capitalism as foundational systemic structures is to mask the ordering and transformative principles at work upon the system. What becomes lost are concerns about the constitution—the genesis, generation, and transformational possibilities—of the global order. Expressed differently, IR/IPE theory is largely descriptive and problem-solving because it is largely neither analytical nor critical (e.g., Rosenau 1976).

How else might we proceed? What other postures can we strike? I adopt a view that is—for lack of a better label, and labels appear to be important in such matters—late-modern postpositivist. Modernism typically privileges the theorist: she or he is either an enormously perspicacious observer (a well-debunked myth) or an especially skilled parter-of-the-veils. In both instances, the theorist occupies a privileged position by means of her or his (supposed) ability to see the world as it is rather than as it appears. Holding a distinction between reality and appearances is a distinctive feature of a modern worldview. The embedded ontological assumption avers that there exists a structure to the world that is independent of the knower (Habermas 1971: 304; Bernstein 1978: 175). More to the point, that structure is orderly and lawlike; these laws and the concomitant order (may) become known by theorists in the course of their scientific investigations. In this manner, theorists are again privileged.

In contrast, postmodernism declares that each individual creates the world in unique, particular, idiosyncratic ways, although the acts of (re)creation and (re)production are always social in character. We constitute the world for ourselves to a marked degree. There is no hard distinction between reality and appearances; reality is not independent of the observer. However, it seems to me that one can accept this postpositivist view of social construction, even applaud it, without adopting the heavy mantle of postmodernism. Postmodernism rejects the foundations of the Enlightenment; postmodernism dismisses philosophical foundations—even condemns them—and thereby reduces the world to the "endless play of dominations"; that is, to the endless succession of worldviews (and their proponents) competing and crusading to dominate social activities, perceptions, and conceptions.[4]

In short, no foundations exist. Without foundations, postmodernism is nihilism, nothingness. Yet we can't stand "nowhere." No matter where we "stand" or what we "see," we must stand somewhere and see from some particular perspective. These are foundations. With foundations, postmodernism is no longer *post*modern. Instead, it becomes critical modernism.

Indirectly, questions about the evolution and development of social institutions and practices are questions about foundations. When we ask how institutions and relations come about, we ask questions about genesis and generation: what generated or constituted these institutions and relations? One can discuss such concerns in the vocabulary of "constitution" and "recursion", and thereby of "agency" and "agents." In this vocabulary, we can consider individual actors, their worldview ("foundations") and practices, and the consequent social structures. This acknowledges yet modifies Giddens's (1984) "duality of structure" and Ashley's (1989: 272–274) "undecidable opposition." Giddens's "duality of structure" describes structured social relations as both the outcome of social practices and as the medium through which social practices are channeled. Thus, social structures possess a dual role: consequence and catalyst. Ashley's phrase *undecidable opposition* refers to the conundrum confronting social theorists: is society composed primarily of social structures and patterns of social relations which generate or constitute social actors, or do the practices and activities of social actors generate and constitute social structures? The choice is undecidable because we clearly understand the duality at issue. This is the agent-structure problem.

I propose herein that constitutive principles mediate the dualistic opposition. Constitutive principles generate or constitute social structures. Agents and their various activities constitute these principles through their patterned, recurrent activities. These behaviors reveal the actors' understandings of the world, and thereby indicate the prevailing worldview and philosophical foundations. Were IR and IPE theorists to move away from description toward critical theory, the subject of "constitutive principles" becomes apprehensible, making efforts to address "generation," "genesis," "recursion," and "constitution" intelligible and tractable. Such a move also brings us to consider conceptual histories (Ball 1989; Ball et al., eds. 1989) as a means for approximating (recreating) agents' understandings.

To make claims about inextricable, mutually constituting agent-structure relations (e.g., Giddens 1984; Wendt 1987) is at best a partial alternative solution. It must be joined to an epistemological view—critical theory—that questions the origins and changes in/of the agents, their activities, and their conceptual understandings. The immediate subject becomes critical theory, and through it, constitutive principles with conceptual histories, and the historically contingent practices and understandings of agents. In the following sections, I address these concerns in turn.

CONSTITUTIVE PRINCIPLES AND PROPERTY

Principles

As several authors note (e.g., Leach 1961: 7; Lukes 1977: 8; Ruggie 1983a: 266, footnote 16), one may distinguish social structures by their "ordering principles"; that is, the principles by which the structures are ordered, arranged, or organized. The term *principles* conveys a sense of axiomatic primacy. Its etymology reveals the notions of origins and basic elements.[5] In the context of structural analysis, principles may be said to represent the essential components establishing the distinctive characteristics of form, organization, and operation. They are the underlying precepts, the originating and actuating sources by which or from which other characteristics are founded or derived. Unlike other concepts, *principles* conveys the notion, *constitution.* Ordering principles analytically describe existing structures; constitutive principles constitute the structures and agents that comprise and construct our world.

Investigating "constitutive principles" contributes to our understanding of "generative structures" (cf., Ruggie 1983a: 266, footnote 16). Constitutive principles generate structures; they generate social relations generally. We may understand constitutive principles as shorthand references to discernible sets of human practices. These practices and activities instantiate the constitutive principles; hence, the structures. As the behaviors of individual agents comprise constitutive principles, so constitutive principles constitute social structures; hence, society.

Social structures are not immutable, primordial entities. The continuous production and reproduction, constitution, and reconstitution of the social world is called recursion. This is the essential quality of the "duality of structure": social structures do not exist without human action; in turn, social structures provide the means by which human action is (re)produced. Structures are the medium and outcome of human activity (e.g., Giddens 1984: 25, 181). By moving from *structure* to *generative structure,* our conceptual awareness embraces *agents* and *agency,* thereby arriving squarely at the agent-structure problem (e.g., Wendt 1987). While Wendt's discussion successfully draws attention to ontological problems, I strive to confront ontological and epistemological issues simultaneously. Wendt identifies a problem; I seek to resolve it.

Property as a Constitutive Principle

Property rights organize a significant variety of constitutive human activity. The variety of social practices described by the constitutive term "property rights" helps to generate the structures of capitalism and the state system. It is impossible to divorce the concept *property as ownership* from the concept *rights to property* (or *rights over property*). As analytical leverage, property rights and property correspond well with Giddens's (1984) notions of rules and resources. Giddens argues that social rules and resources are integral to the constitution and (re)production of society. Property rights are rules coordinating social activity; property is the resource at issue and in turn a resource to be wielded in distributing material advantage.

Property is a particular type of valuable or valued resource, whatever the attributes or motivations for possessing it. Moreover, property rights are a specific form of social rules. Often they are codified as laws into institutionalized legal codes. As a constitutive principle, property contributes to generating what are perceived in the modern era as distinct political and economic realms. Specific manifestations include the structural features of the state system and global capitalism. Also, property rights both contribute to the state system/global capitalism dichotomy and (when understood as rules) help to resolve this particular problem. I do not intend to suggest that the institutions are related, integrated, linked, conjoined, or whatever may be described by any of those words' synonyms. Such terms suggest two separate spheres that are somehow connected to each other. Instead, I refer to a unity: a single, coherent social reality.

Historically contingent understandings of property mediate this unity by marking the degree to which the political and economic realms are separate or distinct. The single, overwhelming, socially definitive character of property—understood as tangible and material, and as best represented by land—had bifurcated into real and mobile forms by approximately 1700. Conceptions of mobile or intangible property arose in dramatic political debate concerning corruption, the transferability of political offices, and credit (see, e.g., Pocock 1985). Credit is immediately comparable to other intangible values, such as insurance and fluidity, and to mobile instruments, such as notes, bills of exchange, and such. Differences between mobile and real property underscore differences between global capitalism and the state system, respectively. The associated shifts in property rights provide for the generation and linking of the state system and global capitalism. Global capitalism is a system of production and exchange based upon the fluid transfer of factor inputs, final products, and capital (as opposed to tangible markers of wealth).

One can understand the state system as a system of territorially based, real, landed property. Consider, for example, the relationship between "a state" and "estate." Both describe an extensive landholding, but both also convey a sense of "status." Sovereign and seigneurial status—conferred from the feudal and early modern titles—were well understood in the early modern period. As an adjective, *sovereign* is a superlative referring to undisputed rank, status, or ascendancy; or to unrivaled quality. These characteristics, applied to a ruler's territory, give us the modern sense of sovereignty and supreme jurisdiction. Thus, we can see that "the state" represents the territorially grounded property rights of sovereign monarchs, especially as these rights and holdings were fundamental in the development of institutional-legal structures for ruling and controlling society.

Thus, property denotes status and authority as it connotes power and political privilege. Control over property and property rights contributes to the constitution of the "political world" by establishing forms of privilege and by reinforcing both material and social asymmetries. Property also denotes the use and disposal of property, and thereby delimits access to production and exchange. Thus, property and property rights help generate the "economic world" as well. These privileges and denotations contribute to control, domination, exploitation, production, and exchange, all of which are clearly understandable as structural features of social relations. Just as clearly they involve social practices.

Historically Contingent Notions of Property

One can trace the significance of property and property rights—indeed, their joint role as a constitutive principle—through the political thought and practice of the classical to modern eras. Over this span, three broad traditions of thought and practice emerge: moral/civic, jurisprudential, and instrumental-utilitarian. Property is central to each.

The dominant moral/civic tradition, at least in Anglo-Saxon scholarship, emphasizes the role that political life plays in developing an individual's personality, the good life, and community interests. By approximately 1450, the traditions of moral and civic virtue had crumbled in the feudal collapse. Jurisprudential conceptions—more Roman than Greek—helped erode the foundations of a moral/civic polity and its social practices and relations. The juristic tradition—which introduced the vocabulary of rights and "things"—placed individuals and objects in counterpoint. The subsequent sociopolitical relations of individual-to-object (juristic) rather than of individual-to-individual (moral/civic) eroded the classical conception of politics and carved from it a distinct "economic" realm. This economic sphere stood in contrast to moral/civic political ideals. At the same time, developing political practices centered upon relations between authorities and subjects, thereby displacing the moral/civic notion of politics as individual-to-individual. Further, legally conceived rights and duties (rather than moral injunctions) expressed the prevailing relations between authorities and subjects.

These distinct realms of social activity—the political sphere (polity) and the economic realm (market)—were grounded in particular, expanded senses of property and property rights. Said differently, these realms are socially constructed and their borders depend to great degree upon the socially established senses of rights to and over property. The spheres took distinctive shape in the clash between moral/civic and jurisprudential notions of property and property rights. These seemingly distinct though related spheres, and the rights to property appropriate in each, contributed to social and material asymmetries involving power, control, exploitation, and domination. Once institutionalized, they introduced the transition to state-building and nascent capitalism.

Centuries later, those thinkers developing liberal thought reified and justified the separation, yet implicitly acknowledged the spheres to be separate but related (see below). The developing coherence of liberal ideology and the unfolding of the modern era are closely related episodes. Together, they are related to differentiation in the notions of property and property rights. The changes marked a distinction between real and mobile property. This was a profound change, but one perfectly in keeping with the productive spirit of the age (Pocock 1985).

This change promoted the growth of global capitalism and a system of competing states. Global capitalism and the competitive state system are distinguishable by the mobile and real conceptions of property, respectively, upon which they rest. These distinctions and separations—as economics from politics and mobile from real property—are socially constructed to serve socially valuable purposes (cf., Walzer 1984). Yet by (socially) constructing a sense of it, we might also understand the modern era as the unity of global capitalism and a competitive state system. Property rights link the (seemingly distinct) spheres into a single, coherent social reality. That coherence is no less "whole" than ancient and medieval understandings of politics and society. By considering property and property rights, we see how the constitutive principles and significant social practices differently constitute and unify the social "wholes" of these eras.

We now come to the crux of the issue of property as it affects the discussion below: property is a constitutive principle. "Property" constitutes social actors and objects and constitutes the relations among them.

The Oxford English Dictionary reveals that the word *property* descends from the Latin word *proprius,* meaning *one's own, proper,* from which derived *proprietat.* The latter means a quality or attribute of a person and, normatively, this implied *a proper or appropriate* characteristic. Such characteristics represent a condition of *propriety.* Property later came to apply to material characteristics of individual personality and so, too, to material possessions, which were regarded as extensions of personality. In short, property came to mean that which is owned by, belongs to, or is possessed by an individual. Here, *property* conveys all of the senses of normative judgment *(propriety)* and personality characteristics *(properties),* extends them to material possessions *(personal property),* and approves the relationship between individual and external object *(proper, appropriate).* Property and property rights are inextricable. Moreover, the broad constellation of concepts encircling *property* and *property rights*— whether etymologically or conceptually related—include the cognates of *possession, own, use, title, domain, rights, right,* and *propriety.* Each suggests specific, relevant, and appropriate rights as well .

Property is a constitutive principle that generates to a considerable degree the organization and dynamics of social relations. In large part, individuals act by reference to the existing assignments and distribution of property rights: the resources and rights at their disposal, and those available to others. In the section below, I illustrate how *property* and *property rights* establish a conceptual grounding for the apparently distinct realms of the state system (politics) and global capitalism (economics).

PROPERTY AND MODERNITY: THE STATE SYSTEM
AND CAPITALISM AS A COHERENT WHOLE

Significant Social Practices

The "crown state" emerged from the "crown" when monarchical families became the purveyors of property rights as part of their alliance with the bourgeoisie in order to organize and administer institutional structures for public governance and rule. Although already well-established, real property was significant because it provided the foundation for the claims by states' rulers to be territorial rights–bearers—that is, landholding sovereigns. By approximately 1700, however, the diversity of social practices involving property created a discernible split in the notion of property rights (Pocock 1957 and 1985:113). Property (and property rights) acquired distinctly real and mobile forms. Mobile property includes intangible resources, such as credit. The evolution of mobile property spurred the growth of capitalism—as distinct from mercantilist state policies—and with it the expansion of a system of competitive states. The split in property (rights) established the conceptual division between the state system (real, tangible property) and the capitalist system (mobile, intangible property). The institution of property rights contributes to the generation and linking of capitalism and the interstate system as articulated structures; differences between real and mobile property contribute to the differences between the two structures.

Prior to 1700, there was no distinction between the state system and capitalism: a bifurcated understanding of real and mobile property was not yet institutionalized. Property meant, primarily, real, landed property; states were central to the development, administration, and enforcement of property rights. Yet leaders and administrators understood the necessarily inextricable character of property's many facets. They also understood that burgeoning institutional orders (proto-states) required resources such as revenue, specie, and specific "national priority" products that were most effectively attained by promoting mobile property and capitalist exchange and production. Simultaneously, expanding capitalist enterprises and fluid resources benefited from a stable institutional order.

This view of property (rights) and concomitant social relations suggests that the origins of the modern state as a territorial entity are based not solely upon sovereignty (cf., Ruggie 1983a) but upon property as its concrete social manifestation. Sovereign states are first and foremost holders of property rights: holders of a grounded stake in the secular social realm. The crucial terrain is the sovereign state. Arguing that the global system is grounded upon the concept of sovereignty actually misses the fundamental point. Sovereignty is the physical manifestation of sovereign property rights to territorial property. As such, it provides the groundwork, if you will, for the international system.

Yet sovereignty is not the definitive feature of states. Rather, sovereignty is a property right that conveys status, authority, and a form of rule. Sovereign property rights define and delimit the extent of landed, grounded, territorial authority. We understand this (original) authority in terms of rights to and over specific land and its occupants, whether animal, mineral, vegetable, or human. Philosophic debates over the location of sovereignty—as in "popular sovereignty"—effectively illustrate the emphasis upon property (use and control) rights. Thus, sovereignty underscores the territorial dimension of inter*nation*al relations, implies a locus of authority, but says nothing about the relations these states and authorities conduct. For that we might turn to the term "seigniorage," which describes the right to coin and print currency, and therefore the opportunity to engage in arbitrage opportunities. *Seignior-sovereign* and *seigniory-sovereignty* are synonymous pairs in their original feudal meanings. Subsequent use has attributed fluid, intangible connotations to the former and material, landed connotations to the latter.

We can also understand that *sovereignty* provides a shorthand label for a form of social rule. The notion of "sovereign as authority" suggests specific social rules and rule-governed behavior, identifiable by consistent social practices and concomitant social structures. The consequence, as always, is a form of social rule. While *sovereignty* signals us to stable patterns of agent-structure relations, but hides the reproductive mechanism(s) from us, *property* allows us to see all of the component variables, their structural consequences, and the reproductive characteristics.

With the development and acknowledgement of mobile property, capitalism becomes a system of fluid exchange, moving beyond its grounded, agrarian dimensions. Crucial to this development is state practice. Policymakers identified goals (interests) and means (policies). Regardless of the chosen goals, a first step was often to centralize authority and create bureaucracies. Indeed, creating and enhancing necessary social institutions in the name of efficiency was a priority. Were not the state and the market just such institutions? Acquiring material and monetary resources posed a particular difficulty, so policymakers fostered institutions that could provide the service. They did so by offering property rights—often in the form of grants, monopolies, charters, use rights, and many other benefits— in exchange for resources, goods, services, and specie. Thus, joint-stock companies date to as early as 1450, become prominent by the 1550s, and become prime movers by approximately the 1650s. As these companies acquire corporate personalities, corporate law blooms and our contemporary understanding of corporations comes into being. Medieval understandings of corporations as polities are transformed to accommodate this new type of social actor. Thus, policymakers, jurists, and lawyers combined to promote—in the state's interest—new forms of largely political actors, competition, and centralization.[6]

As a result, bureaucratic development occurred apace in both England and France in the seventeenth century largely to achieve greater taxation and resource distribution. Efficiency and competitive advantage were the foremost justifications. Of course, the sovereign, territorial groundwork provides sites or vessels from which and to which capital can flow. At the same time, state rulers exercised their sovereign property rights in order to promote capital accumulation and to engage in international competition with other sovereign entities. Indeed, the exercise of sovereign property rights became the key to driving both global capitalism and the competitive state system, as it also became the means of directing the state toward acquisitive and aggressive ends.

For example, in England Queen Elizabeth I knighted international pirates such as Sir Francis Drake for "appropriating" the wealth of others. In France, Louis XIV employed "devil's brigades" to collect taxes at home so that more funds would become available for domestic institutional restructuring, infrastructural development, and international competition. The latter primarily involved military campaigns and economic intrigue. Thus, Louis' finance minister, Colbert, could remark about the king's "monetary war against all European states" that

> Your Majesty has founded companies which attack them everywhere like armies. The manufacturers, the shipping canal between the seas, and so many other new establishments which Your Majesty sets up are so many reserve corps which Your Majesty creates from nothing in order that they may fulfill their duty in this war (quoted in Staniland 1985: 70).

Similarly in England, the last half of the seventeenth century marked the development of a "modern" institutional infrastructure for domestic governance and international competition. The English state comprised an institutional-legal order and an inextricably intimate connection between the state apparatus and competitive "economic" enterprises. The English (and Dutch) joint-stock companies are exemplary illustrations. Their long, celebrated histories and their intimate connections with statecraft and foreign policy offer elaborate examples of the indistinguishable nature of "political statecraft" and "economic production and exchange." The joint-stock companies received monopoly concessions from state policymakers in exchange for conducting activities on behalf of the state and bearing most of the investment risks. In return, the state would earn revenue by taxing the imported goods and their consumption or use. The distinction between political and economic realms (as between public and private) is completely blurred in the aforementioned case of early joint-stock companies formed to conduct state-sponsored piracy (e.g., Drake's raids). Queen

Elizabeth was a personal investor, as, too, were later rulers. Some of the plunder was, of course, returned to investors, but that allocated to the Crown increased the national wealth by threefold over a thirty-year period that overlapped Elizabeth's reign. Other companies performed diverse, complementary activities.

The development of central banks, joint-stock companies, and an institutional-legal infrastructure in England, France, and the Netherlands occurred similarly during the seventeenth century. At one end of this period came the early Dutch and English joint-stock companies, founded in the 1550s, and the establishment of the Dutch central bank in 1605; at the other end of the period came the founding of the Bank of England in 1694 and the failed French attempt in 1719 to create a central bank modeled on the English example. In between came the Cromwellian interregnum, the Dutch-English alliance, England's wars with France, Louis XIV's reign, the Glorious Revolution, and the coronation of William and Mary. The experiences of the English, Dutch, and French contributed to a number of developments: to the formation of nation-states in these territories; to the institution of "the state" and its component institutions and bureaucracies; to systemically competitive state interaction; and to the dynamics of global capitalist production, distribution, exchange, and consumption.

Statecraft and the expansion of capitalism comprise one phenomenon. Rulers use rights over mobile property to service competition with other states; and the competition creates opportunities for the accumulation of capital. National rulers solicited, promoted, and often created large (joint-stock) companies in order to address the chronically destitute, nearly insolvent character of crown/national finances.[7] The crown extended property rights and granted privileges (grants, charters, exemptions) primarily to induce companies to act on behalf of foreign policy interests and to meet needs for national infrastructural development, domestic consumption, or "national interest." In return, the crown attained desired goals and acquired revenue by taxing imports, production, and/or consumption. For merchants, "[t]he advantage of joint-stock ownership in such enterprizes [sic] was obvious; for, while no individual would be prepared to undertake the whole liability, a number of persons, acting together, were willing to provide the funds required" (Scott 1912/1968: vol. I, 461).[8]

In particular, the uncertain distinction between statecraft and economic activity arises in terms of national foreign policies, domestic needs, and national finances. The ostensible purpose of the state was and is to administer and govern society and to help attain social needs. Stated bluntly, policymakers required specific material resources for both the former and the latter. Rulers turned to joint-stock companies to provide each of these seemingly national and political needs. Monarchical rulers used trading and holding companies to further expansive colonial aspirations, and the credit extended by newly created central banks financed military and infrastructural development (e.g., Polanyi 1957; de Vries 1976; Cipolla 1980; Parry revised 1981; McNeill 1982; Andrews 1984). At the same time, the directors of burgeoning commercial enterprises realized that the centralized authority of the state could enhance the climate and circumstances of commerce. Bargains were struck.

For example, in Britain the Crown engaged the Russia Company and the Guinie (later Africa) Company—both founded in 1553—to act directly in the service of the government and to conduct foreign policy in their respective geographic areas. The Russia Company was to open diplomatic and commercial relations with the czar; the Africa Company was to outflank and impede Portuguese and Spanish trade in Africa and to open the way for British slavers.

For Britain's domestic needs, the Crown created new companies or promoted existing ones. The Crown granted charters, patents, monopolies, and other benefits to companies to stimulate production of valued commodities and to develop national economic and institutional infrastructure. Such companies constructed and maintained aqueducts, built bridges, erected and maintained streetlights, constructed metalworks, delivered mail, made paper, linen, wool, silk, soap, glass, and porcelain, formed banks and insurance houses, mined ores, fashioned weapons for soldiers and sailors, and established textile processes to produce uniforms, sails, and ropes (Scott 1912/1968, vol. III).

The sorry state of national, hence royal, revenues provided limitless incentives to promote, co-opt, and piggyback upon successful companies. And their success could be tremendous. For example, between 1609 and 1613, the annual profit for the East India Company fluctuated between 121 percent and 234 percent (Scott 1912/1968, vol. I: 141, 145–146). At the same time, chronic financial crises plagued the British Crown. Such crises dated back at least to the Tudor reign. The deficits became especially pronounced late in the seventeenth century, when the demands upon the Crown state grew dramatically.[9]

After 1700, the institution of mobile property expanded to provide greater fluidity and scope to market exchange and financial services. Thus, production and exchange expanded, then transformed, into a discernibly distinct social realm. The evolution of liberal thought and the modern mind further encouraged the view of these as distinct realms.

The constellation of significant social structures in this heady sociopolitico-economic milieu involved the crown, common law, and the institutions of markets, credit, and banking. Each element in the set may be characterized in terms of agency/agents. The active agents of statecraft included the rulers, their ministers and other officials, as well as military officers. Judges, lawyers, and diplomats comprised the jurisprudential agents. These actors identified and shaped the social practices to be institutionalized as rules and laws. In this era, diplomats were jurisprudents charged with, among other responsibilities, the ability to make (international) laws binding the representatives of participating states. Capitalist agents included large landholders, bankers, speculators, and other members of the community of financiers, producers, and merchants.

I conclude that the modern world is as unified and organically whole as the feudal world. Yet the modern mind conceives the modern world in terms of discrete, separate realms of social activity. Adept at the functional "art of separation," we conceive a world of walls, and therefore perceive the world as a disaggregated mosaic. Nevertheless, a distinguishing feature of the modern world is the intimate, inextricable singularity of capitalism and the state system—or, the intricately, intimately, inextricably connected relations among agents of statecraft, law, and capitalism—as mediated through jurisprudential activity involving property rights.

The Modern Era and Liberal Thought and Practice

Here a problem emerges: if seventeenth century actors plausibly understood their behaviors in terms of a single, coherent social unity, how have we come to regard social spheres in discrete ways? Why do we regard politics and economics as distinct realms?

The jurisprudential tradition encouraged in two ways the emergence of (so-called) distinctly economic activity. First, the notion of rights or control over resources promoted trade, profit, and savings. Second, the legal tradition undermined political participation as the key (sole?) social activity. In short, it presaged the crucial separation of political and economic realms: "Property was a juridical term before it was an economic one" (Pocock 1985: 56). Thus, Andrew Reeve (1986: 10) remarks "that putting boundaries round the political theory of property poses special difficulties, because property as a social institution is a legal, economic, and political phenomenon."

More broadly, the jurisprudential tradition augured several features of the modern world. In distinguishing individuals from objects/things, it raised not only the issue of alienation, but also of control and disposition of *things:* what might one do with her/his *things?* The available choices largely involved *rights.* These rights represented the spectrum of options available to individuals concerning some specified object and/or practice. The concept of rights thoroughly imbues the liberal, modern worldview (cf., Arblaster 1984; Shapiro 1986; Rapaczynski 1986). In a practical sense, the vocabulary and practices of rights were understood as political or social relations. But they were quickly converted into conceptions of "use" with decidedly economic connotations. These bled directly into production, exchange, and accumulation. Thus, we see a social whole divided into discrete components, to which we have attributed independent characteristics. The significance of property in diverse theoretical genres illustrates the division of the social world into discrete (political and economic) realms.

For example, from Plato and Aristotle to von Hayek and Nozick, the concept of property has occupied a central place in political theory. One might similarly refer to the significance of *property* in the "economic" analyses of Smith, Ricardo, Engels, and others. And one might further note the importance of *property* in the "political-economic" explorations of Locke, Rousseau, Marx, Friedman, and the like. To distinguish these theories as political, economic, or political-economic may strike us as odd. From a point of view on *property,* such discriminations are uncomfortable. These divisions are disconcertingly arbitrary, historical products, features of the modern, liberal world: "Liberalism is a world of walls" (Walzer 1984: 315).[10] It is only in the liberal era that political theory could be maintained as a distinct subject from moral theory, economic theory, legal theory, social theory, and philosophy, for example.

To quote Walzer at greater length, he elaborates: "The old preliberal . . . [s]ociety was conceived as an organic and integrated whole. It might be viewed under the aspect of religion, or politics, or economy, or family, but all these interpenetrated one another and constituted a single reality. . . . Confronting this world, liberal theorists preached and practiced the art of separation" (1984: 315). Perhaps the most distinctive separation is that of politics and economics, power and wealth, or more specifically the state and the market. Other distinctions follow in the wake of this central dichotomy: the division of the liberal globe into the state system and capitalism, the divisions between liberalism and socialism/Marxism, and their relative emphases upon market exchange and modes of production, among others.

To quote Walzer again: "The contemporary social world is still an organic whole, less different from feudalism than we might think. . . . The art of separation is not an illusory or fantastic enterprise; it is a morally and politically necessary adaptation to the complexities of modern life. Liberal theory reflects and reinforces a long-term process of social differentiation" (1984: 318, 319).

Property plays a key role in both maintaining and bridging these distinctions or differentiations. By looking at property we can see the "integrated whole," the single coherent social reality. Some of the distinctions—as between real and mobile property—contribute to the seemingly distinct characters of the state system and global capitalism. Yet the shared features of real and mobile property as property contribute to the wholeness and shared social reality of these institutions; that is, to the modern world. At the same time, differentiations in property, for example, represent adaptations to modernity's complexity. The social world was not always divided so. To divide social life into discrete spheres or realms would have been unfathomable in the classical or feudal eras.

Changes in the notions of property and property rights can contribute to the degree to which the world is seen as relatively whole or divided. The modern, liberal mind sees a highly differentiated world. This is a social adaptation. Differentiation contributes to analysis, which dissolves wholes into manageable components. Here we see the scientific method at work at the theoretical/methodological drive toward ever finer description. The presumption holds that the whole equals the sum of its parts. Manageability promotes efficiency and expediency. The latter promote "economic man," the defining feature of which is the replacement of "passions," needs, and loyalties with "interests" that dictate rational, cost-benefit, instrumental decisionmaking. Lost is a conception and appreciation of sets of social relations, of collective needs, outcomes, and responsibilities, and of principles rather than expediency. Lost is the decided ability and willingness to see that whole exceed the sum of its parts. Social and political life—life among individuals—is eclipsed by juridical and instrumental relations between individuals and objects.

Property was a wedge that split the spheres of society, yet it was also a tie that bound them. As a result, the "political" world was changed and the foundation for an "economic" realm (quite distinct from *oikos*) was laid.[11] "Economics" had burst forth from the shadows of restricted household or manorial production to become society's prime mover, as a system of relations between individuals and objects in the service of marketable production. "Politics" as civic virtue and citizen participation was in danger of disappearing beneath the hierarchical shadow of "politics" as a system of relations among authorities and subjects. Political uncertainty contributed to social and cosmic uncertainty.[12]

Separated political and economic spheres, with the former understood as the relationship between authority and deference, outlines to great degree the liberal worldview. The division of these spheres arose from the juristic separation of property from the individual, of property from (solely) the political realm, and of the consequent dissolution of restrictions on productive activity. Thus, "politics" came to comprise the relations between authority and subjects.

Political authority was the source and enforcer of rights; subjects were those who held rights and avowed deference. Subjects (as individuals) held these rights over material objects (things). Chief among these objects was land. Once land became an object/thing tied to individuals by property rights, land became an economic resource. The property that can be used as an economic resource—again, this overwhelmingly meant land—delimits the new economic realm that was carved from the moral/civic notion of politics by the juristic tradition. The economic realm comprises the set of relationships among individuals and things. Pocock (1985: 105) has written that "the increasingly complex and dynamic relationships and processes which we call 'economics' began to surpass in importance the political relations among people, swallowing up the ancient polis as they swallowed up the oikos."

Pocock describes not just two separated spheres, but the relations between them. The new notions of economics were rivaling, if not eclipsing, the seemingly permanent centrality of the political sphere (Wolin 1960). The new economic relations had succeeded in vanquishing the classical view of participatory politics and had replaced it with alienated politics (cf., Marx 1844/1964). Politics was no longer the relations among (equal) individuals, but was becoming the relations of authorities to subjects. This transformation complemented the relations in the economic realm of individuals (rulers) to objects (subjects). The new economics was crafting a political world in its own image.[13]

With these developments in mind, it is unsurprising that liberalism fostered both political and economic theories of property, and that for each, both a moral/civic and jurisprudential justification was offered. However, a new justification, thoroughly modern and capitalist, also emerged: instrumental utilitarianism.[14] This was the logic, practice, and justification for separating to the greatest degree individuals from objects, making "things" into "tools," or "means," in the service of some other goal. The means by which this goal might be attained were rationally chosen and pursued. Instrumental utilitarianism represents the victory of reason over passions, of the success of interests, goals, and opinions over desires (Hirschman 1977).

CONCLUSION: THE IMPLICATIONS

In this chapter I have made the state system and global capitalism subjects of inquiry. As an ontological matter, I argue that they are linked as structures because they share an organizing principle. Yet I move from structuralism to structuration when I discuss property (and property rights) as a constitutive principle that represents actors' understandings and depicts their behaviors in terms of patterned activities. This view combines actor-oriented and structure-oriented representations of human conduct. By looking at sovereignty as a form of property rights, I can tell a different history of the development of the state system, global capitalism, and the modern world.

By focusing upon property as a constitutive principle and property rights as a set of social relations, one can discern—by some views—identifiable political and economic realms. Yet one can also discern the form of their unity. A focus on property rights also illuminates and expands the notion of sovereignty and the groundings of the international system and the modern world.

Political theorists tell us of the ideas that motivate particular forms of rule. Policy analysts tell us of the exercise of rule and the consequent rules. Foreign policy specialists tell us that competition among states differs from political competition within states and that the former requires vigilance; the latter, moderation. Foreign policy represents defense of the form of rule (*politiea*, governance, statecraft) by defense of the institutions (*polis*, the state). The rules themselves are not typically at issue, nor are the purposive reasons that the association or institution of the state exists. Again we get tautology or liberal hindsight: the state exists to provide security and to engage other states competitively. IPE scholars broaden our sense of how states compete and over what they compete. Where do we learn of motives, of purposes, of purposive association? Where do we learn of the apparatus of rule, of its construction, generation, and crafting? How do we learn of global systems? Where and how can distinctively IR theory contribute? Can it? Does it exist? Should it?

By turning to critical theory, and by modifying structuration theory with the introduction of constitutive principles, I intend to illustrate an alternative perspective. By this view, sovereignty is not the defining, constitutive element of the international system, much less the global system. Sovereignty is a claim to rule. Sovereignty is a set of property rights upon which the claim to rule rests. Specifically, the property rights pertain to real, landed, territorial property. The property rights demarcate the boundaries of state authority. The demarcation is territorial; the rights are property rights. They convey authority to rule, hence the right to create and constitute a polity.

This formulation reverses the Aristotelian argument that the *polis* preceeds the *politiea*, bringing the argument more nearly in line with Madisonian thought. Madison was concerned with building a state from scratch. So, too, were William of Orange and Louis XIV. Indeed, so, too, were Henry VIII and Ferdinand and Isabella, for that matter. By looking at property rights, we see the history in a different light and we read it in constitutive and generative terms, rather than teleological or tautological ones.

We see that the institution and corporate entity we call "the state"—the apparatus of rule and statecraft—could not exist without material and intangible support. Conceived organically or ahistorically, the state subsumes all other entities and identities. It is not a polis, but merely a form of rule, indeed a stark apparatus of rule understood bluntly as the chain of command. An ahistorical, liberally—and modernly—bounded reading promotes such conclusions. Yet, if state-*building* becomes a historical issue, we can see that it was not merely a policy choice. It was not a national or social undertaking similar to that of building the pyramids.

State-building was a response to systemic conditions—such as internecine religious conflict, widespread disease and poverty, and frequent famine and hunger that induced centralized authority, formal social institutions, wider spheres of interaction, economies of scale and markets, and the reduction of decisionmaking to expediency and efficiency rather than principle. It is less a matter of the development of states (a state-centered myth) than a matter of the development of a state system. To this extent, state-system building and market-making are in many ways indistinguishable. When we look not at the actors but at the relationships the actors found themselves in and conducted, we sense the motives differently.

In short, the state and market production, trade, and investment became a single, unified, coherent global system. As a coherent social unity, they comprise the modern world. States differ and market exchange knows many forms, yet the state system and global capitalism comprise a single social system. It evolved and developed as a whole, and it continues to do so. Once liberalism displaced republicanism, institutionalized the jurisprudential reckoning of property rights, introduced the vocabulary of rights, markets, and national interest, and absorbed instrumentally utilitarian decisionmaking, we had the modern world. These conceptual groundings or givens—ontologically reckoned and socialized in such notably common terms as "that's the way the world is"—are perhaps the most significant exports of the liberal West. This vision rests on an elaborate constellation of conceptual understandings, many of them implicitly or explicitly concerning property rights. Seen systemically, now globally, the implications for world poverty, repression, and pollution, to name but a few of the problems, are profound.

NOTES

This chapter is a revised version of a paper delivered at the International Studies Association annual meeting in Washington, D.C., March 1990.

1. Nye's *Bound to Lead* (1990) is an excellent example. Borrowing from Gilpin (1981), Nye specifically notes his interest in "war and change," discussing it as an international political topic, which he understands in terms of the balance of power. The competitive state system or the global order become issues only to the extent that changes in the distribution of power *within* the system (synchronic change) occur.

2. Nye (1990) himself makes the point. Looking at the theoretical mainstream, among those concerned with synchronic change *within* the global system, Nye derisively criticizes IR theorists—especially hegemonic stability theorists and neo-Marxians—for "superficially linking" and failing "to spell out causal connections" among the realms of politics (including the military) and economics.

3. Horkheimer offers a similar, albeit more loaded, characterization of critical theory:

By criticism, we mean that intellectual, and eventually practical effort which is not satisfied to accept the prevailing ideas, actions, and social conditions unthinkingly and from mere habit; effort which aims to coordinate the individual sides of social life with each other and with the general ideas and aims of the epoch, to deduce them genetically, to distinguish the appearance from the essence, to examine the foundations to things, in short really to know them (Horkheimer 1972: 270, in Bernstein 1978: 180).

4. We often evaluate the so-called success or scope of these dominations by how extensively they depict, constitute, reproduce, and perpetuate wholly new sets of social relations. Dominant worldviews establish or affect the full range of social relations. Such are "totalizing" worldviews. Liberalism is an example; Christianity used to be. The views of specific political parties are not.

5. The word *principle* is derived from the Latin *principium*, meaning *beginning*, which itself is from *princip-* or *princep-*, both meaning *first part*. Thus, the word *principle* conveys the sense of origins and beginnings and basic elements, or "first parts." Similarly, the word *prime* is a feminine form of the *prin-* root. All of the following words share the same root: principle, prince, principal, prime, primary, prima donna, primal, primate, primitive, primo, primogeniture, and primus (inter pares).

6. Undoubtedly, the dating of these events will not be lost on able readers. For many scholars, the midfifteenth century marks the early transition toward modernity and the modern world. Most notably, scholars mark early signals of the appearance of proto-states and proto-capitalism, often pegging these transformations to the burgeoning Age of Exploration. The Portuguese attack upon the island of Ceuta in 1415 sets an early threshold. By 1480, both England and France were trying to match the successes of Portugal and Spain. The sixteenth century was one of exploration, colonization, and mercantilism. Spain was the troubled champion. Yet by the midseventeenth century, Spanish domination had seriously waned in the face of the unique competition provided by the Dutch, English, and French. If 1648 arbitrarily marks the modern era by marking the institutionalization of a European state system, it also marks a transition toward the differentiated unity of a system of competitive states and global capitalist finance, production, and trade as policymakers acknowledged the virtues of transferring property rights to mobile property—by then acknowledged as a unique form of property—to relative "specialists" in joint stock companies.

7. Wilson (1977:131–132) argues that, in the case of Britain, "[given] the relative backwardness of the British economy and the serious problems that stood in the way of efficient tax collection, government tax revenue was plainly never going to expand sufficiently to cover more than a part of its expenditure." See also Scott (1912/1968, vols. I and III passim); Hannay (1926: 12); Heckscher (1934); Schumpeter (1954); Howat (1974 passim); Kenyon (1978 passim); and Ekelund and Tollison (1981).

8. Clough (1959:153) makes clear the attraction for merchants:

> In brief, in return for a trade monopoly, such companies [were] given the task of performing all the acts of government in those regions under its jurisdiction . . . the right to exercise in this region all the privileges, prerogatives, and powers usually held by sovereign states—to seize and defend territories within its sphere of action, to make peace, to levy taxes, to administer justice, and to make local laws.

9. For example, the British government ran a consistent deficit from 1688–1815 (Wilson 1977: 132, especially Table 5.21). Yet, by about 1680 some joint-stock company directors were forming small banks to loan money to other joint-stock ventures. The East India Company could borrow at 3 percent interest; whereas the Crown often had to pay upwards of 10 percent. By 1694, the Crown encouraged the financiers to establish a national bank—the Bank of England. The Crown used the national bank to handle national financial affairs, to finance infrastructural development, to wage war, and to establish the institutional setting of the modern state.

10. Marx (1844/1964:103) is merely more specific when he remarks that "private property rests altogether on partitioning."

11. It is perhaps ironic that one of the motivations for "economic" activity in this period was that of acquiring (sufficient, necessary) property to entertain the possibility of enjoying the "good life." Unfortunately, the classical notion of the virtuous good life was disintegrating.

12. In this regard, the Cromwellian interregnum merely mirrored the sociopolitical uncertainty following the collapse of the Roman Empire. Filmer, Hobbes, Harrington, and Locke, among others, responded to the circumstances of their times much as Aquinas had in his: "[S]ince authority has disintegrated, and God had withheld His word as to where it was now lodged, the individual must rediscover in the depths of his own being the means of reconstituting and obeying it" (Pocock 1985: 55). The consequence in each case was a focus upon political authority and the subsequent ruler-ruled relationship. Property always played a key role and contributed to social rules and forms of rule.

13. Even so, the notion that politics involved individuals at all was itself disappearing. Over time, authority came to be vested less in an individual than in "the crown" and ultimately in "the state." These are no longer individuals; they are things, although Louis XIV's exclamation *"l'etat c'est moi"* blurs the distinction. Individual subjects too became faceless and uniform since they had lost political personality. They became a group, "the masses," "the rabble." They, too, became things and their participation in politics became a source of fear. Ryan (1987: 39) writes: "Not only Constant, but Mill and de Tocqueville held that negative liberty was threatened by mass society. . . . They were all the more fearful because the threat to liberty that they feared came from the whole mass of the citizens."

14. Although Reeve (1986) and Ryan (1987) write with different purposes and from different perspectives, one can read into their discussions a similar division of the material. Pocock (1985) distinguishes the moral/civic tradition from the jurisprudential in the classical and transition eras, but does not further divide them.

3

Hobbes, Smith, and the Problem of Mixed Ontologies in Neorealist IPE

Naeem Inayatullah & Mark Rupert

Neorealism, the predominant theoretical tradition in the field of international political economy (IPE), has in recent years become a kind of intellectual lightning rod: it has drawn criticism on analytical and political grounds; it has been deconstructed; it has been the object of subtle critiques and caustic polemics. We believe this flurry of critical reflection has, on the whole, been healthy, inasmuch as it has helped to demarcate the implicit commitments and the limitations—both theoretical and political—of orthodox IR/IPE.[1] However, we believe that the activity of critique necessarily entails a positive aspect as well as a negative; that critique should illuminate not just the self-limiting boundaries of past practices, but also the possibilities for the future that are latent in those historical practices. Thus, our purpose here is not just to add two more voices to the critical cacophony of IR/IPE, but to explore what we believe is a novel interpretation of the sources of confusion in neorealist theory, and to revive a discussion of the tensions and possibilities of political economy that animate classical texts such as those of Hobbes and Smith, but which has been submerged in the neorealist appropriation of these texts.

Neorealism is plagued by explanatory inconsistencies that reflect theoretical contradictions at the most fundamental level. We will trace these self-contradictions in the explanatory accounts of one of the most influential neorealist scholars, and locate the sources of these in the antinomy of nature and society that neorealist theoretical arguments have (re)produced through a one-sided reading of the legacy of Hobbes and Smith. These classical texts manifested an unresolved tension between nature and society, "politics" and "economy," thus constituting political economy as a field of dialogue and argumentation. Neorealists have failed to recognize the tensions and possibilities that lie at the heart of political economy, and with which the great texts were centrally concerned. Rather, they have presupposed an untenable dichotomy between society and nature, and transformed each side of this relation into an abstract, self-contained whole that is implicitly taken as *the* fundamental reality—a one-sided ontology into which its complement is subsumed and in terms of which it is then explained. In the process of constructing explanatory accounts on the foundation of such a dichotomized ontological position, they have alternatively privileged one side or the other of the nature/society relation, compounding these twin ontological commitments to form a self-contradictory theoretical argument.

We argue that it is this semiconscious vacillation between natural and social ontologies that produces the fundamental explanatory inconsistencies evident in neorealist accounts of contemporary political economy. Further, we contend that such contradictions will remain an intractable problem for IPE theory unless and until the dichotomization of nature and society is abandoned in favor of a more dialectical view.

In hopes of contributing toward such a movement, we attempt to reclaim the ambiguous legacies of Hobbes and Smith. Through an analysis of their classic works, we demonstrate that each aspect of neorealism's dual ontology rests on a one-sided reading of these texts. We suggest that it is precisely the ambiguities, tensions, and contradictions in these texts that allow us to read them for contemporary purposes. Such a reading starts with a respect for the authors' struggle to make sense of the relation of society and nature, and a critical appreciation for the shortcomings of their attempts to resolve these tensions. Such a reclamation is the object of the first section of this paper. In the second section, we proceed to demonstrate the failure of neorealism to appreciate the ambiguities that underlie the arguments of Hobbes and Smith, and the one-sided reading of their legacies that is thereby produced. The self-contradictions and vacillations of neorealist argument, we contend, are a direct result of these interpretive shortcomings.

It is our hope that a critical reinterpretation of these texts, and of neorealist arguments drawing upon them, can help us to recover latent possibilities for political economy. We point toward the possibility of a political economy that views *nature* and *society* as two aspects or moments of a dialectical relation in process, a relation that is being continually reconstructed (and through which *being* is continually reconstructed), and in which theory and practice, interpretation and critique, are active participants.

NATURE AND SOCIETY IN THE
CLASSICAL PROGENITORS OF CONTEMPORARY IPE

Hobbes

On the basis of his arguments about life in a relatively anarchic "state of nature," Hobbes[2] is often taken to be one of the great founders of the realist tradition in IR/IPE. We wish to suggest that the appropriation of Hobbes as an archetypal realist (along with Thucydides and Machiavelli,[3] one might argue, similarly misunderstood) is a gross oversimplification, and that a critical appreciation of this helps us to understand fundamental analytical self-contradictions within neorealist theory. Our interpretation of Hobbes's *Leviathan* emphasizes the integral role of twin themes that might nowadays be identified as realist, on the one hand, and nonrealist, on the other. These themes, and Hobbes's vacillation between them, will be shown to be a necessary outcome of his dual and conflated ontological commitments.

The intriguing complexity of Hobbes's analysis revolves around a central dualism and his implicit attempts to overcome it. Once he posits the "state of nature" and "society" as opposites, apparently discrete and mutually exclusive, it becomes impossible to construct a bridge between these conceptual islands without incorporating in that bridge aspects of both nature and society. For our purposes, the interesting part of this conflation is that Hobbes will find it impossible to get men from the state of nature to society without introducing into the state of nature significant aspects of sociality.

As his theoretical point of departure, Hobbes constructs a powerful image of a state of nature wherein all human individuals are necessarily embroiled in a war of each against all. Humans, according to Hobbes, are driven by a natural and insatiable impulse toward the acquisition of power. Further, there exists among men in the state of nature a general equality of physical and mental capabilities, such that no individual is sufficiently stronger or smarter than the rest to live without fear of them. Under these conditions, men must view each other with unrelenting suspicion and hostility ("diffidence"), and none can look forward to a life that is anything but "solitary, poor, nasty, brutish and short." Consequently, they will feel themselves compelled to construct some social means by which to exit this horrific situation.

The question we may then pose to Hobbes is: given the conditions you describe, can men have the *ability* to construct any such social means to leave the state of nature? How could such men come together and agree to form civil society? If Hobbes is to negotiate this transition, he must attribute to men the ability to deliberate together and to cooperate in the setting up of procedures whereby a "plurality of voices" can agree to give up their natural rights as individuals and invest them in a man or assembly of men, thus creating the awful sovereign power that makes possible law, morality, industry, and all the virtues of civil society; that is, the "mortal god," Leviathan. These abilities, necessary to leave the state of nature, are grounded in the laws of nature, accessible to all men in common through their faculties of reason. It is this common ability of men to reason, to understand the laws of nature and, voluntarily and cooperatively, to limit their own natural freedom, that allows for the covenant that marks the transition to life in civil society.

Without such capabilities, it would not be possible for men to leave the state of nature. And yet, if men can exercise such abilities in the state of nature, it is difficult to see why they would be so powerfully driven to leave it. If men can engage in collective reasoning and hence can master their common acquisitive impulses while still in Hobbes's state of nature, then Leviathan—the product of this activity—cannot be a necessary condition for such activity to occur. It would seem, then, that the opposition between the asocial horrors of the state of nature, on the one hand, and the security and cooperation of civil society, on the other, have been overstated. The reasons for constructing Leviathan may not be as compelling as they would appear at first glance.

On closer examination, it seems that Hobbes presents us with a dilemma: if we accept the strongly asocial sense of the state of nature (anarchy = diffidence born of natural human impulses, the war of each against all), then the need to get out of the state of nature is clearly established, but the ability of men to work together toward the construction of civil society is undermined. If we accept the weaker, more social understanding of the state of nature (anarchy = decentralized society, governed by common reason and natural law) then the ability to get out of the state of nature can be established, but the compulsion to leave it is undermined. In sum, Hobbes's arguments establishing the need to leave the state of nature precludes the ability to do so, and his statements about men's ability to leave the state of nature vitiate the necessity for them to leave.

One way to avoid this problem is to reconceptualize the relation of society and nature from external opposition to internal relation.[4] For example, we can argue that there is—and must be—some sense of sociality implicitly present in Hobbes' state of nature and that, as a consequence, it is not unambiguously a state of war. In particular, the common ability of men in the state of nature to partake of reason and natural law embodies some latent sociality. This constitutes the latent social ontology in Hobbes's text, an ontology in which internal relations and dialectic are implicit. It may be that the aspects of sociality present in the state of nature are not strong enough for people to be as secure as they might like, but this is very different from postulating a social void that impels individuals inexorably toward Leviathan and civil society. Although less starkly defined, this second interpretation envisions people as having both the ability and the motivation to construct stronger forms of society (but perhaps not requiring the absolute ruler envisioned by Hobbes).

To summarize our discussion of Hobbes, then, we have argued that Hobbes's starting point is a "natural" ontology: humans are seen as presocial, autonomous individuals in pursuit of self-preservation and security in a state of nature devoid of legal authority. But Hobbes's destination in this text is in opposition to his starting point. His goal is to show that the needs of such individuals are best met in a certain form of society—civil society ruled by a Leviathan. The problem for Hobbes is this: given his starting point, how can he describe a process that moves his primordial individuals into such a society? In describing such a process, Hobbes admits to such social characteristics of individuals as the capacity for trust and cooperation—their ability to reason together. This implicit introduction of a social ontology vitiates the hostility and suspicion rampant in the state of nature, and thus allows for individuals cooperatively to take their leave of that condition. Thus, in the context of Hobbes's arguments, the natural ontology that serves as his explicit starting point is necessary to create the compulsion for individuals to leave the state of nature; while its implicit complement, the social ontology, is required in order to allow these solitary individuals to leave the state of nature together. The conflation of natural and social ontologies represents not so much the imposition of an extraneous element upon Hobbes's argument, but rather is necessary to its construction.

Smith

We have suggested above that Hobbes vacillates between his characterization of humans as naturally acquisitive of objects and of power over others and his suggestion that common faculties of reason and natural law allow men to combine in such a way as to leave the state of nature and form civil society under the rule of Leviathan. We suggested that the conflation of natural and social ontologies was integral to the construction of Hobbes's argument. We shall now argue that a similar conflation characterizes the arguments of Adam Smith in his *Wealth of Nations*.

Whereas Hobbes's primary focus was on the relationships among natural individuals in the formation of civil society, Smith focuses his analysis on the relationship of individuals to nature in the organization of production. In moving from Hobbes to Smith, we shift from an analysis centered on the problem of security to one centered on the problem of wealth. For Smith, the fundamental cause of wealth is division of labor, the origins of which are taken to be rooted in a certain "natural propensity" or impulse common to all men (Smith/ed. Cannan 1976: 17). However, in assuming that division of labor and exchange are natural activities for human beings, and that such activities generate wealth, Smith's argument makes it rather difficult to understand the existence of poverty.

Thus, no sooner has Smith grounded his analysis on a natural impulse than this assumption is softened and Smith suggests that there are *reasons* why (some) men begin to "truck, barter and exchange." The reason is that there is not enough wealth in the state of nature, prompting those with an intuitive understanding of economics to specialize—to form a division of labor and exchange in order to increase their aggregate wealth. With this move, Smith transforms his initial presupposition about the origins of wealth from a natural constant into a social variable.

It is important to note, however, that in Smith's world not everyone is able to form a division of labor. In particular, "savages" do not specialize, do not participate in a division of labor, and therefore have no wealth. "Savage nations," Smith suggests in implicit contrast with capitalist Europe, do not have enough wealth to care for their old, young, and infirm (Smith/ed. Cannan 1976: 2). Their needs exceed their production, but producing more requires skill of labor, skill that they do not possess. Such skill can be developed only once division of labor has been "thoroughly introduced."

The poverty of "savage nations," then, can be accounted for by their existence outside of a division of labor. Indeed, Smith does not think of these "savages" as living in nations at all—although he uses the word; rather, he thinks of them as self-subsistent individuals in a state of nature (see Inayatullah 1988: Chap. 3). He lumps these individuals together and calls them a "nation"—a nation of autonomous, self-subsistent individuals living in a state of nature. Such men are poor because in the state of nature their labor is undivided, in the sense that each individual undertakes all the productive activities that are necessary to sustain that person's life. Such undivided, unspecialized labor, Smith argues, is unproductive of wealth, and it is this that accounts for the apparent poverty of "savage nations."

Smith clearly implies that it is poverty that provides the motivation for such "savage" individuals to leave the state of nature and they do this by entering into relationships of specialization and exchange; that is, division of labor. Wealthier societies are assumed to have been thus motivated at some antecedent point when they themselves emerged from the impoverished life of natural savagery. We might then ask of Smith: How was this remarkable transition accomplished, given the natural conditions of poverty and savagery that you describe?

Here we encounter a fundamental inconsistency in Smith's account. As we saw was the case in Hobbes, so in Smith the motivation or need of individuals to escape the state of nature, and the imputed ability to do so socially, contradict one another. For Smith, the motivation to get out of the state of nature requires that man's natural condition should be one of poverty; yet to escape this condition through the creation of a division of labor requires, as we explain below, that individuals in the state of nature accumulate and exchange "surplus."

In order to explain the origins of the division of labor, Smith constructs a scenario that gives us a short account of how he thinks the "trucking disposition" leads to the division of labor (Smith/ed. Cannan 1976: 19). As in the overall plan of the work, this scenario involves a tribe of hunters or shepherds (Smith/ed. Cannan 1976: 2). However, contrary to the initial imagery, in Chapter 2, the hunters or shepherds are not poor.

In a tribe of hunters or shepherds a particular person makes bows and arrows, for example, with more readiness and dexterity than any other. He
frequently exchanges them for cattle or for venison with his companions;
and he finds at last that he can in this manner get more cattle and venison, than if he himself went to the field to catch them. From a regard to
his own interest, therefore, the making of bows and arrows grows to be
his chief business, and he becomes a sort of armourer (Smith/ed. Cannan
1976: 19).

Our bowmaker could make bows or he could go out and catch cattle or
venison. The question is which should he choose. Because he has a natural
talent for making bows, he chooses to concentrate on this task. He thinks
it more efficient to make the bows and exchange them with someone who
is more talented than he at chasing cows. It is important to notice that if he
were less calculating he could choose to catch the cattle himself and still
satisfy his basic needs. The choice concerns how to get the most from his
efforts in a situation where man's relationship with nature is characterized
by abundance. An environment of abundance and not poverty is characteristic of this "savage nation" of hunter-shepherds (or armorers).

As Smith continues his story, understanding of the advantages of specialization and exchange becomes widespread and as a result people
develop their talents and become, variously, house-carpenters, smiths, bra-
ziers, and tanners. All of them, it turns out, live in conditions of abundance: what they exchange is above and beyond what they need.

And thus the certainty of being able to exchange all that *surplus part of
the produce of their own labour, which is over and above his own consumption,* for such part of the produce of other men's labour as he may
have occasion for, encourages every man to apply himself to a particular
occupation, and to cultivate and bring to perfection whatever talent or genius he may possess for that particular species of business (Smith/ed.
Cannan 1976: 19. Our emphasis).

It is not, then, mere impulse or the "trucking disposition" that leads to the
division of labor. Our armorer needs to make some calculations first. He
needs to understand that his labor is better spent on producing bows than
on hunting. He also needs to understand that someone else will, in fact, be
hunting and not making bows. He has to anticipate that this other person
makes the same calculation with regard to his (the armorer's) talent of
bowmaking. Of course, he has to know that the hunter has labored enough
for there to be a surplus when they meet at the end of the day. And he has
to assume that the hunter needs a new bow and has to believe that coming
to agreement on the terms of exchange will not be an obstacle.

In Smith's telling, the origins of the division of labor require two conditions. First, the precondition for specialization and exchange is that there
must exist some surplus that can be exchanged. Second, the propensity to

truck, barter, and exchange is really based upon a sort of social reasoning: the ability to calculate how to get the most out of one's labor given that others are following similar reasoning.[5]

By giving "savages" this capacity for abstract economic reasoning and by putting them in a condition of abundance, Smith is able to provide an account of the origins of the division of labor. The capacity to reason is necessary because it allows men to make the types of calculations that motivate them to exchange. This is clear enough. But is the condition of abundance necessary, or is it merely an artifact of Smith's analysis?

Smith *must* start the account of the origins of division of labor from a condition of abundance and not poverty, for the following reasons. Prior to division of labor, if I require something I would simply make provision for that need myself. I am unlikely to think of making provision for that need by exchange, because this would require a set of additional conditions. One of these is that I must produce in quantities beyond what I immediately need, and then offer this additional quantity in exchange. However, producing a surplus and then seeking exchange seems a roundabout and risky procedure when I can satisfy my needs directly with my own labor.

Perhaps the following Smithian scenario will clarify this kind of dilemma. Assume that I exist prior to division of labor; that I am not yet a specialist; and that there are five activities—hunting, armory, carpentry, smithing, and tanning—that I must perform myself in order to satisfy my own needs. Suppose that I am able to perform all these activities: that I have the requisite skills and materials to feed, clothe, and shelter myself adequately. I am an independent, self-sufficient individual and yet, let us further assume, I live in a tribe of hunters and shepherds.[6] Now suppose I have a particular talent for making bows. Why would I work to produce more bows than I myself require in order to acquire extra meat through exchange? Why—if on the day that I had a hankering for more meat I could use my time and my bow to acquire more meat? Even though I may not be as good a hunter as someone else, I am good enough to have survived up to now. If I choose to become a specialist and use my time to produce bows, not only must I be sure about the exchange process actually working, but I must be willing to give up my independence of other producers and willfully make myself dependent upon (1) my particular skill (bow-making); and (2) the demand of others for my products (their acceptance of my bows in exchange).

For the emergence of a division of labor to be conceivable, then, we must assume that some level of wealth, and the skills requisite for its production, already exist, *prior* to the entry of these Smithian individuals into relations of exchange. Further, Smith's "savages" must all engage in the sort of instrumental calculation that promises greater wealth from further specialization and exchange. They must collectively understand the advantages of division of labor as Smith has described them. For specialization requires that each individual becomes dependent upon his fellows' acceptance of the products he has produced in exchange for other necessities (that his specialized activity has precluded him from providing for himself). In short, the state of nature cannot be understood in terms of the absence of wealth, skill, or social reasoning if Smith's account of the origins of division of labor is to be comprehensible.

Clearly, the opposition between the self-sufficient but impoverished and savage life of natural individuals and the wealth and specialized skill of "civilized" nations is overdrawn in Smith's account. The social relations that define and produce wealth must already exist in the state of nature if Smith's supposed transition to specialized production and exchange is to be possible. As with Hobbes, the method of abstract opposition between society and nature ultimately collapses in on itself. The positing of such opposites makes it impossible to bridge the gap between them; to mediate the originally posited opposition. Yet, such a mediation is what these theorists require their analysis to provide. Thus, the state of nature must be implicitly modified: instead of being the opposite or absence of society it comes to resemble society in significant ways. For Hobbes, the state of nature must come to contain security and cooperation; and for Smith it must contain surplus or wealth, and its inhabitants must be able to understand their situation in these terms. Therefore, the transition depicted by these theorists is not the absolute movement from one logical point (nature: anarchy for Hobbes; poverty for Smith) to its absolute opposite (society: order for Hobbes; wealth for Smith), but movement from a situation that already entails some social qualities to a situation in which these qualities are further developed and rendered more explicit.

These twin conflations of nature and society in Hobbes and Smith, we wish to suggest, are hardly accidental. Implicit and operative in the arguments of each author is an internal relation of nature and society, such that each side of the relation contains aspects of the other, and neither can be meaningfully abstracted from the relation in which nature and society are embedded. Such an internal relation, although explicitly denied in the analysis of each theorist, is actually integral to the process that each attempts to describe. In the next section of this chapter, we will analyze major works by one of the founders of the neorealist tradition of political economy and argue that similar analytical dilemmas arise in the course of these, more contemporary, accounts of political economy. The confusion of neorealism, we then suggest, is no more accidental than was that of Hobbes and Smith.

NATURE AND SOCIETY
IN NEOREALIST POLITICAL ECONOMY

In this section, we will argue that mainstream, neorealist IPE uncritically compounds the world views presupposed by a one-sidedly Smithian understanding of economics and a one-sidedly Hobbesian understanding of politics. Thus, mainstream IPE defines its universe of inquiry and constructs its most important theoretical statements in terms of mixed metaphors that derive from the tradition of liberal social theory.

On the one hand, neorealist scholars of IPE associate "politics" with the system of sovereign states, represented as a Hobbesian state of nature in which nation-states take on the appearance of presocial individuals, struggling for security in an anarchic world. In this naturalized Hobbesian universe, politics is understood in terms of the zero-sum interaction of individual states, competing over relative shares of resources that confer power and wealth. In such a world, the central analytical problem becomes the construction of a system of order among antagonistic individual states.

On the other hand, neorealists associate "economics" with the world market, understood in terms of a Smithian division of labor in which individual members of society can pursue their economic self-interest and, in so doing, benefit the community as a whole by increasing aggregate social wealth. In this one-sided appropriation of the Smithian worldview, the problem of social order apparently dissolves into a world of interdependence in which social interactions take on a more cooperative, positive-sum character. Individuals in such a world are understood in terms of the specialized roles that they play in the division of labor, and hence must depend upon each other for the provisioning of those needs that their own specialized production cannot satisfy, and for the social valorization (by purchase) of the products of those specialized productive activities. The primary analytical problem in such a world becomes the allocation of social resources in such a way as to maximize output and thereby maximize total social satisfaction and wealth.

In constructing his seminal neorealist account of IPE, Robert Gilpin has defined his approach in terms of an explicit dissent from both "liberal" and "Marxist" approaches, which he perceives as one-sided and as overemphasizing the operation of "economic" forces and downplaying "political" factors. Gilpin's explicit point of departure is an assertion of the reciprocal relationships that obtain between "politics"—understood as distributive struggle among naturalized, abstract individuals, competing over relative shares of the resources necessary for power—and "economics"—understood in terms of the production of aggregate social wealth. This model of reciprocity is graphically represented in the top row of Figure 3.1, below.

Gilpin distinguishes his own political analysis from the concerns of liberal economics insofar as the latter generally focuses upon absolute gains in aggregate social wealth. In contrast, Gilpin's political economy is centrally concerned with *relative* gains, for distributional inequalities are a potential source of (political) power over others. It is, then, in these terms that Gilpin understands politics and economics to be *reciprocally determining.*

> The argument of this study is that the relationship between economics and politics, at least in the modern world, is a reciprocal one. On the one hand, politics largely determines the framework of economic activity and channels it in directions intended to serve the interests of dominant groups; the exercise of power in all its forms is a major determinant of the nature of an economic system. On the other hand, the economic process itself tends to redistribute power and wealth; it transforms the power relationships among groups. This in turn leads to a transformation of the political system, thereby giving rise to a new structure of economic relationships. Thus, the dynamics of international relations in the modern world is largely a function of the reciprocal interaction between economics and politics (Gilpin 1975: 21–22; see also 1987: 8–24).

We now propose to analyze this allegedly reciprocal relation as it plays itself out in Gilpin's account of the construction and decline of systems of global political-economic order. We will demonstrate that Gilpin's simple model of reciprocality masks a more complex series of moves in which "politics" and "economics" take on fundamentally different meanings at different stages in the argument, and in which social and natural ontologies are repeatedly juxtaposed and confounded.

An explicit goal of Gilpin's argument for reciprocality is to maintain the importance and autonomy of the political sphere against the encroachments of alleged economic determinism such as that which he attributes to "Marxism."[7] In apparent contrast to such economistic formulations, Gilpin asserts that economic transactions can occur only within a political framework, based upon a systematic distribution of power and wealth among participants. At the international level, the expansion of world market relations must, then, entail some sort of political arrangement among individual states (Gilpin 1975: 33–43; 1977; and 1987: 82, 86–92). Thus, Gilpin formulates in terms of a naturalized Hobbesian worldview the central analytical puzzle of neorealist IPE: "In a world of conflicting nation-states, how does one explain the existence of an interdependent international economy?" (1975: 39).[8]

Chronically insecure, individual states in an anarchic environment may perceive their interests to be best served by increasing their own wealth and power at the expense of others and hence pursue predatory policies of economic nationalism that preclude the growth of cooperation and interdependence.[9] To overcome this problem, Gilpin argues, requires a political solution that economistic theories are unable to grasp (1975: 33–43; 1987: 22, 43–46, 47, 85).

According to this line of reasoning, an international system with a single economically and politically preponderant state is most likely to engender a division of labor. Such a "hegemonic" state has the capabilities to create the environment in which international relations can take on the appearance of a positive-sum game. Its economic dynamism invigorates the world market with innovative technologies, rapid accumulation of capital, and new "leading sectors" of production and standards of consumption. The hegemonic economy can "undercut the static mercantilist conception of wealth" and offer singular economic opportunities to states that choose to engage in economic liberalization (Gilpin 1977: 33; also 1975: 47–59; 1987: 80–111). Thus, the economic capabilities of a hegemonic state help to minimize the disruptive effects of mercantilistic distributive conflict, and can create positive incentives for economic cooperation.

More fundamental from the perspective of Gilpin's one-sided Hobbesian worldview, however, are incentives that encourage such predominant states to reshape the interstate system and *create the political environment of order* in which its economic advantages can be realized. Given the specialized productive capabilities, accumulated capital, and liberal ideology of a hegemonic state, its decisionmakers are likely to believe that an interdependent world economy will serve to enhance its power, wealth, and security. Hence, it may be expected to deploy its power resources to construct the political infrastructure for "specialization, multilateral free trade, and an international division of labor" (1977: 31, 34–39).

In sum, the centerpiece of Gilpin's theory is a model of the political construction of economic order by naturalized abstract individuals, i.e., sovereign states.[10] Given the presence of a preponderant hegemonic state, a set of environmental constraints and incentives are created in which it appears rational—in terms of an instrumental cost-benefit calculus, i.e., logical economism[11]—for such individuals to liberalize the economic relations between them. The fundamental insecurity of the anarchic interstate system may for a time be ameliorated under the influence of a "liberal hegemonic state," possessed of singular economic and political powers and understanding its interests and social role in ways radically different from those of ordinary states. This central thesis of Gilpin's argument is graphically represented as Stage Two of Figure 3.1.

Here, politics appears to shape the social framework for the production and distribution of wealth and, through the creation of a liberalized international economic order, to facilitate the expansion of the total social product. Wealth is seen as socially expandable, and hence economics becomes an object of politics. Gilpin's argument suggests that the political action that allows escape from the relatively anarchic and impoverished state of nature is made possible by a hegemonic distribution of power in the international system. It is this distribution of power that generates the capabilities and the incentives required for the construction of a global liberal order. However, Gilpin's account then confronts the following fundamental problem: How can we understand the apparently extraordinary order-creating capabilities and interests of the hegemonic state, given the

initial presupposition of states as abstract individuals in a condition of natural anarchy?

According to Gilpin's account, the construction of global systems of
order depends primarily upon the power, interests, and ideological vision
of a single international actor, capable of inspiring awe in other states,
transforming the matrix of constraints and incentives they face, and inducing their compliance to a new, specifically liberal, set of rules for international relations. Yet, there is nothing in neorealism's simplified
Hobbesian universe that would enable us to envision an extraordinary individual of the kind required for a hegemonic stability solution—qualitatively distinct from its fellows in both its means and its ends. Hobbes understands the rough equivalence of asocial individuals to be an important
defining condition of the state of nature inasmuch as it gives rise to the
"diffidence" from which proceeds the "war of every one against every
one"; and Waltz (1979) is at pains to argue that an anarchic international
system implies the formal equality and functional similarity of individual
states inasmuch as all sovereign states must seek to secure their own self-
preservation by whatever means they may deem necessary. In light of this
definition of the neorealist universe of inquiry as one of generalized insecurity premised upon essential equivalence among individual actors, how
is it that an actor so unique as a hegemonic state can arise?

Up to this point in his argument, Gilpin has been primarily concerned
with the political preconditions of market relations; but at this juncture he
needs to explain the origins of political hegemony in an anarchic world of
essentially similar individuals. In order to do so, he shifts his analytical
ground: international economic interdependence and the operations of
world markets—until now taken as a problematic outcome requiring explanation in terms of political prerequisites—become key causal factors in
his account of global political order.

Gilpin understands the emergence of "liberal hegemonic states" as a
consequence of the uneven operation of world market forces, which (tem-
porarily) concentrate within the boundaries of a single state new technologies, new "leading sectors" of industry, and new sources of wealth and
power that transform it into the "core" of the world economy and make
possible its extraordinary role in the international system (1975: 47–59,
67–70; 1987: 92–117). Technologically dominant relative to other states
(i.e., "peripheries"), Gilpin's core has both the means and the incentives to
liberalize its international economic relations. In world market trade, its
advantages allow it to reap "monopoly rents" and to accumulate vast profits. These profits may then be invested overseas in ways that intensify economic complementarities between core and periphery. Thus world-market
forces generate the protohegemonic state by transforming it into a core of
the world economy, hierarchically related to less dynamic and therefore
more dependent peripheries.

So it is in terms of this core/periphery relation, in Gilpin's account, that we are to understand the qualitatively distinct role of the "liberal hegemonic state" in the world economy, and the political implications of this role. "The core is principally defined by its performance of certain functions in the international economy" (1975: 48; cf., 1987: 93–97). It organizes the world's monetary system. It manages international trade and encourages commercial liberalization. And the core provides investment capital and an impetus to economic growth for the system as a whole. "In short, the core sets and enforces the rules of economic exchange and development. These rules are accepted by the periphery in part owing to the power of the core and in part because the system generates growth for both core and periphery" (Gilpin, 1975: 48). This aspect of Gilpin's argument, in which the hegemonic capabilities for the construction of order are themselves generated, is represented in Figure 3.1 as Stage One. At this stage of the argument, it would appear that hegemonic power results from the natural operation of a market economy. Ultimately, it is the uneven development of technological advantage in the world economy that accounts for the differentiation of states into core and periphery and that creates the possibility of hegemonic order in an anarchic interstate system. This naturalization of economic forces also serves to explain the impermanence of hegemonic order in the international system, and hence allows Gilpin to explain the persistence of anarchic politics among independent states as the fundamental reality of IR/IPE. For the natural processes of the market economy operate unevenly. While at one time they may serve to concentrate wealth and potential power resources in a particular territorial area or state, at another they will operate to diffuse this advantage, redistributing wealth (and hence power) more evenly across the interstate system. The decline of hegemonic systems of order is then explained in terms of the same naturalized economic forces that generated hegemonic power in the first place. This is illustrated in Stage Three of Figure 3.1.

Having examined each stage in Gilpin's account, let us now bring all three stages of his model together in order to assess the extent to which his theory does indeed portray a reciprocal relationship between politics and economics. The complete three-stage model is illustrated in Figure 3.1. The top line of Figure 3.1 represents the chain of causal claims made by Gilpin; i.e., causal relations in which politics and economics alternatively determine one another. Beneath this apparent causal chain, however, we have represented the alternating ontological commitments that are implicit in Gilpin's causal arguments. Our claim here is that Gilpin's chain of argument is rent by the most fundamental kind of contradiction and, as a consequence of this basic disjuncture, his claim to have made a case for reciprocal determination of politics and economics breaks down. Far from establishing the autonomy of politics, we suggest, Gilpin's theory rests on a dual economism.

Figure 3.1
Gilpin's Three-Stage Model of Hegemonic Order

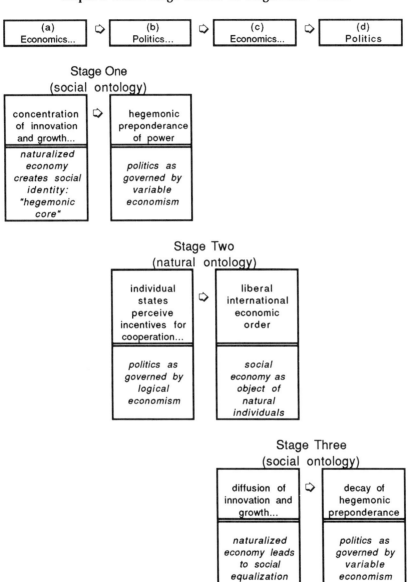

The apparent reciprocity between politics and economics rests upon a confounding of a natural and a social ontology that are fundamentally inconsistent, and in which the terms *politics* and *economics* assume very different meanings depending upon the direction of causality with which Gilpin is concerned. When the direction of causality is reversed, the ontology underlying the argument is implicitly shifted and the terms that Gilpin wishes to relate take on entirely different meanings: the *economics* that determines politics is not the same as the *economics* that is determined by politics, and vice versa. *Politics* is understood alternatively as a sphere of collective activity by naturalized abstract individuals who construct the economy to serve their individual purposes (i.e., politics governed by logical economism); or as being largely determined by the operation of naturalized, exogenous economic forces upon social individuals (politics governed by variable economism).

Gilpin's theoretical point of departure is the characteristic neorealist appropriation of the Hobbesian state of nature, and the problem of explaining cooperation under conditions of anarchy. Accordingly, in the center (Stage Two) of the model represented in Figure 3.1, *politics* is defined in terms of competition and conflict among self-subsistent *natural individuals* (i.e., sovereign states), and *economy* is understood as a *social object*, framed or constructed by the collective action of such abstract individuals, undertaken to serve their particular interests (as yet undefined). In this phase of the argument, politics is understood as being governed by individualistic calculations of costs and benefits, a formal reasoning that (following Ashley) we will refer to as logical economism. It is precisely this instrumental reasoning that determines whether collective action among abstract individuals will constitute a social economy. Logical economism then serves as the link between politics and economics at this stage of the argument, and apparently enables us to understand the economy as having been politically constructed.

However, it then becomes necessary to explain *how* economic relations are constructed by these abstract individuals, and hence to impute to them purposes and capacities for social action. At this point the chain of argument (represented by Stage One in Figure 3.1), the status of *economy* is implicitly changed: it becomes a natural context that determines the politically relevant attributes of these—no longer abstract but now social—individuals. The natural necessity of production and consumption is presumed to generate a sphere of norms, rules, and conventional practices that facilitate communication and cooperative endeavor (e.g., exchange, division of labor) among individuals who no longer appear as abstract monads, but as differentiated parts of the natural economy (i.e., core/periphery). With this turn in the argument, the political identities, motivations, and capabilities of individual actors are explained in terms of their situation within an economy that is no longer an object of political action, a social

product, but rather now itself appears naturalized. Further, the same economic forces that account for the generation of a "liberal hegemonic state"
in Stage One of Gilpin's model also account for its degeneration in Stage
Three. Like extreme weather, the uncontrollable natural forces of the economy blow over and reshape human societies, as well as the identities and
capacities of their inhabitants. Hence, the individual political actors that
had been ontologically primary in the definition of the central analytical
problem (Stage Two) are now seen to be generated by the natural economy, which thus assumes the status of the most fundamental theoretical
entity. In stages one and three, variable economism constitutes the link between "economics" and "politics."

    We wish to emphasize that the *politics* and *economics* that are related
via variable economism (in stages one and three) are not the same entities
as those that are related via logical economism (in Stage Two). This is
demonstrated by the two distinct senses of politics that appear at point (b)
in the model, and the two senses of *economics* at point (c). Although the
stages are meant to interlink so as to constitute a coherent chain of argument explaining the rise and decline of hegemonic systems of order in
terms of the reciprocal interaction of politics and economics, the inconsistent ontological commitments implicit in the different stages of the argument preclude the desired linkages between stages one and three on the
one hand, and the central problem of Stage Two on the other. The different stages of the model entail visions of social reality that are diametrically
opposed. Ultimately, then, Gilpin's claim of reciprocality breaks down,
due to ontological disjunctures that lead, quite literally, to the disintegration of his model.[12]

CONCLUSION: FROM ABSTRACT
OPPOSITION TO DIALECTICAL PROCESS

    We have tried to demonstrate that there is a striking homology be-
tween Gilpin's theories and those of Hobbes and Smith. As with Hobbes
and Smith, we find in Gilpin's neorealism an analytic point of departure
that is inconsistent with the desired destination, and that eventuates in a
confounded ontological position. All three theorists begin with the abstraction of their central units of analysis from any social/historical context
in which they might be embedded. Egoistic individuals (whether in the
form of liberal individuals or sovereign states) are thus naturalized, and
constitute a common presupposition of these theories. An opposition is
then posited between these natural individuals and some social condition
(civil society, division of labor, or liberal international economic order).
The central analytical problem thus framed is how to understand the formation of such social relations in terms of the actions and motivations of

the primitive individuals. In all three theories, some cost-benefit calculation is presumed in which the individuals compare their natural condition
with some form of social existence, and choose the latter on the basis of its
greater utility (in terms of security, wealth, or both). It is in the process of
collectively making this comparison that social relations are transposed
into the putatively natural condition, and the initially posited separation
collapses.

Gilpin is hardly the only neorealist to uncritically reproduce the confounded ontologies of Hobbes and Smith. An ontological framework of
abstract individualism is a defining feature of the neorealist tradition of
scholarship, and when that framework is invoked as a way to understand
social relations (e.g., those of the world economy), the naturalized individuals that constituted the initial presupposition must be imputed, however surreptitiously, with some form of social identity and some capacity
for social action. In other words, having initially created the apparent
problem of understanding social cooperation among abstract individuals,
the problem is "resolved" by implicitly attributing to those individuals
characteristics and capacities for action that they could only have by virtue
of their participation in social relations. Natural and social ontologies are
thus conflated.

Contradictory ontological commitments of just this kind are, we contend, a danger that inheres in the fundamental project of neorealist IPE.[13]
Insofar as neorealists define their project in a form homologous with that
of the classical liberals, they incorporate into their IPE the same basic
problem with which the liberals grappled unsuccessfully. They tend to do
so, however, without an explicit recognition of the fundamental problems
involved, and hence reproduce the liberal conundrum of nature and society, explicitly in opposition while implicitly conflated. Our purpose here
has been to sketch out the outlines of that conundrum, and to trace the
manner of its incorporation into one of the most influential neorealist theories of IPE.

One major implication of this line of argument, then, is that if IPE is
to avoid placing itself in a confounded ontological position, it must come
to grips with its intellectual heritage. This implies a critical rereading of
those works that are so often simply taken for granted as part of the historical backdrop of contemporary scholarship. The meaning of classical
texts such as those of Hobbes and Smith (as well as Thucydides, Machiavelli, and so on) is neither self-evident nor settled, and should be a matter of active debate among scholars of IPE. There is much to be learned
from such a rereading, we contend, not simply about the texts and their
times but also about ourselves and our own situation in contemporary
controversies.

Starting explicitly with asocial assumptions, these texts—and much
contemporary social theory—need the implicit introduction of a social

ontology if the analysis is seemingly to cohere. If this is the case, perhaps we should be unhappy with approaches that assume asocial individuals, problematize sociality, and then smuggle in social relations to do the actual work of the analysis. One alternative to assuming anarchy (opposition) and problematizing cooperation, sociality, and order, would be to do the opposite: assume that humans are inherently altruistic beings and problematize conflict and disorder. For our purposes, such an inversion is primarily rhetorical; we recognize that while the polarities are reversed, the method remains the same. A better method might be one in which both cooperation and conflict are problematized within a historical process. Such a method, we believe, is implicit in the classical texts of Hobbes and Smith, in that it is present in the form of an unrealized, latent possibility.

More specifically, we suggest, on the basis of our own reinterpretation of this heritage, that the opposition of nature and society that underlies the basic analytical framework of abstract individualism should be recognized as a self-limiting analytical device, embodying conservative political implications and generating incoherent explanatory accounts. Instead of an uncritical and one-sided appropriation of the legacies of Hobbes and Smith, we suggest a reading that conceives nature and society as isolated monads, to be brought into an external relation in which one is subordinated to the other; we envision a dialectical political economy in the tradition of Hegel and Marx; a political economy in which nature and society are conceived as two aspects or moments of an internal relation in process.

From a Marxian perspective, the historically developing *internal relation* of human social beings and nature is central to an understanding of political economy. Instead of conceiving nature and society as polar opposites, discrete and mutually exclusive entities, Marx understood them as two aspects of a single process. For Marx, nature and society are mediated through the practice of "objectification"; i.e., the creation of a world of objects through socially productive activity in which human beings, their social lives, and their natural environment are together transformed (cf., for example, Marx and Engels 1970, 48–52, 59–64; Marx 1975: 322–334, 325, 349–350, 355–358, 389–391; Marx 1977: 133–134, 173). Stressing the essential connection between human social life and a natural environment that is apparently separate from and external to human beings, Marx refers to nature as "man's inorganic body" (1975: 328).

For Marx, then, human beings are naturally social, and socially natural, insofar as social interaction with nature (in the form of socially organized productive activity; i.e., objectification) is a necessary condition for the reproduction of all human life. However, the way in which this activity is organized and carried out cannot be determined a priori. The social conditions of productive activity are variable—continually being reproduced or transformed in the productive practices of human beings—and thus can be understood only historically. The organization of productive activity is historically specific, enmeshed in particular forms of social life and the kinds of practices that they support.

It is on this basis that Marx criticizes the representation of social relations that are specific to capitalism as if they were immediately natural and universal, rather than the product of the active mediation of human social relations and nature through productive activity—socially produced and historically mutable. In the representation of (capitalist) social reality as if it were natural and universal, Marx sees a self-limiting form of human understanding in which human social products are abstracted from the process of their creation, and thus are attributed an autonomy and an effective power over human social life that they have by no intrinsic nature. As their products apparently take on a life of their own, human beings are increasingly "subjected to the violence of things" (Marx and Engels 1970: 84). Human social life is then governed by the objects it has created and the mystified forms in which it understands those objects. Social life takes on the appearance of the objective, as human beings are subordinated to the objects they have produced and in that sense are themselves objectified. Marx refers to this distorted, inverse relation of objectification in terms of "alienation" or "fetishism."[14]

From a Marxian perspective, then, the naturalized abstract individualism of the liberals—uncritically appropriated by neorealism—represents a fetishized social self-understanding that is scientifically inadequate and historically conservative. A Marxian dialectical alternative would strive for a critical understanding of the historically specific organization of productive activity (i.e., the particular form in which the internal relation of society and nature is reproduced) in order to make explicit the possibilities for change that are latent in the social relations and practices of the present. Such a Marxian dialectical research program for IPE—critical of the class-based organization of production under capitalism, as well as the modern "political" state, premised upon capitalism's abstraction of politics from the real material life of the community—is evident in the pioneering works of Robert Cox, and those who follow in his tracks (cf., for example, Cox, 1981, 1983, 1987; Gill 1986a; 1986b; Rupert 1990, 1993). It is our contention here that such a research program is progressive (in a theoretical and practical sense) over the neorealist program.

Another possible direction for a dialectical research program in IPE— one with a somewhat lesser emphasis on the importance of production —makes the search for self-identity through contact with the "other" the central motivation of individual humans and societies. In such a framework, the search for contact, communication, and meaning, and not nature-given characteristics of individuals or societies, assumes central importance. These meanings concern the projects of individuals and societies who attempt to create, discover, and realize their identity by various processes of social interaction with others. Such projects may include IR/IPE's familiar obsession with the pursuit of power and wealth, but also religious conversions, gift giving and other ceremonial reciprocity, staging of spectacles, debate, and the pursuit of knowledge.

In recent work, Inayatullah (especially 1991b) attempts to sketch some of the assumptions of such an approach. The sketch includes the following propositions:

1. Each culture assumes that it lives within a greater whole, to which we may refer as "the universe."
2. All cultures try to make sense of the universe and "their" place and role in it.
3. Each culture recognizes, perhaps in a subconscious or intuitive way, that it cannot do this alone and needs the help of those it identifies as "others." This implicit need for the other constitutes each culture's recognition of the particularity of its own vision—a particularity it needs to transcend. The need to sort out what is idiosyncratic from what is universal moves each culture to exploration, dialogue, and learning.
4. In contrast to the implicit need to reach out, there is an explicit opposing force. Each culture is committed to what it considers to be the universal elements of its own vision. It is unlikely to give up these elements. Further, to the degree that a culture conflates specific elements with the whole of its vision it is unlikely to part with even part of its vision. If this is accurate, it may reveal the source of what seems like intransigence; it tells us why cultures are often times unwilling to compare and learn when faced with the understanding of the "other." The need to maintain its own understanding of the universal in the face of other claims to universality moves each culture to egotism, monologue, and proselytizing.
5. Each project of understanding the universe—both as a whole and any part of it—has been historically coconstructed by various cultures. Thus, there is no essence specific to a culture.

When a culture looks at itself, it finds a tension between the particular and universal viewpoints. That is, there is a voice that suggests that "we are only part of the whole." Another voice suggests that "we *are* the whole." In this latter view, one's own culture is mostly taken for granted as universal; and it vies for universality in actual historical space. There is, then, a latent desire in all cultures for physical and temporal extension, a desire that may be actualized to one degree or another. This need not be seen only in negative terms; for example, as imperialism. It may be seen as the need of a particular culture to express and realize its universality. In other words, it may be seen as a part of making sense of the world.

Cultures make sense in a double manner: (1) Each culture tries to incorporate all new and anomalous information into its own (dynamic) formulation and meaning. It therefore tries to make sense of the world by trying to understand it. This, however, is not enough. (2) The world must also be changed so that it corresponds/coheres to that understanding. Otherwise, that culture will not fit into the world; it will become marginalized, outdated, and may well die. A necessary element of making sense, then, is to remake the world so that a particular culture is expressed, realized, and empowered in it.

When a culture looks at another (different) culture, this look also contains the tension between particularity and universality. One voice suggests that the other culture is an important source of knowledge. This outside knowledge is especially important to sort out the contradictions in "self"-perception. Another voice suggests that the outside culture is an idiosyncratic, exotic, nonnormal entity. This same voice suggests that the other culture's need to express its particularity as universal—its need to extend itself and remake the world in order to fit in that world—is a form of imperialism that it may need to check if the world is to make sense.

In sum, all cultures vie for universality but are, in fact, particulars—but particulars that may contain some element of the universal; that is, each culture may see and contribute some important aspect of a future good society. Certainly, they project themselves as constructing or contributing to such a future. These alternative projects or ideas agree in some ways and compete in others. The specific way, and ways, in which cultural projects interact—including the intended and unintended consequences of their interaction—constitutes the history of world political economy. The reasons why parts of some projects find their way onto the world stage while others do not constitutes the theory of world political economy.

In such approaches to IPE, nature and society are not merely opposites. This is because various understandings of "nature" (as well as "society") are themselves social constructions. What is "natural" and what is "social" are valuations that constitute specific understandings of the universe; they reveal the conceptions of a particular culture. This implies that a broad understanding of the antinomies of IR/IPE necessitates placing the neorealist orthodoxy within the ascendance of the culture of which it is a part. Even this seemingly (post)modern insight is there for our reading in a classical text. As Rousseau claims,

> The philosophers who have examined the foundations of society have all felt the necessity of return to the state of nature, but none of them has reached it. . . . All of them speaking continually of need, avarice, oppression, desires, and pride, have transferred to the state of nature the ideas they acquired in society. They spoke of savage man, and it was civil man they depicted (1983 edition: 118).

What is depicted as the "natural state" is often little more than the projection (onto other cultures) of a familiar social ill.

There are (at least) two major strands of contemporary political economy theory that resemble the philosophers described by Rousseau. At the core of their reasoning they continue to treat nature as an entirely asocial space. These two strands are neoclassical economics and neorealist IPE theory—the lineal descendants, respectively, of Smith and Hobbes. In Gilpin's work, these basic antinomies are compounded: an asocial theory of international politics is combined with an asocial theory of international economics. We see this as a double-barreled projection of a twice-alienated culture.

NOTES

1. Following Cox (1981), Ashley (1984), and Wendt (1987) we understand neorealism not in reference to specific theoretical arguments or the works of particular authors, but as a family of arguments sharing a common commitment to atomistic ontology and empiricist epistemology in the construction of IR/IPE accounts. Thus, we would categorize the following important works, among others, as belonging to the neorealist tradition of scholarship: Gilpin 1975, 1977, 1981, and 1987; Waltz 1979, and 1986; Keohane and Nye 1977; Keohane 1980, 1982, 1984, and 1986; and Krasner 1976 and 1978.

2. The analyses of Hobbes and Smith below draw heavily on the arguments of Naeem Inayatullah, *Labor and Division of Labor: Conceptual Ambiguities in Political Economy*, doctoral dissertation, University of Denver, 1988.

3. See, for example, Gramsci's (1971: 125–143, 169–175, 247–253) discussions of Machiavelli, Cox's (1981 and 1983) explications of the implications of these for IR/IPE, and Garst's (1989) reclamation of Thucydides.

4. A concept of internal relations is central to dialectical methodologies. In brief, an internal relation is one in which the interrelated entities take their meaning from their relation, and are unintelligible outside of the context of that relation. Classic examples are master/slave, parent/child, and teacher/student relations. For discussions of the role of internal relations in Marxian analyses, cf., Ollman (1976: 12–40, 256–276); Gould (1978: 1–39, 184 n. 22); and Sayer (1987: 18–23). Another way to think about internal relations is in terms of the Hegelian notion of the "unity of opposites." See, e.g., Stace (1955) and Collingwood (1933).

5. Some of these conditions are noted by Smith when he tries to deduce the origins of money (Chapter 4, 26). But Smith does not present these requirements as possibilities when he attempts to deduce the origins of the division of labor.

6. Smith starts with a tribe of hunters and shepherds but does not say what makes them a tribe. He assumes that something binds them together, but it cannot be the functional differentiation of tasks because this would imply that division of labor has already occurred.

7. Gilpin's discussions of Marxism (1975: 26–33; 1987: 34–41) border on caricature. The rich and varied tradition of Marxian scholarship, of which the economic determinist tendency is hardly representative, is presented as if it were a monolithic doctrine that could be adequately summarized in terms of a few formulas. For Gilpin, as for so much contemporary scholarship, classical Marxism serves as a classical straw man.

8. The following comes as close to an explicit ontological commitment as one is likely to find in works of neorealist political economy: "In the modern epoch,

as the theory of hegemonic stability stresses, nation-states and the conflicts among them are the foremost manifestation of man's nature as a 'political animal.' Far from being mere creatures of economic and historical forces, states are independent actors in economic and political affairs" (Gilpin 1987: 80; cf. 85, 88). However, the apparent single-mindedness of this commitment is dissipated somewhat by the sentence that immediately follows it: "It should be equally obvious that the market and 'economic man' have achieved an independent reality." Gilpin concludes on the basis of this dual ontology that "The dynamics of the international political economy must be understood in terms of the interaction of state and market within their larger historical setting." Confounded as it may be, Gilpin's attempt to specify the fundamental commitments that underlie his theorizing seems to us commendable. Unfortunately, such reflection is not the norm in the tradition of neorealist scholarship. For example, in a footnote to a 1987, coauthored retrospective article, two leading researchers in the field sarcastically ridiculed the explicit concern of other scholars with such issues (Keohane and Nye 1987: 737).

9. In some earlier versions of the argument, this problem was represented in terms of the "free rider" problem of public goods theory, but more recent versions have responded to critics of this approach by softening their identification of hegemony with a public good. Compare: Kindleberger (1973, 1981); Conybeare (1984); Snidal (1985); Keohane (1984, 1986); Gilpin (1987). Other participants in this neorealist intramural debate have directed their attacks at the general correspondence of hegemonic stability arguments with historical evidence: cf., McKeown (1983); Stein (1984).

10. Positing an abstract equivalence among naturalized individuals, based upon characteristics imputed to all in common, is fundamental to the analytical method employed both by Hobbes and the neorealists, and a central aspect of the liberal tradition of social theory (Arblaster 1984). Steven Lukes describes as follows this approach to theorizing:

> According to this conception, individuals are pictured abstractly as given, with given interests, wants, purposes, needs, etc.; while society and the state are pictured as sets of actual or possible social arrangements which respond more or less adequately to those individuals' requirements. Social and political rules and institutions are, on this view, regarded collectively as an artifice, a modifiable instrument, a means of fulfilling independently given individual objectives; the means and the end are distinct. The crucial point about this conception is that the relevant features of individuals determining the ends which social arrangements are held . . . to fulfill, whether these features are called instincts, faculties, needs, desires, rights, etc., are assumed as given, independently of a social context (1973: 73).

In the case of neorealist theory, states are treated as abstract individuals, and ascribed general features such as "sovereignty," "national interest," etc. For Gilpin, the paramount concern of individual sovereign states must always be their wealth and power relative to other such individuals; and changes in the constellation of international economic relations must then be explained in terms of these individual interests. "The security and political interests of states are primary and determine the international context within which economic forces must operate" (1987: 85; cf., 1981: 9). On the individualist presuppositions of neorealist theory more generally, compare: Ashley (1983, 1984); Keohane (1986); and Wendt (1987).

11. We have borrowed the terms *logical economism* and *variable economism* from Ashley (1983). "Variable economism involves the one-way determination of

political outcomes, as measured in terms of political variables, by variation in economic variables" (1983: 466). *Logical economism,* on the other hand, "is the reduction of the practical interpretive framework of political action to the framework of economic action: the reduction of the logic of politics to the logic of economy" (1983: 472).

12. Although the juxtaposition of multiple, distinct ontologies would be neither surprising nor troublesome for postmodernist thinkers, one might expect a "realist" tradition—which defines itself in terms of its ability to soberly observe and practically manipulate *the* real world—to view such a theoretical condition with greater dismay. In light of their fundamental commitment to a univocal real world, the existence within their arguments of multiple and inconsistent worlds threatens to vitiate scientific norms of coherence to which neorealists generally subscribe. We are grateful to Fritz Kratochwil for effectively, if also obliquely, prompting us to specify the context and scope of our critique.

13. Although constraints of space and time prevent us from extending this paper's critical analysis to the works of other major neorealist scholars, we will suggest here that the theory of the international regimes is not invulnerable to criticisms such as those we have leveled at the theory of hegemonic stability: cf., for example, Keohane and Nye (1977); Keohane (1980, 1982, 1984, 1986).

14. On alienation, see: Marx and Engels 1970: 52–54, 84, 91–93; Marx 1975: 322–379, Marx, 1977: 990, 1002–1018, esp. 1003–1004, 1016. For fetishism, see: Marx 1977: Ch. 1, esp. 164–165, 167–168, 174–175; also 980–990, 998, 1003, 1005–1008.

4

Timeless Space and State-Centrism: The Geographical Assumptions of International Relations Theory

John A. Agnew

The representations of space we use in everyday life to signify our political, religious, and moral outlooks, such as left and right, central and marginal, in and out, beyond and within, have become so familiar to us that they go largely unquestioned. The use of spatial metaphors in more formal academic thinking is, if anything, even more taken for granted. Yet the spatial representations of the social sciences are important at the level of "common sense" in reifying among general populations what might otherwise be unusual or even preposterous ideas. The key premise of this chapter is that representations of space are particularly important elements in how the social sciences, specifically as shown by the field of international relations, define and limit their conceptions of social and political processes. Representations of space, therefore, are not isolated, idiosyncratic, or marginal aspects of the social sciences. Rather, representations of space are deeply embedded in these intellectual fields and intertwined with associated representations of scale (Sack 1980). In the context of this chapter space is understood as referring to the presumed effect of location and spatial setting—or *where* social processes are taking place—upon those processes; and *scale* refers to the spatial level—local, national, global, at which the presumed effect of space is operative.

In the contemporary social sciences, two interpretive communities conceive of space and relate space and scale in distinctive ways (Agnew 1992a). The first sees space as, or becoming, *national*. In other words, space is viewed in terms of a series of blocks defined by national-state boundaries in which a "modern" national culture and society displace "traditional" or residual local ones. From this point of view, social and political phenomena occur in essentially similar ways throughout the territories of particular national states but differ between states. This usually implicit representation of space as a "coming together" is dominant in such fields as political sociology, political history, macroeconomics, public administration, and, as we shall see later in this chapter, the field of international relations.

A second and smaller interpretive community views space as *structural*. From this point of view, the spatial effects of particular geographical entities such as nodes, districts, regions, areas, etc., are fixed by their relationships or interaction with one another. Thus an industrial core area (or city) is paired with a resource periphery (or hinterland) in terms of a structural relationship of superiority/inferiority. This representation of space as a "keeping apart" is characteristic of much academic geography, including both spatial analysis and regional geography, as well as some varieties of regional anthropology, economic history, and neo-Marxist sociology (especially world-systems theory). There are important differences across these fields in the scale at which core/periphery structures are regarded as operating. For example, city/hinterland relationships, central city/outer city differences, and city hierarchies are important in urban geography whereas global core/semiperiphery/periphery relationships are key to world-systems theory.

Neither of the two interpretive communities has shown much self-consciousness about its representations of space and scale. They are hidden geographies. Both are open to serious questioning, as I have attempted to show elsewhere (Agnew 1992a). But the absence of much explicit discussion of space in the social sciences has misled some commentators into declaring the conventional social sciences as *spaceless:* guilty of privileging time over space (e.g., Soja 1989), when in fact they are organized around key representations of space.

Apart from some pathbreaking papers by Walker (1984, 1990) and Ashley (1988), the representations of space in mainstream international relations theory have not received much attention. The purpose of this chapter is to open up debate over how geographical space is represented in contemporary international relations theory. All major forms of international relations theory, classical realism, neorealism, and idealism, share a focus on "the state." Less well known is their associated conception of the state as a peculiarly territorial entity. I argue that this conception involves three geographical assumptions that have together created an image of international relations as either actually fragmented among competing states or, for idealists, potentially unified in a global superstate. If the geographical assumptions are problematic, however, as I endeavor to show, then the image of international relations that they reproduce may also be open to question.

THE TERRITORIAL STATE
AND INTERNATIONAL RELATIONS THEORY

In political theory, definitions of the state have two aspects. One involves the exercise of power through a set of central political institutions.

The other entails the clear, spatial demarcation of the territory within which the state exercises its power. The former aspect has been uppermost in discussions of state/society relations and the "relative autonomy" of the state in relation to other putative causes of social life. In the field of international relations, however, the second aspect has been predominant. It has been the geographical division of the world into mutually exclusive territorial states that has received most emphasis from students of international relations. Indeed, the term "international relations" implies a focus on the relations between territorial states in contradistinction to the processes going on within state boundaries. State and society are thus related within the boundaries, but anything outside the state relates only to other states.

The historical development of this bifurcation in the meaning of the state has not been well explored. One point of origin surely lies in the association between ideas of organic nations of definite ethnic provenance and sharply defined spatial sovereignty that developed in the seventeenth and eighteenth centuries, when the modern European state system was coming into existence. There is another, more ancient, root, rediscovered at that time and passed down to our century. The founders of European civilization in ancient Greece were deeply attached to the concept of the polis, the politically autonomous city. Political interest was focused on the internal life of the city. "The outer world was only significant if it threatened invasion or promised plunder" (Mazzolani 1970: 16). The virtues of Aristotle, as MacIntyre (1981: 152–153) suggests, presuppose "the now-long-vanished context of the social relationships of the ancient city-state." The pursuit of the virtues (and virtue) was at that time impossible beyond the confines of the polis. The grounding of the modern territorial state in a presumed continuity with the ancient Greek city-state underscored the interior/exterior distinction, even as pursuit of the virtues, in the classical sense, was abandoned.

Another more recent point of origin for the peculiar fixation with bounding states and societies in neatly divided spatial packages lies in the intellectual division of labor that emerged in the aftermath of World War I, when international relations was first established as a separate field of study. The international was theorized as separate and distinct from the national or domestic, requiring a more homogeneous and uniform conception of the state as an actor than that adopted by students of "domestic" social life, and restricted to studying and offering advice on managing the relations between territorial states (Carr 1939).

This division is evident in both "idealist" and "realist" forms of international relations theory. In the former, international institutions, interstate cooperation, and international law are viewed as constraints on the anarchy of international relations. Each nation-state has its own interests, and the purpose of international law and "regimes" governing international transactions is to provide a set of rules for international conduct that reduces the possibility of recourse to military force (Neff 1990: 4). For Neff, states are the sole real actors in international relations, and they compete rationally with one another in the pursuit of power, especially military power. Though the realist school can be divided into various streams of thought—for example, minimalism, fundamentalism, and structuralism (Doyle 1990) or descriptive (Carr), axiomatic (Morgenthau), and theoretical (Waltz) (Rosenberg 1990)—it is united upon these key premises.

In recent years, the realist school, broadly dominant in the field for many decades, has come under challenge. In particular, there has been a shift away from an exclusive concern with military or security relations toward interest in economic processes and the internal factors, such as domestic coalitions of business and other interests, affecting foreign policy. The realist view, however, drawing its intellectual legitimacy from its presumed origins in the writings of Thucydides, Machiavelli, and Hobbes, and neorealist derivatives of it, giving much more emphasis to economic relations than classic realism, remain intellectually dominant within the field of international relations as a whole. One measure of this is Vasquez's (1983: 162–170) estimate that more than 90 percent of the hypotheses examined empirically by students of international politics through the early 1980s had been realist in conception. The focus on relations between *territorial* states continues to be at the heart of contemporary international relations theory. This can be seen by summarizing some recent writing by two influential—and distinctive—theorists: Kenneth Waltz (1979) and Robert Keohane (1984).

Waltz first established his realist view of international relations with the publication of *Man, the State and War* in 1959. In this work he compared three "images" of the origins of war—human nature, the domestic constitution of states, and the international system. He concluded that the third of these was the best basis for a theory of war. His later work continues this emphasis by focusing on the "structures of inter-state relations" and totally excluding the internal character of states from the purview of international relations. For Waltz, the structure of the international system has three features: it is anarchic, without any higher authority; states all perform the same functions and are equivalent units; and there is an unequal distribution of capacities and resources among states. From these key features he draws a number of inferences, in particular that the balance of power is the central mechanism of the international system and that at any specific moment the overall system's shape is determined by the nature and number of its "great powers." After 1945, the international system thus involved a bipolar balance of power between two great powers in contrast to the multipolarity of the early nineteenth century.

Waltz's account of international relations rests firmly on the view of the territorial state described previously. First, he takes the national-territorial conception of the state to its logical extreme in his claim that international relations should be studied only at the systemic level. The argument that states are constrained by the system is not at issue. What *is* at issue is Waltz's stronger claim that "internal" processes of states can be excluded altogether from the theorization of international relations. Second, Waltz's system of territorial states is structural and ahistorical. If the examples chosen by Waltz are a guide to his thinking, territorial states have been around at least since the time of Thucydides. He pays no attention to the distinctiveness of the modern international system and its roots in the expansion of markets and growth of military competition in the sixteenth and seventeenth centuries. "The state system" thus has an existence outside the historical contexts in which it has evolved.

The question Keohane (1984) seeks to address is the orthodox idealist one of how cooperation is possible in the international system in the absence of a dominant or "hegemonic" power. Much of Keohane's analysis relies upon the concept of *regimes*—"rules, norms, principles, and decision-making procedures"—governing the institutionalization of the international economy, especially trade and finance, since World War II. In this framework, the behavior of states is, therefore, not only the result of the competitive pursuit of power. Rather, there are important incentives for cooperation; the regimes and formal international institutions that result can significantly restrict state conduct.

The territorial state, however, remains the central actor. The pattern of international economic relations is seen as determined largely by the policies of states and states' relative economic importance and decline. There is no sense of the state in its "state/society aspect" and hence of the social and economic processes within state boundaries that shape state policy. Moreover, unlike some of Keohane's previous writing in which he argued that nonstate actors (such as multinational corporations) were eroding the power of states, in this work there is little explicit attention to the global socioeconomic system in which individual states are situated.

The privileging of a national-territorial conception of the state that is characteristic of international relations theories, as illustrated by such different writers as Waltz and Keohane, rests on three geographical assumptions that are theoretically and empirically problematic. First, the territorial state has been viewed both as existing prior to and as a physical container of society. As a consequence, society is restricted by definition to the national level. This assumption is common to all types of international relations theory. Second, the use of domestic/international or national/foreign polarities has served to obscure the interaction between social processes operating at different scales; for example, the link between the globalization of certain manufacturing industries with production facilities located in different countries and the deindustrialization of regions within countries where these industries were once concentrated. This assumption has been particularly important in neorealism's fixation upon the national economy as the fundamental geographical entity in international affairs. Third, national spaces have been reified as set, or fixed, units of (secure) sovereign space. This has served, in particular, to dehistoricize and decontextualize processes of state formation and disintegration. Classical realism and idealism both rely heavily upon this assumption. It can be regarded as the rock-bottom geographical assumption of international relations theory that underwrites the others.

From an analytic point of view, the "territorial trap" is set in three ways, therefore; and it operates empirically when at least two are combined. Avoiding one provides no guarantee of avoiding the others, especially the third. The third, then, is particularly powerful. In the last instance, state territorial sovereignty is the determining assumption. The assumptions and how they combine are now examined in more detail.

THE TERRITORIAL STATE AS CONTAINER OF SOCIETY

Most international relations theorists (perhaps most social scientists) mean by *society* the social order or organization within the territory of a state. Thus, we commonly encounter such phrases as *American society*, *Italian society*, etc. Such alternative formulations as *social system* and *social formation* are also usually thought of in terms of territorial definition associated with particular states. Mann (1984), a strong supporter of the contemporary relevance of a state-centric definition of society, has pointed out, however, that the pertinence of state boundaries to what is meant by society is by no means self-evident. The case he makes is historical. Prior to modern times, society was not state-defined. But today "states are central to our understanding of what a society is" (Mann 1984: 212). This is because "where states are strong, societies are relatively territorialised and centralised." Moreover, "The territoriality of the state has created social forces with a life of their own." These include "the existence of a domestic market segregated to a degree from the international market, the value of the state's currency, the level of its tariffs and import quotas, its support for its indigenous capital and labour; indeed, its whole political economy is permeated with the notion that 'civil society' is its [the nation-state's] territorial domain" (Mann 1984: 212 and 210).

The state-defined society, therefore, is "the product of the usefulness of enhanced territorial-centralisation to social life in general," as groups in civil society (dominant economic classes, churches, military elites) "entrust power resources to state elites . . . because their own socio-spatial basis of organisation is not centralised and territorial." However, as Mann is quick to add, "This has varied considerably through the history of societies, and so consequently have [sic] the power of states" (Mann 1984: 210–211).

To Mann, then, the territorial state-society relationship is a historically contingent one. In particular, the modern nation-state system "resulted from the way expansive, emergent, capitalist relations were given regulative boundaries by pre-existing states" (Mann 1984: 209). But the territorial states took on a new meaning and significance as they came to have an increasingly key role in the structuring of social processes. The territorial state was "prior" to and a "container" of society only in this particular historical context (also see Poulantzas 1980).

The nation state, based on a circumscribed territory, involved the creation of a unified and homogeneous space in which the various aspects of social practice—culture, knowledge, education, employment—were rationalized and homogenized. This state was never simply an Hegelian "rational unity." Its spatial exclusivity was crucial to the incorporation of social practice under state regulation. But because space was subordinated to the state and became, in Lefebvre's (1991: 281) terminology, "classificatory" and "instrumental," the state's spatial unity and internal homogeneity were taken for granted as a "reality" of social life in general. One key weakness of Hegelian idealism may be its "timeless" conception of state-centered space. As Lefebvre (1991: 279) notes: "For Hegel space brought historical time to an end, and the master of space was the state." The recent claim about "the end of history" in light of the end of the Cold War and the great ideological struggle it entailed (Fukuyama 1989) involves a fairly straightforward association between an Hegelian-like fusion of a liberal state with society and the fading of social movements, in particular "international communism," presumably oriented toward undermining this identity. Making the identity, however, is not only characteristic of iconoclastic Hegelians. It is an inherent feature of much modern social thought.

How has the historical contingency of territorial state-society been turned into a transcendental necessity as in international relations theories? I have argued elsewhere (Agnew 1989) that since the nineteenth century a principle of what Smith (ed. Cannan 1976: 191) calls "methodological nationalism" has prevailed in the social sciences. Irrespective of their other differences, and in varying degrees, important figures in the development of the social sciences, such as Marx, Durkheim, and Weber, all accepted state boundaries as coextensive with those of the "societies" or "economies" they were interested in studying. More particularly, to a thinker such as Durkheim, the territorial state was both creator and guarantor of the individual's natural rights against the claims of local, household, occupational, and other secondary groups. The state thus came to function both as an "enforcer" of natural order and as a "container," through the territorial definition it provides and the "statistics" it collects, of empirical observations about social and economic processes. The categories used by the state for collecting statistics came to be the main operational categories of the empirical social sciences.

The intellectual division of labor that emerged in the rapidly expanding universities of Europe and North America in the late nineteenth century reinforced this sense of reality. Fields such as sociology, political science, and economics had in their origins the practical interests of the state in, respectively, social control, state management, and the national accumulation of wealth. At their roots, therefore, they were national in focus.

This was the intellectual context in which the social sciences became oriented toward the territorial state as a "natural" unit upon which to base their claims to generalization. Reference to local or regional settings, except as "case studies" of presumptively nationwide processes, or to global social processes, as distinct from inter*national* relations, was largely closed off by the "nationalizing" of social science and its subservience to the territorial state. This sense of reality has been reproduced in the field of international relations by the tendency of theorists to restrict society to a national-state scale. Only inside the state is there the possibility of social order: outside is anarchy.

THE DOMESTIC/INTERNATIONAL POLARITY

Regarding territorial states as the nodes of international relations, many theorists adopt what can be thought of as a version of abstract individualism. Its theoretical origin lies in Hobbes's world of "war-of-all-against-all," in which territorial states are understood as individuals struggling against one another for wealth and power. From this point of view, the territorial state is viewed in classic mercantilist terms as a single, abstract individual; a domestic economy, understood as an identity, in an environment of international anarchy. This is an especially important feature of so-called neorealist theory (Milner 1991).

Mercantilism was a set of practices and policies followed by many European states in the seventeenth and eighteenth centuries. It was never a coherent economic theory or doctrine. Perhaps its most important characteristic was an overt economic nationalism. This was based on the assumption that the world's wealth was basically fixed in size and that, consequently, one state's gain could only come at the expense of another state's loss. States were thus locked into a permanent and deadly competition for wealth and trading advantage. In the context of the seventeenth century's general economic stagnation, this perspective had a certain plausibility. However, the view that national economies were the basic building blocks for economic activity in general became strongly grounded in the economic and political philosophy of the time. We are its inheritors. Liberal political economy from Adam Smith on provided an alternative, but it has always been vulnerable, especially during periods of stagnation or depression, to charges of depoliticization of resource allocation and devaluation of place and social solidarity (Agnew 1984; Neff 1990).

The territorial division of labor under early industrial capitalism, however, was strongly organized on a national basis. The leaders who built many nation states, from Hamilton in the United States to Bismarck in Germany to the Japanese oligarchy of the Meiji restoration, all used economic policy to buttress their political ambitions. Over time, however, the increasing mobility of capital and the decreasing importance of transportation costs have produced a geographical pattern of economic activities not readily captured by national-level representations of economic characteristics or performance (Massey 1984; Smith 1984).

But despite this trend in spatial practice, the subordination of the economic to the political in an essentially mercantilist formula is still characteristic of the major realist and neorealist international relations theories. This is perhaps most obvious in contemporary treatments of the so-called U.S.-Japan trade dispute, in which the two territorial economies are regarded as the major economic actors. In fact, its major features are intra-industry and intracompany trade and investment flows; not interterritorial competition (e.g., Mastanduno 1991). The historically contingent nature of state-economy relations thus continues to be collapsed "into a single, abstract unity" (Rupert 1990: 429) in which the long-term complementarity of wealth- and power-seeking by territorial states is assumed a priori. E. H. Carr (1939: 116) attempted a historical grounding for interterritorial competition when he asserted, during a very abnormal time in recent history, that: "We have now therefore returned, after the important, but abnormal, *laissez-faire* interlude of the nineteenth century, to the position where economics can be frankly recognized as a part of politics." Carr thus characterized the interimperialist rivalry of the interwar "twenty years' crisis" as representing the normal condition of international relations.

The rigid separation of the domestic from the international entailed by this view serves both to identify a field of study ("international relations," separate from the "domestic" social sciences) and, more significantly from an intellectual point of view, to eliminate the possibility of seeing the territorial state and its power as dependent upon the interaction of global and more local (including national) processes of social structuration. In this connection, Cox (1981) suggests that states are in a constant condition of reconstruction in the intersection of global and domestic social relations. From this point of view, showing how the domestic and the international come together under different historical conditions (rather than separating them in permanent opposition) then becomes the overriding task for the social scientist.

Cox (1987) identifies three "historical structures" of world order over the last two hundred years in which the position and importance of the state have been distinctive. The first of these world orders was constructed in the period 1789–1873, with the political, economic, and ideological ascendancy of Britain. The older mercantilist system was supplanted by the norms and practices of liberal capitalism carried into the world by British businessmen and politicians.

The second world order was one of "rival imperialisms" (1873–1945), in which state economic intervention expanded, international rivalry grew, and nationalism intensified. In this period, there was open conflict for domination among states, largely through territorial expansion, but no one state was hegemonic in the way Britain had been in the previous period.

The third world order (1945 to the present) is one in which interstate competition and conflict has been largely transformed through U.S. reconstruction of the industrialized capitalist states along liberal democratic lines. The new "neoliberal state" characteristic of this order seeks "its security as a member of a stable alliance system and its economic growth as a participant in an open world economy. Its task [is] to adjust the national economy to the growth of the world economy, to facilitate adaptation rather than to protect existing positions" (Cox 1987: 219–220). The "embedded liberalism" (Ruggie 1983a: 198) of the United States, with older historical roots but more immediate origins in the peculiar political economy created by the New Deal and U.S. involvement in World War II, thus became globally ascendant, as the United States became the world's hegemonic state. A new integrated global economy was constructed under U.S. supervision. Since the late 1960s, this world order has been under strain as the three main geographical pillars of the liberal world economy, the United States, Western Europe, and Japan, have become increasingly competitive with one another, although in a context of increased interdependence (Van der Pijl 1984). The recent problems of the U.S. national economy, especially those that can be traced to alleged unfair foreign competition, especially from Japan, presage a further challenge to the tenets of embedded liberalism, both domestically and internationally, as groups with economic interests at different scales (global, national, regional, local) mobilize to strengthen policies that better serve their particular interests (Rupert 1990: 450–451).

Whatever the specific merits of Cox's periodization, the major point is that the domestic/international couplet constitutes a shifting interaction rather than a fixed polarity. How misleading the conventional mercantilist view can be is illustrated by one statistical item that many people in the United States (and some elsewhere) have spent much time worrying about since the early 1980s: the U.S. trade deficit. In terms of the national books, the deficit was $144 billion in 1986. If the trading and investment activities of U.S.-owned companies abroad and foreign firms in the United States are included, however, the huge deficit becomes a surplus of $77 billion. By comparison (see Table 4.1), the two figures for Japan (national and ownership-based trade balances) are much closer. The difference shows how much more U.S. firms are involved outside their national boundaries than are Japanese firms. Most important, an "ownership-based" measure of trade' raises the basic question of how "international" transactions should be thought of in an increasingly nonmercantilist world economy in which perhaps 40 percent of trade between countries is now carried on *within* companies (Reich 1991).

Table 4.1   Conventional and "Ownership-Based" Trade Balances, United States and Japan (U.S.$ billions)

	U.S.	Japan
Exports [1]	224	146
Less intra-firm transfers	123	60
Plus local sales to foreign MNCs[a]	267	3
Plus sales by home-owned MNCs abroad	777	150
Equals total "foreign sales" [2]	1145	239
Imports [3]	368	114
Less intra-firm transfers	191	65
Plus local purchases from foreign MNCs	445	58
Plus purchases by home-owned MNCs abroad	446	90
Equals total "foreign purchases" [4]	1068	197
Conventional trade balance [1] - [3] =	−144	+32
"Ownership-based" trade balance [2] - [4] =	+77	+42

Source: Data reworked from Julius 1990: 81.
[a] Multinational corporations.
Note: Figures for United States are from 1986; figures for Japan are from 1983.

A wide range of nongeographical factors now determine the competitiveness of firms in many industries: access to technology, marketing strategy, responsiveness to consumers, flexible management techniques (Julius 1990: 82). All of these are the assets of firms, not areas. Large firms grow because of their success in deploying their internal assets. Multinational firms cannot be readily restricted from switching their relatively mobile assets from place to place or country to country. Indeed, states now compete with one another to attract these mobile assets to their territories. In this new world of space-transcending industry and finance, who is regulating whom?

STATE SOVEREIGNTY AND NATIONAL SPACE

If, as the previous two sections allege, *society* and *economy* have been largely assimilated to the territorial state in international relations theory, so has the concept of *security*. This term has been applied to the survival and maintenance of the sovereignty of the state over its territory, rather than, for example, to human, cultural, or ecological security. The total sovereignty of the state over its national space in a world fragmented into territorial states is regarded by all of the orthodox theories as a major underpinning of international relations.

But the idea of state sovereignty is a relatively modern one. It emerged in late medieval Europe in the face of the collapse of the well-established principle of hierarchical subordination. In premodern communities, there were few fixed boundaries between different political authorities. Communities were united by allegiance and personal obligation rather than abstract individual equality or citizenship in a geographically limited territory. Similarly, with respect to time, the present was understood as a repetition of the past rather than as an unfolding of novel events in a cumulative or progressive sequence. Time was known only to be cyclical—seasonal, annual, natural (birth, lifetime, death). Space was organized concentrically around many centers depending upon political and religious affiliations. The term *sovereignty* was formally associated with the authority of the monarch (Poulantzas 1980).

The modern state replaced this plurality of hierarchical bonds with an exclusive identity based upon membership in the "imagined community" of the nation (Anderson 1983). In other words, "the principle of hierarchical subordination gradually gave way to the principle of spatial exclusion" (Walker 1990: 10). Older hierarchical arrangements in Europe involving church and empire, feudal obligations, and theological claims gradually gave way to an identification of citizenship with residence within a particular national space. Sovereignty shifted from the person of the monarch, identified with a "divine cosmos," to the territory of the state and its political institutions (Collins 1989). In political theory, the central problem became the political control of the individuals released from their customary obligations under religious—dynastic authority. Older religious-dynastic communities could rely on a chain of command extending from God, through the sovereign and the links of political obligation, to the humble subject at the base of the pyramid of power. Modern political theory has had to develop an alternative subjectivity. By and large, this has involved the emergence, from Hobbes to Rousseau, Kant, and Hegel, of the individual self-conscious subject constrained in a variety of different ways by the rationality of the state and the market. In particular, with Hegel, arguably the most important philosopher of the modern state, the individual becomes an agent only through the state's definition and enforcement of individual property rights—one "capable of owning, acting according to private will, entering into contract, establishing [a] career, accountable legally and morally for stealing from others, and worthy of being held responsible individually for the successes and failures in [their] life" (Connolly 1988: 118).

In this construction, only the state could guarantee the harmonization of society. Only within the territorial boundaries of the state could the self-conscious subject of modern history emerge. This, in turn, gave rise to a spatial demarcation between places in which "authentic politics"—the pursuit of justice and virtue—was possible and places where it was not. The latter were "outside" the boundaries of the territorial state. As Walker puts it at greater length:

> Inside particular states we have learned to aspire to what we like to think of as universal values and standards—claims about the nature of the good society, freedom, democracy, justice, and all the rest. But these values and standards have in fact been constructed in relation to particular communities. They depend on a tacit recognition that these values and standards have been achieved only because we have been able to isolate particular communities from those outside—an isolation that implies the continuing legitimacy of war and violence (1990: 11–12).

The politics of nonspatial affiliation, especially class, have been almost impossible to organize in this context. Imagined national communities have proven much more robust than imagined categorical communities. "In one country" may well be their collective epitaph. But identity is not intrinsically national—territorial. If social practices are not largely restricted within tightly defined territorial boundaries, then identity, too, can expand beyond these limits, as noted later in this section. As yet, however, the possibility of an individual existing "securely" outside the tightly bounded spaces of "modern" territoriality is not open to conventional theories of international relations. Consequently, "security policy" is not a form of politics at all. It involves the recognition of a world "out there" where claims concerning justice and virtue give way to claims about realpolitik and the use of force. Danger and insecurity are associated with the world beyond the boundaries of the sovereign territorial state. Security thus becomes the defense of a particular spatial sovereignty.

This relationship of security to spatial sovereignty has four important consequences for international relations theory. First, it has led to the definition of political identity in exclusively nation-state terms. This can be seen as progressive in the sense that state sovereignty involves an active embrace of popular membership or citizenship as opposed to hierarchical subordination by empires, superpowers, or multinational corporations (Wolin 1960). However, in the contemporary world there is a remarkable flowering of alternative political identities of a regional, ethnic, and sectoral (gender, ecological, etc.) character, related in part to the threats to "national security" from changes in military technology, global ecological problems, and resistance to bureaucratic government. Increasingly, orthodox thinking about security must engage with shifting sensibilities about political identity (Dalby 1991).

Second, and related to this exclusive definition of political identity, is a rigid separation between those people within the national space pursuing "universal" values and all those outside practicing different, and inferior, values. This is the so-called problem of the "other," in which the people of other states are represented and incorporated into a world of other sovereign states—some as "barbarians," who though uncivilized and dangerous can be coexisted with; some as "heretics," dangerous dissenters who threaten the stability of the state system and who can be dealt with only through vigilance or conversion; and some as "primitives," those who have not yet "developed" and who await incorporation into the "community of nations" (Rosow 1990: 294–299). In the contemporary world, however, these "others" are less easily marginalized and mystified than in the past, even as classic representations of them persist. In particular, massive international migrations, the emergence of middle-level or regional "superpowers," and the deterritorialization of communications media combine to limit the confinement of "others" in spatial reservations. In this context it has become increasingly obvious that the spaces occupied by the others have always been connected to the rest of the world, including its so-called civilized territories. They have not been separated or autonomous. As Gupta and Ferguson (1992: 4) remark: "The presumption that spaces are autonomous has enabled the power of topography to successfully conceal the topography of power."

Third, and most vitally, the security-spatial sovereignty nexus involves viewing the state "not in its historical particularity, but abstractly, as an idealised decision-making subject" (Ashley 1988: 238). The actual processes out of which states have emerged are obscured in favor of an ideal-type territorial state. Consider, for example, the different processes of expansion and incorporation through which the modern territorial states of Britain, the United States, and Germany were created. Britain was produced by the conquest and dynastic inheritance of adjacent territories by a succession of English monarchs over a period of six hundred years. The United States came about through the settlement of a vast continental tract by free immigrants from Europe and slaves from Africa engaged in an expansion that took only about one hundred years. Germany as a modern state was created in the midnineteenth century by the incorporation of many small, German-speaking principalities into a Prussian-dominated *Reich*. Each of these constitutes a territorial state but with distinctive origins, scale, and founding mythology. The ahistorical bundling together of these states and the lack of attention to the creation of the spaces in which sovereignty has been vested constitute "silences" about the foundations of international relations that are of profound significance.

Fourth, and finally, the principle of state sovereignty "denies alternative possibilities because it fixes our understanding of future opportunities in relation to a distinction between history and progress within statist political communities and mere contingency outside them" (Walker 1990: 14). The only alternatives for political organization are either continuing fragmentation into territorial states as we know them or integration into some global superstate. This rests on the view that government through states is necessary because of the axiomatic untrustworthiness of human beings. In Dunn's (1979: 23) words, "If men (sic) were to be safe in each other's company, they needed a fundamentally external guarantee of their security—a familiar Hobbesian argument." But as Dunn points out, this is an argument not without its own problems. The main objection was stated by Locke in suggesting that the trustworthiness of *government* remained the larger question: "This is to think that Men are so foolish that they take care to avoid what Mischiefs may be done them by *Pole-cats* or *Foxes*, but are content, nay think it Safety, to be devoured by *Lions*" (quoted in Dunn 1979: 24).

This mode of thinking has had one particular consequence. Geographically variegated, as opposed to territorially homogeneous, forms of political community have been eliminated from consideration by the close association of security with spatial sovereignty. This reflects the persisting tendency to view the autonomy of "intermediate" or nongovernmental organizations and associations as a threat to the vital interests of both individual liberty and the nation-state (Frug 1980: 1089). Indeed, eradicating the power of intermediate groups was for long seen as simultaneously advancing both the interests of individuals and state interests. Powerful "subsidiary" bodies could be seen as representing a threat to the monopoly of sovereignty exercised by the national state. To permit more than two sovereigns to function within the one territory would create *imperium in imperio*, a dispute over jurisdiction. Moreover, individual liberty could only be guaranteed when there was a limited possibility of coercion and interference by other organizations in state protection and regulation of individuals. Yet, nonstate forms of political community can be defended in terms of their contribution to political freedom and the pursuit of the good life. For example, the arguments for the stimulus to democracy provided by membership in local primary groups made by Jefferson and de Tocqueville rest upon this position.

THE TERRITORIAL TRAP

There is a historiography to the three geographical assumptions. The first two are relatively modern, dating in their current construction from the nineteenth century, even when they have older intellectual sources. They can be thought of as interacting with the older and more fundamental assumption of state territorial sovereignty. But they do so in different ways.

In the first place, sovereignty as construed by contemporary international relations theory implies a relation of similarity among all states in which differences in social and political practices are defined and demarcated by state territorial boundaries. The first geographical assumption, therefore, is closely tied to the assumption of state territorial sovereignty, because the state-society identity is possible only on the assumption of state sovereignty. This is the way in which the understanding of sovereignty is shared by bureaucratic and popular cultures; practices based upon sovereignty such as citizenship, emigration and immigration, policing, trade, national defense, and diplomacy are so pervasive that society is easily defined by them (Milliken 1990). It is "common sensical" to see the territorial state as the container of society when the state is sovereign.

State sovereignty is also intrinsic to the second geographical assumption, the domestic-international polarity. It is the state's resolution of the "problem of order" within its territorial boundaries that separates domestic society from international anarchy. Outside the state's boundaries there is only struggle for power between the "individuals" of international relations: sovereign states. There is an essential conflict of territorial interests in which one state's gain is always another state's loss, unless, at least in idealist accounts, they can negotiate a temporary regime of cooperation over their antagonistic interests.

The territorial trap, therefore, is circular and cumulative. The geographical assumptions are not linear and additive. They interact to produce mutually reinforcing accounts of international relations, be they realist, neorealist or idealist, that are state-centered and in which the space occupied by the states is represented as timeless. International relations theory is thus put beyond history by its geographical assumptions.

EMERGING SPATIAL FORMS

It has only recently become possible to question the geographical assumptions upon which much conventional wisdom in the social sciences relies. From one point of view, this is because the intellectual movement loosely described as poststructuralism has produced a variety of theories that argue for a deterritorialized and socially heterogeneous conception of culture in a postmodern world (e.g., Lyotard 1986). From another, the modern world has changed and is changing materially and as a result the assumptions upon which we base our understanding of the world must change also (e.g., Cox 1987). These views are not necessarily in conflict, although from the logic of the analysis and the examples in the previous sections it should be clear that I come closer to the second view. Representations of space are not "merely" epistemic; functions of how one "just happens" to think. They are related to the dominant political and material conditions of different eras (Williams 1977; Berman 1982; Kern 1983; Smith 1984; Harvey 1989; Lefebvre 1991).

The international relations theories of writers such as Waltz and Keohane came to dominance during the Cold War, when their geographical assumptions, whatever their limitations, could be seen as having a certain validity. Over the past twenty years, however, spatial practices, the ways in which space is produced and used, have changed profoundly. In particular, both states and nonstate actors now operate in a world in which national boundaries have become culturally and economically permeable to decisions and flows emanating from networks of power not captured by territorial representations of space.

The signs of a new spatiality departing from the forms characteristic of conventional representations of space are everywhere (Agnew 1992b). At one end of the scale is localization or fragmentation. The Soviet Union, which was in part an effort to meld many regional ethnic groups into one state, has broken up. Emerging replacement states are trapped between the desire to acquire the accoutrements of statehood (flags, militaries, currencies, and so forth) and the need to collaborate economically with one another. Yugoslavs—the citizens of former Yugoslavia—argue violently over national differences so fine to the outside observer that New York City neighborhoods could as easily justify separate statehood. French-speaking Quebeçois openly advocate separation from the mainly English-speaking part of Canada. In nominally secular India, radical Hindus suggest that the country should become more Hindu, initiating a renewal of historic regional, religious, and linguistic enmities. In many countries, social classes and established political ideologies appealing to "class interests" have lost their value as sources of identity. Regions, religions, and ethnicity challenge national states as the loci of political identity. Increasingly, the links between the places of everyday life in which political commitments are forged and the states that have structured and channeled their political activities are under stress. New loyalties everywhere undermine the state's political monopoly.

At the other end of the scale, in talks on the General Agreement on Tariffs and Trade countries negotiate about opening up trade in services that would involve them admitting into their territories both more foreigners and "foreign" ways of doing business. Foreigners are already migrating internationally at a rate never previously experienced in modern world history. In Europe, the dominant political issue of the time is the movement toward a more unified European Community and the degree of formal political unification this should entail. The world's financial service industries are increasingly globalized, operating around the clock without much attention to international boundaries. Many manufacturing industries have branch plant and research facilities scattered across the globe rather than, as in the past, concentrated in clearly identifiable regional clusters. Even the most sacrosanct of national powers, the power to wage war, is no longer exclusively national. The 1990–1991 war between the United States and Iraq involved the United States in a major exercise of coalition building, cost sharing, and use of the United Nations that smacked more of collective security than unilateral action by a single nation-state.

How has it been possible for the contradictory spatial forms of fragmentation and globalization to emerge together? The most important point is that globalization is not synonymous with economic and political homogenization. The globalized world economy is based on the transnational movement of all the potentially mobile factors of production: capital, labor, and technology. As this has occurred, largely under the influence of U.S. hegemony since World War II, localities and regions within states have become increasingly vulnerable to disinvestment and "restructuring." Prior to the acceleration of globalization in the late 1960s and early 1970s, and under the rigid military blocs of the Cold War, equalization of incomes across national territories, regional economic policies, and state repression, produced increased homogeneity at the national scale. However, increasingly mobile capital, the abandonment of regional policies in the face of pressures to increase national aggregate competitiveness, and the decline of state socialism as an ideology have given rise to *increased* spatial differentiation, or uneven development within states.

Wolin (1989: 16–17) captures the major point eloquently when he writes:

> Compelled by the fierce demands of international competition to innovate ceaselessly, capitalism resorts to measures that prove socially unsettling and that hasten the very instability that capitalists fear. Plants are closed or relocated; workers find themselves forced to pull up roots and follow the dictates of the labor market; and social spending for programs to lessen the harm wrought by economic "forces" is reduced so as not to imperil capital accumulation. Thus, the exigencies of competition undercut the settled identities of job, skill, and place and the traditional values of family and neighborhood which are normally the vital elements of the culture that sustains collective identity and, ultimately, *state power itself* (my emphasis added).

Consequently, economic interests have been redefined from national to regional and local levels. Political identities have also become increasingly complex and less anchored in singular national identities (Agnew 1992b). Increasing numbers of people live in what Said (1979: 18) has called "a generalized condition of homelessness": a world in which identities are less clearly bonded to specific national territories. Refugees, migrants, and travelers are the most obvious of the homeless; at least in the national sense (as opposed to the housing problem of "homelessness"). But the issue is more general:

> In a world of diaspora, transnational culture flows and mass movements of populations, old-fashioned attempts to map the globe as a set of culture regions or homelands are bewildered by a dazzling array of post-colonial simulacra, doublings and redoublings, as India and Pakistan apparently re-appear in post-colonial simulation in London, pre-revolution

Teheran rises from the ashes in Los Angeles, and a thousand similar cultural dramas are played out in urban and rural settings all across the globe (Gupta and Ferguson 1992: 7).

From this point of view, globalization has provided the context for fragmentation. Without the first the second could not occur.

Of course, the territorial nation-state has persisting strengths. National political identity is still strong across much of the world. Mann's (1984) society-defining state is still not exhausted, despite attempts in the 1980s at spreading a gospel of universal privatization of public services. A legitimation crisis is always a real threat when in a more competitive global economic environment states must reduce their social spending. Military force is still largely organized by individual states. In a world with more porous economic boundaries, states must compete with one another to attract and keep capital investment by providing attractive "business climates." A dominant state, such as the United States, has the continuing ability to resolve its domestic economic difficulties through manipulation of the world monetary system, even as it becomes more beholden to it. Finally, the state has a continuing normative appeal. As Wolin (1960: 417) was at pains to emphasize in his classic work, *Politics and Vision:* "To reject the state [means] denying the central referent of the political, abandoning a whole range of notions and the practices to which they point—citizenship, obligation, general authority. . . . Moreover, to exchange society or groups for the state might turn out to be a doubtful bargain if society should, like the state, prove unable to resist the tide of bureaucratization."

The main point is not, then, that the nation-state is in a process of terminal decline. It is that the social world in the process of emergence cannot be adequately understood in terms of the fixed national spaces of conventional international relations theory.

The nation-state, in any version that would fit the minimum criteria for statehood in the twentieth century, is in fact no older than the eighteenth century (Hobsbawm 1990). This is so despite the best efforts of international relations theorists to find it in the Greece of Thucydides or in the Italy of Machiavelli. The European medieval world was a world of local and hierarchical allegiances. In England, as late as the Elizabethan period, the dominant "world picture" was still that of "an ordered universe arranged in a fixed system of hierarchies" (Tillyard 1943: 13). Great power was exercised by small places: city-states such as Venice, Florence, and Lubeck were "global" powers. This may not occur again, although the emergence of Singapore and Hong Kong as important international financial centers is suggestive. What is more important to note in the present context is that the spatial scope of social and political organization is not set for all time. The territorial state is not a sacred unit beyond historical time. The state-centrism of conventional international relations theories assumes exactly that.

CONCLUSION

By means of three geographical assumptions, the territorial nation state has come to provide the foundation for conventional international relations theories—realist, neorealist, and idealist. The first of these is the assumption of the territorial state as existing prior to and as a container of society. The second is the division of the domestic from the international. The third, and most fundamental, is the reification of national spaces as fixed units of secure sovereign space. Each of these geographical assumptions is increasingly problematic. Social, economic, and political life cannot be contained within the territorial boundaries of the nation-state through an assumption of timeless space. Changes in military technology, especially nuclear weapons and their delivery systems, growing global economic and ecological interdependence, and complex population movements challenge the geographical bases of orthodox international relations theory. More and more, the critical theoretical issue has become the historical relation between specific *forms* that political organization can take, of which the territorial state is only one type, and the broader social and economic structures and *geographical worlds* (or forms of spatial practice) in which these forms of political organization must operate (as, for example, in Cox 1987). In this context, however, it becomes important to examine, as this chapter has done, not just how theory is produced by its particular geographical assumptions, but also why the territorial state of orthodox international relations theories is a historically contingent, rather than transcendentally fixed, component of actual "international relations."

NOTE

I would like to thank Stephen J. Rosow, Gearoid O. Tuathail, and Mauro Palumbo for helpful comments.

PART 2
THE CONSTRUCTION OF
IDENTITIES:
FEMINIST REWRITINGS

Reginas in International Relations: Occlusions, Cooperations, and Zimbabwean Cooperatives

Christine Sylvester

In 1988, I began a study of "women," "production," and "progress" in two provinces of Mashonaland, Zimbabwe, focusing on the ways women are defined in relation to official notions of progress in and across several sectors of production in that new country. During one portion of the research, I became acquainted with two silkmaking cooperatives located on the outskirts of Harare, the capital, both operated entirely by people called women and both engaged at that time in negotiations with the European Economic Community over funding. There, in geospaces far removed from the central concerns of professional international relations (IR), I learned something about the ways "our" IR theories block certain agents and forms of cooperation from occupying the privileged inside of the discipline. This chapter is about the cooperative occlusions from cooperation that mark theories of IR and international political economy (IPE) and about some cooperative resistances to occlusion that take place beyond our usual frames of vision.

REGINAS AND REGIMES: SITES OF OCCLUSION

Several years ago, Friedrich Kratochwil and John Ruggie pointed out that the theoretical emphasis on regimes, then solidifying in a corner of IR, brought into relief two sides of one coin. It enabled us to begin to appreciate the effects that regularized forms of cooperation could have on states. It also enabled us to see the ways in which regimes could become relatively autonomous from the states that created them (Kratochwil and Ruggie 1986: 760).

A parallel double-casting of a different sort was emerging around the same time in feminist literatures. It was becoming clear, on the one hand, that the move to bring gender sensitivity to bear on IR was revealing previously unrecorded sites of people called women in the world (as

109

underpaid producers in the world-system of capitalism, as commodity logos, as beneficiaries of global tourism, and so on). On the other hand, it was exposing the cooperative autonomy of IR theory and its regimes from the female-bodied and -monikered reginas who evoked places and tasks domestic; that is, some realms of identity were denied relevance to places deemed international (Enloe 1989; Sylvester 1993b). The same could not be said of Eugenes—those male-bodied images and tasks assigned to people called men. Those shadows stalked the land and dominated, albeit in unacknowledged ways, the scripts of IR. We might say that certain cooperations ruled.

Within contemporary IR/IPE theory, three perspectives offer seemingly contrasting views of cooperation in international relations. Neorealism tells of states inhabiting an anarchic system and striving therein to survive—that is to say to maintain identity via territory—through self-help rather than through processes of cooperation with others. Neoliberal institutionalism telescopes the ways in which an anarchic system harbors incentives for states to cooperate with each other by establishing regimes— "principles, norms, rules, and decision-making procedures around which actor expectations converge in a given issue-area" (Krasner 1982: 186). A focus on multilateralism now emphasizes relations among three or more states on the basis of generalized principles of conduct, an indivisibility among members of a collectivity with respect to the range of behavior in question, and a diffuse reciprocity that elevates the importance of cooperative institutions to the system (Ruggie 1993: 10–11). Peering through gender-sensitive lenses at just these three approaches to cooperation, we find that the differences between them all but disappear when we consider their shared cooperations on behalf of socially constructed Eugenes and their cooperative occlusions of reginas.[1]

Neorealist Minimalists

Kenneth Waltz's *Theory of International Politics* raises the question of how there can be "an order without an orderer and . . . organizational effects where formal organization is lacking" (1979: 89). Borrowing heavily from microeconomic theory, Waltz answers that order forms spontaneously from the self-interested, self-helping acts and interactions of states bent on surviving in a system that has no central authority. Put differently, in situations where each system-unit has sovereign rights of autonomy from the governing norms of every other unit, the formation of an overarching governance system is impossible. Coordination of separate and independent state actions, however, is possible. When "states retain their autonomy, each stands in a specifiable relation to the others. They form some sort of an order. We can use the term 'organization' to cover this preinstitutional condition if we think of an organization as simply a constraint"

(Waltz 1979: 100). To Waltz, the organization of order revolves around balances of power, international economic divisions of labor, hegemonic states of great capability "called on to do what is necessary for the world's survival,"[2] and war—"often mistakenly taken to indicate that the system itself has broken down" (1979: 109, 195–196).

Neorealism, the broad theoretical offshoot of Waltz's reasoning, posits that "structural constraints cannot be wished away, although many fail to understand this." Moreover, the constraint of governance-less existence in international relations should not necessarily be wished away: "[a] self-help situation is one of high risk—of bankruptcy in the economic realm and of war in a world of free states [but] it is also one in which organizational costs are low" (Waltz 1979: 109, 111). To venture beyond the deep structural imperatives of mere organization into the realm of "willingness of states to work together," says Joseph Grieco, requires a reduction in conditions that alarm realist states; for "a state will decline to join, will leave, or will sharply limit its commitment to a cooperative arrangement if it believes that gaps in otherwise mutually positive gains favor partners" (Grieco 1990: 1, 10). The emphasis on egoistic states helpless at working together very purposively evokes a minimalist orientation toward cooperation in international relations.

Less-Minimalist, Neoliberal Institutionalism

Neoliberal institutionalism allows that states in anarchic international relations can and must cooperate under certain conditions or face the consequences of unfettered ego (such as the crashing restrictions on trade that attend uncoordinated intercontinental air travel; beggar-thy-neighbor policies, or global resource depletion). There can be cooperation under anarchy, under the security dilemma, among egoists, and after hegemony (cf., Axelrod and Keohane 1985; Jervis 1978; Axelrod 1981; Keohane 1984) because:

> as everyone understands by now, rational egoists making choices in the absence of effective rules or social conventions can easily fail to realize feasible joint gains, ending up with outcomes that are suboptimal (sometimes drastically suboptimal) for all parties concerned (Young 1988: 1).

Moreover, Robert Keohane distinguishes between "crude," realist-force models of hegemonic stability, which equate power with leadership, and the forms of asymmetrical cooperation that a willing hegemon promotes to achieve order. He says: "Unlike an imperial power, [the hegemon] cannot make and enforce rules without a certain degree of consent from other sovereign states" (1984: 46).

"Cooperation," to the neoliberal institutionalist, however, is a very restricted concept that presupposes an original and perhaps more authentic condition of no cooperation. It is "the use of discord to stimulate mutual adjustments" (Keohane 1984: 46). "Discord" is the day-to-day consequence of inhabiting an anarchic system. "Mutual adjustments" lie in institutions that can "reduce verification costs, make relationships more iterated, and facilitate punishment for cheaters" (Grieco 1990: 33), all of which lower the likelihood that a state will be double-crossed by other states once it warily enters international contracts (Keohane 1984: 97). In turn, "conventions . . . enable actors to understand one another and, without explicit rules, to coordinate their behavior" (Keohane 1989: 4).

Reciprocity is one such convention. It informally regularizes expectations among states and helps to hold anarchy in check when formal institutions cannot be rationalized. Diffuse reciprocity, in particular, enables states to reach the point where each can "contribute one's share, or behave well toward others, not because of ensuing rewards from specific actors [specific reciprocity, as in two states agreeing to reduce tariffs], but in the interests of continuing satisfactory overall results for the groups of which one is a part, as a whole" (e.g., as when a state is accorded unconditional most-favored-nation status) (Keohane 1989: 146). However, diffuse reciprocity cuts two ways: it can whittle away at defensiveness and thus affect key norms of state behavior, and it can expose diffuse reciprocators to exploitation if they cooperate in the absence of strong norms of obligation (as when a country free-rides on future concessions made among its partners). A history of satisfaction with regime-coordinated reciprocity on specific issues can minimize the probability of exploitation and double crosses by defection-minded states and help maximize the possibilities for relational forms of autonomy in the system—relationships in which participants gain or deepen their identity in the process of working with others. Relational autonomy stands in contrast to the reactive form of autonomy that neorealists implicitly respect, whereby relationship is denied in order to achieve and maintain identity.[3]

In neoliberal institutionalism, regimes lie in between "conventions" and perfect conditions of "diffuse reciprocity" in deepening the institutional "governance" characteristics of the anarchic system. At the same time, if states are self-interested actors, owing to the system being without formal governance, then the full play of regime-oriented relational autonomy can never be. States will be inclined to cheat and defect as long as the costs of doing so are not excessively high. Accordingly, "if cooperation is to emerge, whatever produces it must be consistent with the principles of sovereignty and self-help" (Keohane 1989: 132). In this final recourse to reactive autonomy, the would-be neoliberal difference from neorealism ends up affirming neorealist foundations of IR.

Less-Minimalist Multilateralism

John Ruggie maintains that "there is a widespread assumption in the literature that all regimes are, ipso facto, multilateral in character [and yet] this assumption is egregiously erroneous" (1993: 12–13). Regimes can encompass only two states and they can lack the generalized principles of conduct that would make a multilateral security regime, say, incorporate a "norm of nonaggression, uniform rules for use of sanctions to deter or punish aggression, and . . . collectively sanctioned procedures for implementing them" (Ruggie 1993: 13). Multilateralism is a generic form of modern institutional international relations that manifests diffuse reciprocity (such that the good of the group is valued), draws on generalized principles of conduct, and results in a group that is indivisible.

In the post–World War II world, multilateralism has figured prominently in the organization of the Western economic order, thanks initially to the U.S. effort "to project the experience of the New Deal regulatory state into the international arena" (Ruggie 1993: 32). Yet "much of the inventiveness within multilateral arrangements today is coming from the institutions themselves, from platforms that arguably represent or at least speak for the collectivities at hand" (Ruggie 1993: 34). The European Community illustrates this trend in a most visible manner; but so also do groups of multilateral players who, for example, keep the issues of global warming alive internationally (cf., Benedict et al. 1991). This phenomenon of institutionally directed agenda-setting is difficult for neorealism to see, let alone accommodate. By contrast, it seems to be the neoliberal institutionalist vision come to life, only not in the causal sequence that that school would recognize (i.e., with specific reciprocity between states leading to diffuse reciprocity that encourages states—the leaders of the band— to demand more regimes and to extend diffuse reciprocity).

For multilateralism, cooperation is not simply instrumental, such that states adjust their policies to account for others when it is cost-effective to do so. Cooperation "depends on a prior set of unacknowledged claims about the embeddedness of cooperative habits, shared values, and taken-for-granted rules" (Caporaso 1993: 82). These claims draw attention to the conventions that neoliberal institututionalism acknowledges, and reach beyond them. Sovereignty is not a concept that is sensibly applied to a single state or to numerous states in isolation from one another [so much as it] is inherently a relational concept." In other words, the anarchic system of sovereign states is "a forum as well as a chessboard" (quotations from Caporaso 1993: 78).

Because mainstream IR favors the study of state rationalities and interests, it has neglected multilateralism, with its reflectivist and relational bent (Caporaso 1993: 78). Also, one might add, it has neglected some postneoliberal institutionalist possibilities for exploring relational versus reactive forms of autonomy in international relations. Relational autonomy presupposes sociality and involuntary ties, such that we can imagine eviscerating our notions of separate and wary states that are disconnected in international realms of politics from domestic socialities. Yet when the emphasis is on "preconscious, taken-for-granted understandings" (Caporaso

1993: 83) we also become aware of the many ways that even relational forms of cooperation may be narrow and exclusive, such that some groups are indivisible vis-à-vis others: they have encrusted certain "natural" principles of conduct and these create and deepen diffuse reciprocities, but only between themselves. Arguably, reginas have been frozen out of certain regimes through understandings that endow the worlds of Eugenes with taken-for-granted relevance to international relations.

GENDERED COOPERATIONS?

Even as the literature on cooperation becomes less minimalist, it retains an occluding tendency that weakens its scope of engagement with the worlds assigned to reginas. Simply put, these theoretical approaches do not conceptualize sociality and power as having something to do with gender relations. Purveyors of cooperation and noncooperation in IR try to establish difference from each other, but they uniformly share disinterest in the possibility that a field's views of cooperation cooperatively draw on a limited set of human experiences. Neoliberal institutionalism lionizes regimes without examining the extent to which there is a gender regime in international relations that prevents activities we associate with reginas from informing IR theory. That gender regime may also block certain bodies from international relations, allowing them in only as visitors who have no "embassy" to protect them in a taken-for-granted, rule-governed sphere of "men."[4] Neorealists speak of the absence of cooperation in anarchy without questioning the absence of gender anarchy in the supposedly anarchic system. That is, Kenneth Waltz does not qualify his structure-bound IR with a sense that "man's" authority is ubiquitous in the international relations that IR theorists produce. Fascinating possibilities for probing the habits and shared values of gender cooperation in IR seem to elude even the reflectivist multilateralists. Friedrich Kratochwil argues that "the predominance of realism in its various forms has made it difficult to explain the not inconsiderable amount of cooperation in general" without himself even briefly noting that the field is locked into gender cooperative and occluding forms of multilateralism that no one questions (Kratochwil 1993: 445).

Feminist theorizing focuses on the flaws in mainstream scholarship that appear when we ignore the range, depth, and relevance of hierarchical gender relations. *Standpoint* feminism, for instance, posits that theorizing would change profoundly if it were launched from the perspectives of women's lives and then built into "a morally and scientifically preferable grounding for our interpretations and explanations of nature and social life" (Harding 1986: 26). Excluded ones, this argument goes, can see through the smokescreens of "objectivity" to identify the group-preserving qualities that insiders may defend as (really) the universals of life. From that basis of insight, one can struggle to elaborate one's vision, correcting for distortions within it, and produce a series of successor projects to science that offer the possibility of more complete and inclusive knowledge of social dynamics.[5] Feminist *postmodernism,* by contrast to the standpoint perspective, often explores the power and authority that would enable constructs such as "cooperation" to be defined as they are in the mainstream of IR and rehearsed across ostensibly different theories. It encourages scholars to read the canonical texts and their mantra-like pronouncements with a sense of the silenced voices and double meanings that contest, esstrange, and unravel the privileged commonplaces of our field.[6]

These two (of many) feminist approaches have their differences. Yet would either one pronounce any particular domain of sociality as anarchic? For something to be taken as true, most feminists believe it must be constituted as true within some authoritative community that pronounces "the rightful governance of human action by means other than coercion or persuasion" (Jones 1993: 161). Standpoint feminism draws attention to an authoritative community called patriarchy, which projects masculine standpoints on gender, states, regimes of international political economy, and theories of IR. Under patriarchy, anarchy hides by making commonplace the many different ways that people called men dictate the status of activities associated with "women." The postmodern turn in feminism facilitates analysis of the knowledge-power moves that delineate an authoritative boundary of inside/outside and of countervailing knowledge and power that refuse such boundaries. Anarchy is definitely possible in a postmodern world, but only as a by-product of numerous social refusals of dominant discourse, and not because there is a lack of authority in some domains.

Turning the tables, standpoint feminist explorations of cooperation in international relations would start by describing the ubiquitous presence of professional men and norms of masculinity in the world we study and among the studiers (Tickner 1992). Male dominance ensures that many aspects of the theorized system are controlled, ordered, and ruled within the discourse of anarchic relations. The invisibility of "women" in international relations—or one could say the evacuation of "women" from a global human habitat—is one such manifestation of control. Gender power in IR is fixedly unipolar; it is also fixedly untheorized as such. One might say that there exists in IR circles a generalized principle of masculine standpoint that exemplifies diffuse reciprocity among ingroup members and that can result in multilateral indivisibility on the issue of what is true international relations. Relational autonomy reigns among insider colleagues. Toward those outside the group there is a reactive autonomy that, of course, occludes passage inside (Walker 1992).

One could argue, from a care-centered feminist perspective in particular,[7] that "much of the fabric of communal connectedness is lost in the male-rule, instrumental model" of international relations relative to what could be a "search for contexts of care that do not degenerate into mechanisms of blind loyalty" (Jones 1993: 160). Yet one must be careful. The construction of gender-linked standpoints relies on some communal connectedness within each gender group. The scope of connection is purportedly more gender-restricted in a masculine world than it is under feminist standpoints. But standpoint thinking adheres to a notion of truth that is carefully delineated from dangerous external forces.[8]

Meanwhile, practices in international relations willy-nilly defy theorized boundaries of truth and spoil models of inside/outside knowledges. For instance, the felled Berlin Wall symbolizes a situation in which a realist state does not persist with the usual forms of sovereignly separate authority and, instead, becomes connected with the standpoint of another—with painful consequences.[9] Seemingly intractable conflicts between Israel and neighboring Arab states may have been perpetuated "cooperatively" through a politics that lies in between the oft-rehearsed divide (Northrup 1989). Multilateral Europe chugs disjointedly toward unity like a family that tries to reduce internal conflict by establishing lines of authority in spite of periodic defections.

The postmodern turn in U.S. feminism prepares us for boundary transgressions such as these without attributing them to the triumph of feminist standpoint in international relations. There may be multiple standpoints that qualify as feminist, but to thinkers in the postmodern vein all such standpoints may erroneously suggest that a series of truths can be excavated if one digs deeply and hermeneutically enough (Brown 1991). What if we have multiple and mobile subjectivities that make it difficult for "women," or "men," or their standpoints to exist coherently? What if genders are oppositional categories that dump residual tasks on certain groups, leaving others free to participate in crafting humanist enterprises of Western history, such as the state, the market, and international relations?[10] Thus, what if "women" is the residual assignment signifying values, traits, and places that are not deemed public? People called women may seek fulfillment within their assignments and therefore make the invented seem true. But could we not say that "women" is the sum total of the stories various groups in society tell about "women" and the constraints and opportunities that are built around those stories? And is not the gender picture crisscrossed and hyphenated with other assigned identities—class, race, age, ethnicity, and nationality identities?

In posing these questions, we do not end up dashed against the rocks, reduced to elegiacs. The postmodern turn may mean that sisterhood eludes, but it also means that the male-crafted statecraft (Ashley 1989) of international relations/IR eludes, too, dissolved into an admittedly taken-for-granted, but porous, boundary that is subject to deauthorizing activities. To say it differently, the suggestion in all these queries is that the wall of cooperations that holds a field autonomous from women is comprised of less-than-robust practices. But how to proceed with the subversions that are encrusted in gender instabilities?

World-traveling to "women's" cooperatives in Zimbabwe provides some clues. It suggests, a propos of feminist standpoint thinking, that we must keep an ear tuned to what people called women report about their lives, because some stories, whether authentic or not, have been silenced in the IR literature (Lugones 1990). We must also recognize that groups of people do not necessarily stand fixed and timeless in their identities. Our selves can shift into previously unrecognized quadrants of subjectivity, or burrow new quadrants, as we listen to that which has been thought alien. Uma Narayan admonishes us to refuse the thesis that

> those who are differently located socially can never attain *some* understanding of our experience or *some* sympathy with our cause. . . . Not only does this seem clearly false and perhaps even absurd, but it is probably a good idea not to have any a priori views that would imply either that all our knowledge is always capable of being communicated to every other person or that would imply that some of our knowledge is necessarily incapable of being communicated to some class of persons (Narayan 1989: 263–264).

The story in the next section of this chapter gives credence to this plea. It features Zimbabwean women speaking about their silkmaking cooperatives as they become entangled in identity-shifting negotiations with international donors. A strange cooperation emerges across differences. The chessboard becomes a forum in places unauthorized as sites of IR/IPE. People who have no canonical right to narrate issues of international cooperation do so anyway. Subjectivities become mobile. Funds are dispensed to the "wrong" identity. To relate the story, to dance to distant music, is to reduce some boundaries of IR to jelly.

COOPERATIONS IN ZIMBABWE

There is a mood of anxious hope radiating from the small silkmaking cooperatives gathered in the urban township of Mabvuku. Dressed in their good clothes, the women talk nervously among themselves as they await the arrival of a delegation from the European Economic Community that will, perhaps, pronounce the words the women tell me they have been waiting for a year to hear—that Mabvuku and its sister cooperative in Glen Norah are worthy of a Z$200,000 grant to expand their operations. Meager wares, machinery, and inputs are on careful display. Nearly half the small room is taken up with cartons of graded silkworm cocoons. In one corner stands a rickety handloom readied for a demonstration and a spinning wheel loaded with silk thread. Rudimentary wall hangings, greeting cards crafted from cocoon parts, and a few nicely made articles of silk clothing stand out on the unpainted walls.

As I survey the surroundings, two European women arrive with great fanfare. These are the patrons of the cooperatives, the Greek women responsible for starting and funding the producer-cooperatives at the rate of Z$70,000 to Z$80,000 over a two-year period. They are obviously the center of gravity here, and as one breathlessly greets me the other makes suggestions for improving the display. Nervous energy goes into last-minute details.

A more typical day at the cooperative is busy but less frenetic: "The silkworms eat so much that we have to struggle to find enough mulberry leaves to satisfy them. Every day of feeding season, five of us take a public bus into the suburbs. We go house to house looking for mulberry trees and asking permission to take some leaves. The people there think we are mad. We stuff our bags and return, where another group spends the afternoon cleaning dust and water off the leaves—the worms are so fussy. With money from the European Community, we hope to get five hectares to plant our own trees and solve the problem of traveling so much.

"This cooperative is not good yet because we have the problem of finding leaves and little production. But we have learned new skills of weaving and crochet and operate like a family. The Greek women have been kind in sharing skills and social workers from the Harare City Council help. We have learned to be self-disciplined, because of a regular work schedule, and if resources become available the project will prosper and we can hire more people. Then we'll make many things, like mulberry jam and tinned mulberries. The cooperatives will keep poultry and expand the weaving."

A more typical day is also filled with high expectations: "We'll build a factory in the future and employ men and women, although the women will manage it because the men know they have no knowledge of silk. We have many plans. It took the Ministry of Cooperatives so long to process our papers for registration that some of us were discouraged. Our possibilities for EEC funding were held up. Maybe now it will be OK."

But this is not a typical day:

"Yes, yes we understand you have been undergoing training," says one of the two male EEC representatives. "But what about the administration of these cooperatives if the two Greek women leave Zimbabwe?"

"What about establishing prices? Who does that?"

"Have you considered the costs of fencing your new land?"

"Have you had the land surveyed? Precisely how much land is required for your project?"

"Can you get the spinning equipment you need in Zimbabwe?"

"How will you market your products?"

"Can you compete in export markets?"

The Greek women answer all the questions. The local women sigh. They tell me they can neither read well nor do sophisticated mathematics.

A month later, I interview one of the EEC representatives from the Mabvuku Inquisition:

"We haven't given out any aid to Mabvuku and Glen Norah because we're waiting for the government of Zimbabwe to put together a program proposal for us on this. All our funding requires evidence that the government is willing to help the project to succeed by following through on its promises for land or sales outlets. The relevant ministries have taken well over a year on this."

"We plan to fund the two silk cooperatives separately because we want them to compete. If you're not competitive, you'll fail in six months."

"It's good to have the Greek women involved. We calculate that their advice to the cooperatives is worth about Z$1,000 a month—they're saving us money."

A year later, I return to the European Community office in Harare. The original evaluation team for the silk cooperatives has left. "Ah, the silk cooperatives. You know them? Then you know that they are risky ventures. We funded them a while back, but I would never have funded them myself. Silk is a new product in Zimbabwe and we don't know if there is a market. Plus I don't like the idea that the whole thing is held together by two European women. If they decide to leave Zimbabwe, the cooperatives will fall apart. I know that."

"Then why did the EEC fund them?"

"It was all so well orchestrated as mainly a Greek-to-Greek thing. That evaluating officer you spoke to last year was Greek you know. Plus, the team had been to those cooperatives so often. It was all like family."

* * *

When Zimbabweans threw off the yoke of Rhodesia and its absentee landlord, Britain, in 1980, the party-government of ZANU–PF promoted producer-cooperatives as one way of bringing the poor into modern "production" despite national conditions of sluggish growth. However, the government waxed ambivalent about the importance of socialist cooperatives to an economy that was based more conventionally on large-scale farming, manufacturing, and mining. This ambivalence led cooperatives into a tragically ironic, migratory existence within government authority. Cooperatives first came under the purview of the Prime Minister's Office. Then they were transferred to a ministry that dealt with lands and resettlement, as though all cooperatives were agricultural in nature, which is not the case. In 1986, an independent Ministry of Cooperatives was formed, but less than two years later it was merged with Women's Affairs and Community Development; in effect, "cooperatives" were assigned to "women." Cooperatives were then separated from Women's Affairs and turned over to a new ministry, Cooperative and Community Development. Throughout this process of creeping defection, at least three hundred "women's" cooperatives were forced to struggle for survival in a setting analogous to issue anarchy, owing to the waning interest of the resource hegemon.[11]

But there has been more to producer-cooperation in Zimbabwe than government whim. Cooperatives are spaces where what is produced is not always what a government has in mind nor what development economists count as production. One bit of production entails cooperatively generated knowledge. Zimbabwean "women" who join cooperatives often tell me: "Here we help one another to think our own thoughts," or "Here we learn skills without fear," or "Here we do things by ourselves without doubting." Since knowledge is "produced by individuals in actual settings, and [is] organized by and organizing of definite social relations" (Smith 1990: 62), cooperators produce knowledge together. They cooperate, not because they are experiencing discord among themselves as they try to operate in an anarchic-seeming economy, they cooperate because they are social actors who can draw on shared values and embedded cooperative habits.

Along with knowledge, cooperatives produce a range of commodities, from school uniforms to soap, for markets that are often limited to one village or school. Their isolation from the large trade, monetary, and capital concerns that occupy theorists of IR and IPE means that the activities of cooperatives do not feature as starting points for theory. Supposedly, the action lies beyond such local, within-nation activities. But look again.

"Women" who are "cooperators" in Zimbabwe have one foot in a world resonant with neorealism, where competition is valued above cooperation; one foot in a nostalgic realm of used-to-be-household politics, where "international" and "domestic" did not cooperate; and a hand in the till of donor agencies, where multilateral funds are funneled to local projects. This means that these "women cooperators" are simultaneously inside and outside international political economy; inside and outside international-local regimes of aid and development; and inside and outside domestic-international arenas of managerial responsibility. It also means, as a result, that their situation and responses to it warrant attention as part of our study, of cooperation in international relations.

So also do the responses of agencies that have resources for cooperatives. In the course of my study, I recorded a variety of cynical comments from donors about both "women" and "cooperatives," as well as remarks (mostly "women" development agents) that indicated considerable resistance to the negative remarks. The following is only a sampler (rather than sample) of what I heard:

1. "Cooperatives are seen as where you go when there is nothing else to do. They're dumps for the marginal and the unemployed. If you're in a cooperative, you're a failure" (male representative of an international development organization).
2. "Men are threatened by women forming cooperatives. They might not bring in that much money, but they don't want women getting involved. Women, on the other hand, persevere" (woman representative of an international development organization).
3. "Women have always known that they were powerful, but we have been made to feel unpowerful. Now we appreciate the need to exert power. Before, marriage was a profession, Within it, women were given petty managerial responsibilities. What we want is to be on an equal basis with men, because as it stands now, even when women talk sense, their statements are rejected" (woman representative of the Ministry of Cooperatives).
4. "When I think of cooperatives, I think of men" (male representative of an international development organization).
5. "A cooperative has to be more than a family registering. It must be viable" (a local, woman consultant).
6. "All this emphasis on women. It seems too much. I don't approve of separate activities for women. They can always just join the men."
   "Can men always just join the women?" (Silence.) (Discussion with a male official from Mashonaland East Department of Cooperatives.)
7. "We tend to speak of cooperatives as a strategy, but we do not see that people can be pawns in the game" (local woman consultant).

Local "women" cooperators come into "international relations" through these oftentimes reluctant donor agencies. The donors do not usually cooperate with cooperators in determining a project for funding. Rather, they articulate general principles, norms, and rules governing eligibility for funds and expect cooperatives to cooperate with them in a patron-client relationship that legitimates the Western sense of proper business techniques.

The European Economic Community's Microprojects program is especially strack. Prospective recipients of funds must demonstrate the technical, financial, and economic feasibility of their projects and provide assurances that long-run operating costs will be available locally. The projects must also fit into one of several categories of donor priority and satisfy a lengthy list of standards, one of which is that proposals must be written, and written in English, even if project members are not literate or English-speaking. The rules are authoritative. Only serious business enterprises will be funded. Yet in the case under consideration here, the EEC gave generous project funding to cooperatives that insisted on a "family" identity (and we have already seen the opinion that "a cooperative has to be more than a family registering").

Local Meanings of Cooperation

Arguably, the members of the cooperatives hold two approaches to co-operation simultaneously. The first approach is instrumental: one must be proper patrons and cooperate with a donor in order to garner the funds needed to pursue projects. Members anoint the Greek sponsors to handle this form of cooperation and themselves hold back in silence during the EEC inquisition. One can think one's own thoughts while allowing others to speak the words that donors expect to hear because the second meaning of cooperation is noninstrumental. A good cooperative operates like a good family. The co-op teaches skills to its members and nourishes their dreams. It is, in effect, a relationally autonomous site of connection and nurturance, where members are strengthened to handle discord that threatens from out beyond; i.e., not from within. But families in Zimbabwe are no more or less idyllic than families located elsewhere.[12] Discord is common. Cooperation, however, as shaped by these "women," has to do with shared training in what they think of as a sheltering environment vis-à-vis the "out beyond." Their embeddedness in social spaces helps the cooperators to attain a state of diffuse reciprocity, *from whence members initiate the cooperative effort*.

Of course, some IR theorists will argue, righteously, that the cooperatives are not states operating under conditions of anarchy and self-help! But just as multilateralists question the sacred tree of anarchy in IR, there is a larger theoretical lesson to be pondered here. Perhaps domestic norms of cooperation, fixedly located beyond anarchy, are really inside IR, where they can dispel the mesmerizing effects of rehearsed anarchy. The inside, in other words, could have broader parameters of cooperation than many theorists of IR/IPE notice, precisely because states are embedded in ongoing and historical relationships. James Caporaso tells us that the basic question "is not how to cooperate and to derive rules, norms, and sociality from a rule-free, normless state of nature. Rather, the starting point is a social conception of the actors." (Caporaso 1993: 77–78). I would add that that social starting point makes it possible for multiple subjectivities to exist in empathetic conversation with each other, such that rigid and otherly norms of eligibility can accommodate an outlaw family.

The Outside and Inside Meet

We now confidently return to the story of Zimbabwean cooperatives as the story of marginalized insiders to IPE. The Greek sponsors loom into view as insider-outsiders. They are cast by the "women" in a parental-familial role and will, in fact, never receive tit-for-tat reciprocation for their considerable financial and training efforts. That is how it is in "families." Moreover, their trainees develop "own thoughts" on how to build an extended family—a factory that they themselves will run "because the men know they have no knowledge of silk." (Presumably the Greek patrons will be part of the "family," but they are not explicitly mentioned.) The cooperators resist the oversupervision of a standpoint as they take in the standpoints of these empathetic others.

Meanwhile, their patrons face oversupervision from other outside quarters. They face, first, a certain loss of racial authority by working closely with the African "other" in a country that tolerates considerable de facto segregation (of "cultures," the whites say). Second, as "women" they are suspect in donor circles: "I don't like the idea that the whole thing is held together by two European women." And yet, like the women cooperators, they too escape oversupervision; in their case by having one foot inside the cooperatives and the other inside the camp of EEC kith-and-kin. The first placement makes it difficult for the second foot to get a too-tight colonial grip on them and on the cooperatives through them.

The EEC donors also use a Greek-to-Greek "family" relationship to justify (or simply rationalize) funding for these particular cooperatives. Such funding of a cooperative—using family norms—however, is a highly irregular way for multilateral lending agencies to bring the poor into modernity. Some shifting of identity, some mobility among multiple subjectivities, to enable those inside the rules to draw on the outside realm of "family" for meaning and justification—much as the cooperators slipped the boundaries between "cooperatives" and "families" in order to "make many things."

We can say that the resultant cooperations challenge a local subtext in which *all* cooperators are "failures," people who have not made it as sovereign individuals in the valued anarchy of the marketplace. They also face-off simultaneous oversupervision and invisibility in the theories that purport to explain cooperation, or the lack thereof, in international relations. Rather than presenting us with homegrown theory per se, they surprise us, not the least by showing us how reginas in a local situation are affected by regimes affiliated with the international political economy; and how reginas, in turn, can influence the policies of regime members.

AND SO?

It is an accident, one supposes, that there are Greek patrons in Zimbabwe who can develop links with Greek representatives from international relations in order to configure a family authority that overcomes strack rules. Is it an accident that participants in two cooperatives have a family-style diffuse reciprocity among themselves before they seek specific reciprocity with the EEC? One cannot say. Is it accidental that the metaphor of "family" figures into the explanation for the EEC decision to fund the two silkmaking cooperatives? Or did a "strange" conversation take place in this Zimbabwean locale, such that "family" emerged as the point of tangency across difference? Do actors involved in international relations take their cues from socialities that exist beyond the carefully demarcated realm of the international? Does international relations operate with isolated self-helpers or with socially embedded groups that connect on the basis of shared "outside" symbols? All of this is fertile research terrain.

Gender weaves in and out of the stories of cooperation in Zimbabwe and in IR. Gender is often associated only with "women," who are entreated to join those who are the ungendered humans, no questions asked, in an enterprise of theory-building that cannot include them. The invitation to drop gender as a way of knowing hides the already wielded power to exclude through gender-privileged cooperations, a power that affects the field's theory about cooperation. The multilateralists alone seem to understand that "rules, norms, and habits of cooperation [are not] exclusively . . . something external to agents (states), something that agents 'bump into' or 'run up against' as they interact with one another. Instead, they recognize that these practices are often constitutive of the identities and power of agents in the first place" (Caporaso 1993: 78).

Yet gender is an identity, for both "men" and "women," in international relations that even the multilateralists powerfully occlude. They "not-see" postmodern feminist resonances in their call to rethink the "problem of cooperation," usually portrayed as a game of strategic interaction, in favor of a model of decision featuring "debate, communication, persuasion, argument, and discursive legitimation." They overlook gender generally, even as they "do-see" that "the international system is not just a collection of independent states in interaction" (Caporaso 1993: 78).

If we are to promote the idea that "the international system is a forum as well as a chessboard," it is imperative to admit gender into the discussion. This means that not only should the reginas of Zimbabwe speak alongside states, regimes, and multilateral agencies that are themselves the local agents of international political economy, it is also appropriate to query *masculine* gender as an identity that carries power and taken-for-granted assumptions about cooperation. We must look outside IR for the inside, and that "outside" includes those whose lots in life are unchronicled and subversive: "We have many plans. It took the Ministry of Cooperati[on] so long to process our papers for registration that some of us were discouraged. . . . Maybe now. . . ."

NOTES

I prepared this chapter as I was beginning to explore links between my Africanist and feminist IR identities. I have subsequently elaborated the analysis presented here for *Feminist Theory and International Relations Theory in a Postmodern Era* (Cambridge University Press, 1994), and have returned to this piece with a new eye. I thank the Center for International Studies, University of Southern California, for a senior visiting scholar award in 1991 that enabled me to spend time thinking and writing about intersections that should be studied as everyday sites of international relations.

1. These approaches do not exhaust the universe of possibilities for cooperation in mainstream IR/IPE. Ruggie (1993), for instance, suggests that we could speak of bilateralism and imperialism as generic institutional forms of cooperation in international relations. There is a longer tradition of so-called idealist writings that emphasizes the possibilities for cooperatively bringing the domestic rule of law governing liberal Western states to bear on international relations. See the overview in Suganami (1989). There are also functionalist and neofunctionalist writers of the international organization tradition who placed their faith in the formal processes of coordination undertaken by international governmental and nongovernmental organizations. See the overview in Ruggie and Kratochwil (1986). The approaches I discuss here simply seem most current in the field.

2. Indeed, although hegemonic stability theory can seem to focus on cooperative aspects of international relations (that is, on states cooperating with a hegemon in creating regimes) in fact, "the most that can be said about hegemonic power is that it will seek to construct an international order in *some* form, presumably along lines that are compatible with its own international objectives and domestic structures. But in the end, that really is not saying very much" (Ruggie 1993: 25).

3. See Nancy Hirschmann's (1989) discussion of relational and reactive autonomy. For an application to IR, see Christine Sylvester (1992).

4. For a further discussion of "women" as visitors to international relations, because their homes are assigned elsewhere, see Sylvester (1993b, 1994).

5. For an elaboration of the feminist standpoint, see Hartsock (1983). For an application of it to IR, see Tickner (1992).

6. See discussions of feminist postmodernism in Flax (1990) and Harding (1986). Elshtain (1987) uses elements of this approach.

7. This take on feminist standpoint is found in Gilligan (1982) and elaborated and expanded in scope by Tronto (1987).

8. Kathy Ferguson (1993: 12) refers to this as the hermeneutic project of standpoint that calls upon "some version of an ontology of discovery and an epistemology of attunement."

9. One could argue, along with neoliberal institutionalism, that a history of discord between the East and West German states boiled over for the people of East Germany once the Soviet empire began to unravel, leading to cooperation. Still, the image of "women" pushing baby carriages through the Wall and living to tell their tales cannot be accommodated in neorealist and neoliberal institutionalist frameworks, which are peopled only with decisionmakers, government authorities, and an occasional statesman. For in this case, groups of people (momentarily) usurped the authority of state groups, and the latter, unable to weather the onslaught long enough to seek cooperation with the West, expired. For two glimpses of "women" in the German merger, see the exchange between Martina Fischer/Barbara Munske and Soja Fiedler in Sylvester (1993a).

10. See Riley (1988) for the question of whether "women" exist. See Ferguson (1993) for a discussion of mobile subjectivities.

11. For additional discussion of cooperatives in Zimbabwe, see Christine Sylvester 1991a. For an overview of Zimbabwe's political economy, including gender issues in the territory, see Sylvester (1991b).

12. When I speak of families in this context, my frame of reference is the heterosexual family. I am aware that this is a stereotype of *family* and yet am also aware that homosexuality among Africans in Zimbabwe seems to exist underground, sealed off by a relentless homophobia in the local culture.

6

Latin American Voices of Resistance: Women's Movements and Development Debates

Marianne H. Marchand

Very few new ideas about "development" have emerged during the last ten years. Unlike the 1970s, no major conceptual debates have dominated the field.[1] At the same time, the 1980s will claim their place in history as the decade that brought about a dual revolution of liberal democracy and free-market economics. Is it a coincidence that the absence of major "development" controversies occurred during the period when the Reagan revolution and the revolution in Eastern Europe took center stage? I will argue in this chapter that the answer is no.

The production of knowledge (in this case: "development" concepts) is not an autonomous, ahistorical process; rather, it is embedded in prevalent sociopolitical and economic (as well as cultural) forces and structures. As Rob Walker points out:

> [There is a] recognition that the categories and languages in which it is now possible to speak about global problems and political practices incorporate historically specific interests. Although there is no shortage of information about the state of the modern world, it is exceptionally difficult to turn this information into liberating human practices. Information is created largely by elites and for elites. Dominant forms of knowledge and information presume some things are important whereas others are less so. Knowledge and power are intimately associated (1988: 10).

However, a recognition that the production of knowledge is largely an affair of elites begs the question: What about the other groups in society?[2] Are they, and have they been, involved in attempts to resist, as well as transform, prevalent development policies? If so, can we recover their silenced voices?

In this chapter, I will explore what forms of resistance have emerged that challenge new development policies based on neoconservative, free-market economics. Geographically, the analysis will be limited to Latin America. With dependency theory, the region generated one of the most important theoretical challenges to modernization theory during the late 1960s and 1970s. Concurrently, Latin America became the site of neoconservative economic experiments (Foxley 1987). The decade of the 1980s, in turn, brought the debt crisis, and in its wake more democratic forms of government. In sum, Latin America provides an excellent backdrop for my analysis.

In Latin America one does not need to search long to find "sites of resistance" against the new orthodoxy of development. During the last two decades, so-called social or popular movements have entered the political arena throughout Latin America. These movements mostly emerged in response to political repression (under authoritarian regimes) and economic policies (i.e., neoconservative experiments and structural adjustment policies). A closer look at these movements reveals that a majority of the participants were poor women (some estimate their participation as high as 70–80 percent). In addition, a large portion of these social movements deal specifically with women's concerns.

Against this background, this chapter will focus on two specific questions: (1) What kind of practices have Latin American social movements used in resisting dominant development policies? (2) Are these forms of resistance "gendered" practices? In other words, does the female participation rate affect what forms of resistance are employed?

It is impossible to give definitive answers to these questions. However, I will try to establish whether certain patterns (of resistance) exist and also make suggestions as to whether these questions will be worth exploring further. In the remainder of the chapter, I will first provide an overview of the current state of development debates within academic circles. Then I will focus on Latin American social movements and, in particular, how they have been approached in the literature. Finally, I will analyze how these popular movements have tried to resist and challenge dominant development discourses.

"DEVELOPMENT" AND THE "END OF HISTORY"

From its inception, the field of development studies has had to deal with the recurrent question: How do we conceptualize development? To date, no single definition of development has been agreed upon. However, most specialists now concur that we cannot reduce development to a simple measure of growth in gross domestic product (GDP) per capita. Despite partially successful attempts by dependency theorists and international organizations[3] to challenge (previously) dominant interpretations of development, the meaning of *development* is now more than ever at issue. On the one hand, there is the urgent need to reassess our understanding of "development" and "underdevelopment." This is illustrated by the fact that many Third World countries are currently worse off than they were twenty years ago,[4] confronting economic recession, a debt crisis, a food crisis, and an environmental crisis, as well as rising malnutrition and infant mortality.

In addition, it has become virtually impossible for inhabitants of industrialized countries any longer to dismiss the underdevelopment problematique as a foreign phenomenon from which they will be spared. Increasingly, the boundaries between "domestic" and "foreign" have become blurred. The fate of so-called developed nations has become tied to that of the "underdeveloped" (Hamilton 1990). Recent examples of a growing awareness about this new interdependence have been concerns voiced about the ties between the destruction of the Amazon rainforest and global warming. Even President George Bush himself testified to the new awareness when he linked the fate of Kuwait to standards of living in the United States. In addition, many scholars now claim the existence of "Third World enclaves," in the form of inner-city ghettos, pockets of rural poverty, Indian reservations, and so forth, within the First World (Stavrianos 1981).

On the other hand, the seemingly justified calls for rethinking our development strategies have taken a back seat in the face of another 1980s phenomenon, the Reagan revolution. Despite the various development crises mentioned above, the "capitalist path of development" was being presented, with renewed vigor, to Third World countries as the only possible route out of a situation of underdevelopment.[5] The renewed insistence on capitalist development as the only viable solution should be seen in the context of the largely successful attempt by the Reagan administration to reconstruct U.S. supremacy on the basis of anti-Keynesian economic liberalism, consisting of supply-side economics combined with monetarism (Augelli and Murphy 1988).[6] The United States was able to reestablish itself by defeating a weakened Third World counterhegemonic bloc (weakened because of internal contradictions) built upon the interests of the OPEC countries and the quest for a New International Economic Order.

The effects of these changes reverberated into international civil society. First, they entailed the demise of dependency theory to the point where (former) *dependentistas* or sympathizers do not believe in dependency theory anymore (see, for example, Blomström and Hettne 1984; Booth 1985; Randall and Theobald 1985; Kay 1989). Also, politicians such as Jamaica's former prime minister, Michael Manley, and Venezuelan President Carlos Andres Perez, who in the 1970s heralded dependency theory and Third World activism, have now rejected it under the new circumstances. The decline of dependency theory has been accompanied by a reassertion and resurgence of modernization theory "new style," i.e., with an anti-Keynesian thrust.

Moreover, in the wake of the recent changes in Eastern Europe, modernization theory can now, finally, after almost four decades, claim victory in the Cold War of development theories. This victorious claim was actually made by Francis Fukayama in his now famous article, "The End of History?" where he states:

> But the century that began full of self-confidence in the ultimate triumph of Western liberal democracy seems at its close to be returning full circle to where it started: . . . to an unabashed victory of economic and political liberalism. The triumph of the West, of the Western *idea,* is evident first of all in the total exhaustion of viable systematic alternatives to Western liberalism (1989: 3).

This is not to say that intellectuals in Latin America are accepting modernization theory's renewed dominant position without opposition; but discussions about development are now taking place within a different economic and political climate. First, the mere scope and urgency of the Latin American debt crisis has prompted scholars to look for immediate and concrete solutions (as far as that is possible!). Second, the region's collective return to democracy is being highly valued among Latin American scholars. The memories of what life was like under repressive, bureaucratic, authoritarian regimes have convinced many that reaching policy decisions by consensus is extremely important. This has led to a reluctance to engage in ideological debates. For example, Sergio Bitar, a Chilean economist who advocates a neostructuralist approach, emphasizes the similarities between neostructuralists and neoconservative (or monetarist) principles before even analyzing their differences:

> With respect to principles, when the general statements formulated by the advocates of the liberalizing/privatizing system are compared, a strong similarity is observed with the positions of the neo-structuralists. Both the "mainstream" thinking in Latin America and the new structural adjustment theories of the World Bank attach priority to speeding up the growth rate, the eradication of extreme poverty, improving efficiency and competitiveness and increasing exports (1988: 48–49).

In sum, current development debates do not so much address the question of *whether* adjustment programs should be implemented, but rather *what kind* of adjustment policies should be chosen. What we witness are technical disputes between advocates of orthodox and heterodox policies, not a fundamental debate about underlying, basic assumptions (e.g., Meller 1991). In Imre Lakatos's terms, the "hard core" of modernization theory is not being challenged; these disputes take place in its "protective belt" (1970).

LATIN AMERICAN SOCIAL MOVEMENTS AND "DEVELOPMENT"

Despite modernization theory's apparent victory in the Cold War, the debates surrounding the meaning of development have not disappeared.

This time, however, we need to look beyond the academic community to find sites of resistance that challenge the underlying assumptions of modernization theory new style. In the 1980s and 1990s development debates have been taken to the streets in Latin America. Critical social movements or popular movements have voiced resistance against the socioeconomic and political consequences of dominant development models. Their resistance has taken many different forms, ranging from strikes, soup kitchens, neighborhood actions against landlords, land invasions, and demonstrations, to food (IMF) riots and even the ballot box.[7] In other words, presently it seems that any Kuhnian paradigm shift is more likely to result from challenges produced by social movements than from technical disputes among Latin American intellectuals.

The literature on popular movements, which has been at least as prolific as the movements themselves, has tended to focus on two questions. First, various authors have gone to great lengths to differentiate among social, political, and popular movements. Analytically, one can distinguish social movements from political movements on the grounds that they work within civil society and act in defense of specific sectoral interests (Tamayo 1990: 121). Political movements, on the other hand, go beyond immediate sectoral interests and direct their attention at the state (Tamayo 1990). Popular movements largely coincide with political movements. The only difference is that popular movements specifically "comprise a struggle to constitute the 'people' as political actors" (Foweraker 1990). Despite attempts to draw strong demarcation lines among various types of movements, a closer reading of the literature reveals that, in practice, authors often refer to the same or similar movements even though they label them differently (Eckstein 1989; Foweraker and Craig 1990; Hellman 1990). In view of this, trying to distinguish among social, political, and popular movements appears to be a difficult, if not futile, exercise. In addition to this pragmatic reason for not differentiating the various movements, Foweraker claims that there is a more serious, conceptual one: "so-called social movements cannot exist in a separate social sphere that allows only 'external' relations with the political system" (1990: 5). Throughout this chapter, I will use the terms social, political, and popular movements interchangeably, especially since most movements incorporate a combination of social, economic, and political concerns.

The question of autonomy is the second theoretical issue on which much of the literature has focused. A majority of the authors assume that popular movements derive power from their ability to keep their distance from other political forces in society and resist the temptation to create alliances with the latter. As Judith Adler Hellman notes, "some analysts . . . insist that the incorporation of autonomous social movements into broader political movements represents the loss of an authentic popular voice" (1990: 10). I agree with these analysts that the capability to act independently or autonomously creates a certain power for popular movements.

However, this viewpoint entirely overlooks other sources and forms of power, one of which is derived from a movement's ability to influence and change, through its practices, dominant discourses on, for instance, "development." From this vantage point, we should not assume a priori that popular movements are best off by preserving their autonomy. Depending on local circumstances, popular movements might well gain politically and enhance their power by creating alliances with other political forces, either at home or abroad, or both. An excellent example of a movement that successfully created alliances with other political groups and thus became more powerful is the rubber-tappers movement in Brazil. The rubber-tappers not only reached out to native Americans living in the Amazon, they also entered into cooperative relationships with the Brazilian labor party (Partido dos Trabalhadores) and urban, mostly middle-class, environmental groups, as well as the international environmental community. The effect so far has been a calling into question of Brazil's development policies, which emphasize rapid industrialization and an expansion of cash-crop agriculture. The alternative presented by the rubber-tappers and their allies is the creation of "extractive reserves" in the Amazon that would enable sustainable development of the forest (Mendes, 1989).[8]

For a popular movement, the obvious danger in creating alliances lies in the possibility of being co-opted by a political organization, such as a labor union or political party, and thereby losing any say in issues that are on the movement's agenda. However, I agree with Hellman's view on this issue:

> The concern of analysts of social movements for the survival and continued independence of the movements they study is an understandable outgrowth of their observation that grassroots movements may, and often have, disappeared from the scene as autonomous actors once they give their formal support to, formally ally with, or in some other fashion cast their lot with political parties. But this position overlooks the possibility that movements can influence parties or contribute to the rise of new political formations, radicalizing and transforming political programs and dictating an agenda of new issues—a phenomenon that has actually occurred in Mexico and Brazil as in France, Italy, and West Germany (1990: 11).

To date, the general literature on social movements has not addressed the questions that are the focus of this chapter: (1) Can the practices (of resistance) by social movements influence dominant development discourse(s)? (2) Are these forms of resistance "gendered practices?" However, feminist studies of Latin American women's movements have discovered some interesting patterns.[9] The fact that women, and in particular women who are poor, actively participate in the public sphere of Latin American society is a novelty. This has induced several scholars to search for reasons why these women suddenly became so active and to analyze the extent to which politics changed due to their participation (Jaquette 1989; Alvarez 1990; Safa 1990). According to these analysts, a variety of reasons contribute to increased women's participation in the public sphere.

Paradoxically, the Roman Catholic church in Latin America has laid the groundwork for increased women's participation in the public sphere. In the wake of Vatican Council II (1962–1965), the region saw the emergence of liberation theology. In an attempt to create a church for the poor, advocates of liberation theology developed Christian base-communities, the participants in which were mostly women. Within these base-communities, much attention was given to the process of *concientización*.[10] Due to their exposure to this process, poor Latin American women not only became increasingly aware that their poverty was primarily a result of society's socioeconomic and political structures, they also gained a sense of self-empowerment. As Alvarez argues in the case of Brazil, women's participation in popular movements is clearly a "spin-off" of the *concientización* process that took place within the Christian base-communities:

> The political and institutional transformation of the Brazilian Catholic Church proved to be a critical factor in the genesis of contemporary feminism. As in other Latin American nations, during the 1960s and 1970s, sectors of the Brazilian Church gradually turned toward the poor and against the military regime. Actively promoting the organization of the popular classes, creating "new communities of equals" among the "People of God," the progressive Church also provided a vital organizational umbrella for the opposition and cloaked its activities with a veil of moral legitimacy. . . .
> Though originally created as "women's auxiliaries" to Christian Base Communities (or Sociedades de Amigos de Barrio) during the late 1960s and early 1970s, women's community organizations soon took on a political dynamic of their own. Poor and working-class women began organizing around their immediate survival needs, which were sometimes neglected by "mixed" neighborhood groups (1989: 21).

It is interesting to note that in countries where liberation theology has been well represented, women's movements are also very prominent (e.g., Brazil, Nicaragua, Peru).

Whereas liberation theology was instrumental in raising women's consciousness, immediate concerns about economic and political survival made women become active in the public sphere. As early as the mid-1970s,[11] poor and working-class women started to feel the impact of development policies that emphasized rapid economic growth without redistribution of wealth. For them, economic hard times were translated into the inability to fulfill their traditional roles as wives and mothers. According to Alvarez, "in keeping with their socially ascribed roles as the "wives, mothers, and nurturers" of family and community, women of the popular classes were among the first to protest the authoritarian regime's regressive social and economic policies" (1989:21). Being unable to feed their families, in particular their children, many women decided to engage in a variety of survival strategies, such as creating soup kitchens, neighborhood committees, and so forth, to cope with the situation.

Women entered the public sphere in response not only to economic hard times, but also to political repression. The most salient example is that of the *Madres de Plaza de Mayo*. For *Las Madres Locas,* being the caretaker of the family went beyond feeding the children. According to Navarro (1989), when female relatives of "the disappeared" could not get any information about their loved ones from the police, the military, or any other government agency, they decided to go public with their personal grief because they felt it was their duty as wives, mothers, sisters, and lovers.

Helen Icken Safa argues that the entrance of Latin American women into the public sphere is not just a response to political and economic crises in the region. According to her, rapid economic development over the last two to three decades has fundamentally changed the distinction between public and private spheres. Women, perceiving that "their traditional sphere" was under siege, responded by entering the public domain:

> While many studies trace the origin of these [i.e., women's] movements to the current economic and political crisis in the region, I believe they are indicative of a broader historical trend toward the breakdown of the traditional division between the private and public spheres in Latin America. The private sphere of the family has always been considered the domain of women, but it is increasingly threatened by economic and political forces (1990, 355).

How do we interpret these individual and collective practices through which Latin American women have resisted and challenged the effects of their governments' development policies? More importantly, how do these women interpret their own acts of resistance? Two issues stand out. First, many women involved with social movements consider their actions to be apolitical! Second, most of these women reject the label "feminist." They insist that their movements are "feminine" movements, even if they pursue such issues as child-care or women's health (Schmink 1981; Chuchryk 1989; Alvarez 1990).

Why do women who are active in neighborhood committees and soup kitchens, who demonstrate for child-care and against rising cost of living, who go door-to-door with petitions for a local health clinic, consider themselves to be apolitical? Teresa Pires de Rio Caldeira's study (1990) of women involved in a number of Sao Paulo's social movements provides an explanation. For her article "Women, Daily Life and Politics," Caldeira interviewed Paulista women about their motivations for joining social movements. She also asked them about their views on a variety of political issues. What she found was that in the minds of these women, involvement in a social movement becomes a "gendered practice." They define social movements as a new female sphere in which they can legitimately participate. As a result of their participation in social movements, women develop a new identity, which

> contrasts with two other experiences: that of the traditional housewife and that of the man of politics. The situation of the housewife enclosed within the four walls of her home, frozen in time, totally dependent on the man—obviously a negative characterization—is offset against an "opening to the world" achieved by participating in local movements and associations such as the CEBs [i.e., Christian base communities] and SABs [Society of the Friends of the Neighborhood]. Thus, women's new identity is established through the practices of these movements, which contrast with the traditional: they encourage women not to stay alone at home all day but to go out, to learn, to participate (Caldeira 1990: 64).

Paulista women have carved out this new, positive female identity not only in opposition to the old, negative image of the housewife who is staying at home alone, but also in contrast to "typical male activities in the public sphere." According to the women interviewed by Caldeira, their public actions are not political. Their involvement is for "the good of the community," because the "immediate interests of the neighborhood" are at stake. In their own words, these women are participating in the sphere of "woman-talk" (Caldeira 1990). In contrast, politics is characterized as a male sphere where participants (politicians and the like) are in it for their "own personal interests." Politicians are thought to pursue remote or foreign issues that do not have anything to do with the daily lives of these women and their families (Caldeira, 1990).

Why do these women insist that their actions are apolitical? As Caldeira points out, by thus defining their participation in social movements, these women legitimize their entrance into the public sphere to those who might otherwise object:

> In general, women who participate do not work outside the home and on several occasions we were told how they were prevented from doing so by their husbands, alluding to all types of masculine and feminine stereotypes. Their participation in the community or in campaigns for specific demands, however, is neither disapproved of nor prohibited, although it can cause domestic problems, and this is because the space for the new experience has opened precisely on the basis of a widening of women's traditional and legitimate role. They are responsible mothers, housewives, participating in a space for women only, which is thus not considered dangerous. Preserving participating as a female space (in contrast to the masculine space of politics) can therefore be considered as necessary to the strategy of legitimizing activism in the public world without creating excessive conflicts in the private sphere (1990: 65).

Similarly, insisting on the apolitical nature of their public actions allowed women to oppose policies of the authoritarian regime under which they were living. Examples of this practice abound. In the case of *Las Madres de Plaza de Mayo,* as Marysa Navarro (1989) explains, the Argentine military junta did not recognize the public denunciations by the Crazy Mothers[12] about their disappeared relatives as a political act, let alone a serious political threat to the regime's stability; not, at least, until it was too late. Under a regime whose answer to any political act was repression, through their weekly gatherings at the Plaza de Mayo these women managed to create a new political space right under the regime's eyes.[13] For the longest time, the political nature of their actions remained invisible to the authorities (Navarro 1989). Although the participation of women in social movements is often not perceived as political, the effect of their engagement in public activities has been to transform and redefine the boundaries between the public and private spheres, as well as those of male and female identities (Caldeira 1990).

There are similarities in the reasons why women insist on the apolitical nature of their actions and their rejection of the feminist label. In Latin America, the term *feminism* is often rejected because it evokes images of a middle-class, intellectual movement; it is perceived as yet another form of Western (in particular Anglo-Saxon) imperialism. For an account of this in Chile, see Chuchryk (1989). Especially, those movements made up of women from marginalized socioeconomic backgrounds are given the description "feminine" by their participants.

According to Maxine Molyneux (1985), the distinction between *feminine* and *feminist* movements lies primarily in the nature of the issues that they address. Feminine movements tend to focus on gender-related questions or practical gender interests. An example would be women who engage in collective action because they feel that their families' livelihood, and thus their own traditional female roles, are being threatened. On the other hand, feminist movements are concerned with gender-specific or strategic gender interests. In Molyneux's words,

> Strategic interests are derived in the first instance deductively, that is, from the analysis of women's subordination and from the formulation of an alternative, more satisfactory set of arrangements to those which exist. These ethical and theoretical criteria assist in the formulation of strategic objectives to overcome women's subordination, such as the abolition of the sexual division of labor, the alleviation of the burden of domestic labor and childcare, the removal of institutionalized forms of discrimination, the attainment of political equality, the establishment of freedom of choice over childbearing, and the adoption of adequate measures against male violence and control over women (1985: 232–233).

However, both Patricia Chuchryk (1989) and Sonia Alvarez (1990) show that the distinction between feminist/gender-specific and feminine/gender-related interests is not as clear-cut as Molyneux wants us to believe. For instance, self-proclaimed feminine movements regularly address issues such as sexuality and women's legal rights (Chuchryk 1989: 164). And Alvarez (1990) points out that in Brazil feminine and feminist movements are cooperating very closely. In sum, as with the Paulista women insisting that their actions are apolitical, it is important to understand why women reject the label feminist under certain circumstances.

As noted above, women can legitimize their involvement in feminine movements on the grounds that it is an extension of their traditional female roles: to participate in a feminine movement is to try to improve the living conditions of the entire family. Because feminine movements fall within the scope of the traditional female sphere (at least in the justification for their existence), male relatives of women participating will not feel threatened in their position.

While the cultural conditioning of *marianismo*—the female counterpart to machismo that lends women moral and spiritual superiority—denies Latin American women full participation in the public sphere as equals to men, it serves at the same time as a source of empowerment (see Stevens 1973). In particular, poor, urban women have, therefore, focused on expanding the female sphere by creating new female spaces in the public domain, instead of pursuing equality with men by trying to eliminate what are perceived to be cultural boundaries between male and female spheres.

This is not to say that in Latin America there are no women who consider themselves to be feminists or who are involved in traditional politics. Nor does it mean that when individual women insist on the feminine and apolitical nature of their activities, their male relatives will not object to their participation in social movements. However, many women from poor, urban backgrounds successfully participate in social movements by using these legitimizing strategies.

For this analysis, what is most important is that the majority of women in social movements recognize their activities as gendered practices. This is true for the objectives of the participants (to improve the immediate needs of the community), for their justification (to protect their families' livelihood), and for the means (allowing them not to interfere with traditional political channels).

Next, a short dedication: I dedicate the last section of this chapter to a unique, innovative "gendered practice"—one already used by a few women involved in social movements. In this practice, poor, Latin American women give their oral testimony to an intermediary (ethnographer, journalist, social scientist) who then edits and publishes the testimony. Unfortunately, the practice has thus far attracted little or no attention from political scientists. By discussing this practice in more detail, I hope to bring about the recognition that testimonies are powerful political documents that challenge and resist dominant development policies in the region. Because the giving of testimony is a strategy employed by women involved in social movements, the practice should be studied within the context of other strategies pursued by popular movements.

TESTIMONIES AS VOICES OF RESISTANCE

Many academic disciplines, ranging from literary studies to history, have given consideration to life-histories/testimonies as a "phenomenon." However, for the purpose of this chapter, debates in the fields of anthropology and Latin American literature have most to offer. From a review of the literature on testimonies/life-histories generated by both fields, it appears that the two terms overlap. What is a *testimony* for a scholar of one field is a *life-history* for the other. A closer reading reveals that testimonies are a subcategory of life-histories. A life-history can be defined as "any retrospective account by the individual of his life in whole or in part, in written or oral form, *that has been elicited or prompted by another person*" (Watson and Watson-Franke 1985: 2). A testimony (or *testimonio*) distinguishes itself from the general category of life-history by its denunciatory nature. In the illuminating words of John Beverley and Marc Zimmerman:

> The word [i.e., testimonio] suggests the act of testifying or bearing witness in a legal or religious sense. That connotation is important, because it distinguishes testimonio from simple recorded participant narrative. In Rene Jara's phrase, testimonio is a "narracion de urgencia"—a story that *needs* to be told—involving a problem of repression, poverty, subalternity, exploitation, or simple struggle for survival, which is implicated in the act of narration itself (1990: 173).

The openly political nature of testimonies has been traced to the Cuban Revolution. In the Revolution's wake, accounts by people who had participated in the 26 of July Movement and Che Guevara's guerrilla activities were published, "in part as a form of propaganda for armed struggle directed toward a progressive general public, in part as a kind of cadre literature internal to the revolutionary organizations themselves" (Beverley and Zimmerman 1990: 174). Since then, testimonial literature has broadened its scope. It now includes narratives by individuals from a wide variety of marginalized groups in Latin American society. From a literary perspective, "testimonio is a fundamentally democratic and egalitarian form of narrative in the sense that it implies that *any* life so narrated can have a kind of representativity. Each testimonio evokes an absent polyphony of other voices, other possible lives and experiences" (Beverley and Zimmerman 1990: 175). In sum, I will use the term *life-history* to refer to the generic category of recorded participant narrative; *testimony* will denote life-history of a political, denunciatory nature.

Life histories/testimonies have generated many debates among anthropologists and students of Latin American literature.[14] For anthropologists, the debate has focused on the question of whether life-histories are a better format for representing (other) cultures. Advocates have argued that life-histories are the new format that ethnographic texts should follow, because it allows the "anthropological subject" to speak for herself and to represent her own society. Critics, however, have pointed out that the ethnographer still holds the power of production. When creating the text, the ethnographer engages in contextualizing/representing the informants' voices and through these actions either validates or delegitimizes them. At particular moments, it is not clear whose voice is speaking (Clifford, 1986).

The field of Latin American literature has addressed testimonies from a different vantage point. The first problem that has attracted the attention of these scholars is the issue of authorship in testimonies. It could be argued that the anthropologists' questions about representation have been reformulated by literary scholars into questions of authorship. The literary question, Who is the real author? overlaps with the anthropological questions, Who is speaking/Whose voices are we hearing? Within Latin American literature, a consensus appears to be emerging that the problem of authorship will remain largely unresolved. The most one can do is to impose, unilaterally, a single authorship onto the text or assume that the text has been written by multiple authors (Jara and Vidal 1986; Behar 1990; Beverley and Zimmerman 1990).

Scholars of Latin American literature are also involved in a second, more fundamental, debate surrounding testimonies. As, in anthropology, the critique of colonial discourse touches the foundations of the discipline, so does this debate in literature. The question being raised focuses on whether testimonies reflect what is called the truth or are fiction (Jara and Vidal 1986; Beverley and Zimmerman 1990). Why is this question so problematical? In literary terms, the discursive dilemma that emerges can be formulated in the following opposition: if one considers testimonies to be truthful, then *they can only be nonliterary* documents; on the other hand, if one assumes that testimonies are literature, *they have to be fictional.* As Clifford (1986) notes, this opposition is grounded in the opposition of science versus literature, which emerged during the Renaissance period and culminated in the project of the Enlightenment. Against this background, Beverley and Zimmerman (1990) really problematize the disciplinary boundaries of (Latin American) literature by assuming that testimonies are simultaneously fact and fiction.

As an outsider, one can discern in the above overview of the two debates how (self-)imposed disciplinary boundaries prevent the two disciplines from conversing—as exemplified by the overlap between questions about authorship and representation. In the next section, I explore whether the existence of these same discursive/disciplinary boundaries has silenced or marginalized particular issues. In other words, what are the "important questions" that have thus far remained unasked?

From this vantage point, it is interesting to note that no one has yet seriously considered the question as to *why* "informants," like Elvia Alvarado, Domitila Barrios de Chungara and Rigoberta Menchu, have *agreed* to give their testimony! I argue that this "oversight" is grounded in the notion that Latin American women who decide to give their testimony do not actually have the "independence" or "autonomy" to make a decision about whether or not to participate. There is also the implicit assumption that the informant lacks any ability to steer the interview with the anthropologist and, thus, have her own voice heard. Latin American women are denied subject status.

Three well-known testimonies, *I . . . Rigoberta Menchu; Don't Be Afraid Gringo*; and *Let me Speak!* (given by Rigoberta Menchu, Elvia Alvarado, and Domitila Barrios respectively), clearly contradict this denial of subject status. All three women made a conscious decision to tell their life story. In a foreword to *Don't Be Afraid Gringo*, Elvia Alvarado explains to the reader why she decided to cooperate:

> So here comes this gringa [i.e., editor and translator Medea Benjamin] asking me to tell our story. "Why should I get myself in more trouble?" I said to myself. "Better keep quiet and send this gringa back where she came from."
>
> But then I decided that I couldn't pass up a chance to tell the world our story. Because our struggle is not a secret one, it's an open one. Even if you are a gringa, I thought, once you understand why we're fighting, if you have any sense of humanity, you'll have to be on our side (1989: xiii).

Similarly, Domitila Barrios and Rigoberta Menchu provide reasons as to why they decided to speak about their lives.[15] [See Burgos-Debray 1984; Benjamin (1989); Barrios (1978).]

Moreover, it does not mean that, once an informant has made the decision to cooperate, she is entirely powerless. As Daphne Patai (1988) shows, women who are being interviewed often ignore questions by the ethnographer and tell their story the way they want to. This is as much true for women who are political activists, like the women whose testimonies are listed above, as for women who are not involved in social movements (Burgos-Debray 1984; Patai 1988).

Another important aspect of these three testimonies is that Rigoberta Menchu, Domitila Barrios, and Elvia Alvarado did not sink back into anonymity after they were visited by the ethnographer. All three women have relatively high profiles, due to the activities in which they are engaged. Domitila Barrios and Rigoberta Menchu have addressed audiences in Latin America, Europe, and the United States. If they disagree with representations of their communities or themselves in the testimonies, they are in the position to have their own representations of their societies heard. In other words, these women effectively assumed "power of production."

From the perspective of these three women, the silenced question (Why did they agree to give their testimonies?) is more important than the issues raised by anthropologists and Latin American literary critics. All three women are primarily concerned with "getting their message out." Rigoberta Menchu explains this concern in the following passage:

> Therefore, my commitment to our struggle knows no boundaries nor limits. This is why I've traveled to many places where I've had the opportunity to talk about my people. Of course, I'd need a lot of time to tell you all about my people, because it's not easy to understand just like that. And I think I've given some idea of that in my account (Burgos-Debray 1984: 247).

For women, such as Domitila Barrios, Elvia Alvarado, and Rigoberta Menchu, testimonies provide an important tool in their struggles. In today's Latin American societies, one needs to gain access to the privileged world of the "written word" in order to influence public debate. As elsewhere, the project of modernity has entailed the demise of oral tradition to pass on messages and influence public debate (Beverley and Zimmerman 1990). In Latin American societies where illiteracy is high, especially among women, privileging of the "written word" only reifies the marginality of "those already marginalized." In sum, giving one's testimony becomes a political act; part of a larger struggle. Expanding on a phrase coined by Paul Ricoeur,[16] one could argue that the text is not just a paradigm for meaningful action; the text *becomes* meaningful action.

It is clear that, in contrast to literary criticism that has diverted its focus from author-intentionality, we are not able to downplay an author's intentions in testimonial literature.[17] The three women whose testimonies we are discussing share a common purpose. Through their testimonies, they intend to delegitimize dominant, if not hegemonic, discourses on human rights, "development," and so forth. They feel that, in order to address the livelihood of their families and communities, they need to link the apolitical world of their immediate community concerns to the political world of remote, impersonal interests. The testimonies serve to influence middle-class public opinion at home as well as the international community. As such, testimonies become an integral part of these women's practices to resist and transform the dominant discourses. In sum, testimonies have become new tools of resistance in a highly text-oriented, postmodern world; tools that can also give "power of production" to poor and working-class women in Latin America.

CONCLUSION

In this chapter, I have argued that the real development debates over Latin America are taking place in the streets of the region's cities. Social movements, in other words, are becoming major actors/participants in these debates. However, it is not often recognized that a majority of the participants in these social movements are women. It is, therefore, imperative to study the special contributions made by Latin American women in this area.

On the basis of this chapter's analysis, I conclude with three suggestions. First, that through their practices of organizing soup kitchens, neighborhood committees, demonstrations for disappeared relatives, and so on, poor, urban women in Latin America have resisted and challenged dominant development policies in a variety of ways. Most importantly, their practices convey that meaningful development takes place at the local or community level, and that it should be humane or nonrepressive, and encompass all groups in society. From this perspective, designing grand, orthodox or heterodox, development policies does not entail meaningful development. Instead, the meaning of development is being defined and redefined at the grassroots.

Second, that social movements in their attempts to resist and challenge the effects of dominant development policies tend to engage in "gendered practices."[18] Women participating in these social movements are generally responsible for this. They are legitimizing their collective actions as apolitical and feminine, thus creating a new female space in the public sphere. Were it not for the "gendered nature" of these practices, many women would probably not have been willing to participate in social movements. Obviously, I am not arguing the existence of an intrinsically "gendered practice": the question of whether a practice is male or female is being defined by the cultural context within which it takes place.

Third, that one of the most unique and innovative practices resisting and challenging dominant development policies is, in my view, the giving of oral testimony. Unfortunately, political scientists have thus far not recognized that these testimonies are extremely powerful political documents. Women who have agreed to give their testimony approach it in a very utilitarian fashion. Testimonies become (one of the) tools in their struggles to resist and delegitimize dominant development policies. They provide the functionally illiterate with access to the otherwise inaccessible, privileged high-tech world of the written word.

It appears that the giving of oral testimony is also becoming a female practice. The most well-known testimonies to come out of Latin America have all been given and recorded by women. Does this mean that, through their testimonies, poor and working-class women in Latin America will be able to create a female space within our text-oriented world and assume power of production? Only if we start to recognize such testimonies for what they are: political documents.

NOTES

I wish to thank Kate Sonderegger and Cindy Weber for their helpful comments on an earlier version of this chapter.

1. My argument here is not so much that no debates occurred at all, but that they did not attract as much attention as did the controversies between modernization theorists and advocates of dependency theory. In other words, no new major concepts were introduced during the decade of the 1980s.

2. It is important to note that, in principle, I reject any rigid dichotomy between elites and masses. It is very well possible that someone with a specific socioeconomic background and status "objectively" belongs to the elites. However, the same individual might be interested in subverting elite practices (we can find examples of this phenomenon among the *dependentistas* during the 1970s). It is more useful, therefore, to distinguish between those interested in preserving and continuing existing sociopolitical and economic structures and those wishing to subvert them and to create discursive space(s) so that previously silenced voices can be heard. This distinction is based on Walker's discussion about peace and justice (1988).

3. During the 1970s, the World Bank and USAID introduced the so-called basic needs approach directed at the "poorest of the poor." Furthermore, international agencies have also developed alternative indicators for measuring development, such as the Physical Quality of Life Index and the Human Development Index.

4. Even when we rely on conventional standards for measuring "development."

5. Theoretically, one would have expected exactly the opposite: because the "prescribed medicine" of capitalist development policies had failed so dismally, a questioning, or even a rejection, of the development theories that informed these policies seemed in order. In practice, this did not occur.

6. I have more fully elaborated this argument elsewhere (see Marchand 1992).

7. To get an idea of the variety of popular movements that have emerged in the last two decades in Latin America, see, for instance, the collections of articles edited by Eckstein (1989) and Foweraker and Craig (1990). In particular, the articles by Walton (1989), Tamayo (1990), and Zermeño (1990) focus on the popular movements that have emerged in the context of the debt crisis and ensuing austerity measures.

8. To date, a few areas of the Amazon rainforest have been turned into extractive reserves, most notably in Rondônia, which is Chico Mendes' home state.

9. As, to a lesser extent, have studies of women involved in social movements.

10. *Concientización* is the central component of a method developed by Brazilian educator Paulo Freire in *Pedagogy of the Oppressed* (1970). It involves a process of developing critical thinking or consciousness-raising and subsequent actions that are informed by this raised awareness.

11. The exact moment varies among Latin American countries. It mostly depends on the economic situation of a country. Also, the fact that 1975 marked the beginning of the UN Decade for Women meant that money for "Women in Development" projects started to reach the region in the mid-1970s. This funding,

targeted at small-scale "women's projects," might inadvertently have worked as a catalyst for popular women's movements!

12. The label, "Crazy Mothers," of itself indicates that these women were not taken seriously.

13. The Casa Rosada (the Argentine presidential palace) is located at the Plaza de Mayo.

14. The following debates are discussed in much more detail in my paper, "Latin American Women Are Speaking on Development: Are We Listening Yet?" (Marchand 1991).

15. In the case of Rigoberta Menchu, it is the ethnographer Elisabeth Burgos-Debray who refers, in the introduction, to the reasons for giving testimony.

16. The phrase referred to is in a chapter title, "The Model of the Text: Meaningful Action Considered as a Text," in Ricoeur (1981a).

17. As Beverley and Zimmerman (1990) argue, one is not even able to assume that the ethnographer has (post)colonial designs. It is more likely that the ethnographer engages in the project out of (political) solidarity.

18. That is to say, most of the actions by social movements can be defined as female. I make the exception of food riots, which—because of their violent nature—can be defined as male.

PART 3
THE CONSTRUCTION OF IDENTITIES: ADVANCED CAPITALISM

7

Foreign Policy and Identity: Japanese "Other"/American "Self"

David Campbell

The emergence of Japan as an economic power in the postwar era has been a source of considerable marvel. With output equivalent to only one-twentieth of the United States gross national product (GNP) in 1945, and surpassing its own prewar levels of industrial production only as recently as 1959, Japan saw its wealth grow to one-half of U.S. GNP by the 1980s (Krasner and Okimoto 1989: 117). While the indices used to measure economic power vary, Japan's strength is often signified by its extensive capital exports to the United States (which effectively underwrite half of that government's annual budget deficit), its status as the world's leading producer of automobiles, the fact that the world's top ten international banks and largest stock exchange are Japanese, and its global position as the primary foreign aid donor (Schlossstein 1989: 426–427).

The marvel of Japanese economic power has become a considerable source of concern in the United States. Although the interpretation of Japanese economic power as a threat to the United States is not peculiar to the late 1980s and early 1990s—it having been a source of official concern and policy action in the first Nixon administration (Leaver 1989: 430–432)—what is unique about this current period of concern is the way the imagery and language of threats has come to dominate the corridors of power in Washington and pervade the cultural domains beyond.[1] Japanese economic power was popularly considered a greater national security threat than Soviet military power, even by 1990.[2] Advertisements for the automotive industry have emphasized height differences between U.S. and Japanese consumers (to suggest that Japanese cars will be too small), constructing scenarios concerning families visiting "Hirohito Center" in New York (referring to the Rockefeller Center, now part owned by Mitsubishi), and boldly displaying pictures of samurai in aggressive postures (e.g., *New York Times,* July 11, 1990). Publishers are receiving (and not hesitating to print) an array of fiction and nonfiction manuscripts either critical of Japanese practices or with Japanese characters cast in the role of the

147

villain (*New York Times*, July 18, 1990). Hollywood has been far from immune to a similar trend (witness the Michael Douglas film, *Black Rain*). And U.S. citizens of Japanese ancestry have been publicly reproached for "their" role in "buying up America."[3]

There are a number of possible ways to come to an understanding of this phenomenon. What I want to consider here is what the problematization of Japan as a national security threat says about the United States. Accordingly, this chapter examines the discourse of danger surrounding Japan; what Dorinne Kondo has called the "insidiously persistent tropes that constitute the phantasm 'Japan' in the contemporary United States" (1990: 301). In considering this discourse, two themes that have applicability beyond the immediate case being examined here need briefly to be articulated. The first is the need to reconceptualize *foreign policy,* such that its connection to the boundaries of meaning and identity—rather than simply the borders of territory—is brought to the fore. The second is the importance of a well-established yet historically specific discursive economy of identity/difference to the formulation and interpretation of U.S. foreign policy (see Campbell 1992a). Each of these themes challenges some cherished assumptions about the settled nature of identity and the state in the discourse of international relations. It is with a consideration of those topics that we have to begin.

IDENTITY, THE STATE, AND FOREIGN POLICY

Contemporary scholarship in international relations (IR) has been for the most part content to see foreign policy explained as a state-centric phenomenon in which there is an internally mediated response to an externally induced situation of ideological, military, and economic threats (Rosenau 1968; McGowan and Shapiro 1973; Hermann et al. 1987; Smith 1985: 46–47; Caporaso et al. 1987). There are a number of ways in which this understanding can be subject to critical scrutiny. One is to consider the constituted and permeable nature of the boundaries that have been central to the modern world, and the effort thus required to impose an interpretive discipline on the ambiguity of the subject matter. By giving priority to the discursive practices implicated in the construction of social space and subjectivity, we can ask: How did foreign policy come to be understood solely as the bridge between sovereign states existing in an anarchic world, a bridge that is constructed between two prior, securely grounded, and nominally independent realms?

In addressing this question critically, we begin with a fundamental assumption: Identity is an inescapable dimension of being. Indeed, no "body" could be without it. Whether we are speaking of personal or collective identity, "it" is not fixed by nature, given by God, or planned by

intentional behavior. Rather, identity is constituted in relation to difference. Equally, difference is constituted in relation to identity, such that the
problematic of identity/difference contains no foundations that are prior to,
or outside of, its operation. Therefore, whether we are talking of "the
body" or "the state," or particular bodies and states, the identity of each is
performatively constituted. Moreover, this constitution of identity is
achieved through the inscription of boundaries that serve to demarcate an
inside from an *outside,* a *self* from an *other,* a *domestic* from a *foreign.*

In the specific case of "the body," the border between internal and external is "tenuously maintained" by the transformation of elements that
were originally part of identity into a "defiling otherness" (Butler 1990:
133). There is no originary or sovereign presence that inhabits a predis-
cursive domain and gives the body, its sex, or gender a naturalized and unproblematic quality. Understanding the gendered identity of the body in
these terms means that we regard it as having "no ontological status apart
from the various acts which constitute its reality," and that its capacity to
act as a regulative ideal is a consequence of the performances that make it
possible. Gender can thus be understood as "an identity tenuously constituted in time, instituted in an exterior space through *a stylized repetition of
acts*"; an identity achieved "*not* [through] *a founding act, but rather a regulated process of repetition*" (136, 140–141, 145).

Choosing the question of gender and the body as an exemplification of
the theme of identity is not to suggest that, as an *individual* instance of
identity, the performative constitution of gender and the body is prior to
and determinative of instances of *collective* identity. In other words, I am
not claiming that the state is analogous to an individual with a settled identity. To the contrary, I want to suggest that the performative constitution of
gender and the body is analogous to the performative constitution of the
state. Specifically, I want to suggest that we can understand the state as
having "no ontological status apart from the various acts which constitute
its reality"; that the identity of any particular state should be understood as
"tenuously constituted in time . . . through a stylized repetition of acts,"
and achieved, "not [through] a founding act, but rather a regulated process
of repetition." In this context, where the boundary of the body—the parameters of its identity—is "tenuously maintained" by the transformation of
elements from the inside into a "defiling otherness," we can speak of foreign policy as one of the many practices implicated in the performative
constitution of the identity of the state.

Although dependent upon specific historical contexts, we can say that,
for the state, *identity can be understood as the outcome of exclusionary
practices in which resistant elements to a secure identity on the "inside"
are linked through a discourse of "danger," with threats identified and located on the "outside."* The state—emerging as the ground of identity—
achieves its form through discourses of danger that rely on strategies of

"otherness," or practices of differentiation. Through the disciplining consequences of the discourses of "danger"—warning us what to fear or how they are different—the self as "the state," is ordered. "We" come to know ourselves only by distancing and differentiating our self from theirs. The practices that make this possible, and the relationship between the self and the other that results, can be understood as "foreign policy."

Foreign policy (conventionally understood as the external orientation of preestablished states with secure identities) is thus to be retheorized as one of the boundary-producing practices central to the production and reproduction of the identity in whose name it operates. However, we have to be careful in specifying the exact nature of the relationship between state-based foreign policy and political identity. Foreign policy cannot be seen as constituting identity de novo. To explicate this we need to draw a distinction between two understandings of foreign policy. The first is one in which *foreign policy* can be understood as referring to all relationships of otherness, practices of differentiation, or modes of exclusion that constitute their objects as foreign in the process of dealing with them. In this sense, *foreign policy* is divorced from the state as a particular resolution of the categories of identity and difference and applies to all confrontations between a self and an other located in different sites of ethnicity, race, class, gender, or geography. Operating at all levels of social organization, from the level of personal relationships through to global orders, *foreign policy* in this sense has established conventional dispositions in which a particular set of representational practices serves as the resources from which are drawn the modes of interpretation employed to handle new instances of ambiguity or contingency. In other words, the first understanding (*foreign policy*) has provided the discursive economy in which the second understanding (Foreign Policy) operates. This second understanding—Foreign Policy as state-based and as conventionally understood within international relations—is thus not as equally implicated in the constitution of identity as the first understanding. Rather, Foreign Policy serves to reproduce the constitution of identity made possible by *foreign policy* and to contain challenges to the identity that results (Campbell 1992a: chaps. 2,3).

But there is more to *foreign policy*/Foreign Policy than the simple demarcation of a border. Because identity is multilayered, possesses texture, and comprises many dimensions, the demarcation of an inside and an outside, giving rise to the boundaries of the body or the state, has an axiological dimension through which the social space of inside/outside helps constitute a moral space of superior/inferior.[4] It is in this axiological dimension that the body can be understood as being more than a suggestive analogy for the constitution of state identity, for the demarcation of the inside and the outside that gives rise to the state is accomplished, in part, by gendered discourses of power.[5] Manifested most obviously in Machiavelli's discussion of *virtu* and *fortuna*—where *virtu* signifies the discipline and mastery needed to confront and do battle with *fortuna*, the feminine alliance of powers that cannot be understood or controlled and which threaten man and his life—these discourses of power are insinuated in hierarchies pivotal to establishing both the boundaries and conduct of politics, such as strong/weak, rational/irrational, public/private, sane/insane, order/disorder, reason/emotion, stability/anarchy, and so on. In each of these, the first term is "masculine" and superior to its "feminine" subordinate (Brown 1988; Showalter 1985; Merchant 1980; Lloyd 1986). As we shall see below, these figurations play an important part in the interpretation of Japan as a national security threat to the United States.

JAPAN AND THE DIMENSIONS OF DANGER

To appreciate the extent to which the entailments of identity are implicated in the interpretation of the threat from Japan, we need to examine those issues commonly cited as the basis for the understanding of Japan as a danger to the United States. In the discussion that follows, however, the aim is not to counter this representation with a realm of fact; rather, the aim is to illustrate that within what the proponents of the threat perception would consider to be the realm of economic fact, there lies the possibility of a competing narrative about U.S.-Japan economic relations. The possibility of constructing such a competing narrative establishes the space within which the argument about the entailments of identity can be pursued.

Central to the argument about a Japanese threat is the claim that the bilateral trade deficit between the two countries is the result of unfair practices and closed Japanese markets. But in the more than twenty years since 1970, the United States has had a trade surplus with Japan only once (1975); and by 1984, the United States had a trade deficit with OPEC, Canada, the EEC, Latin America, Taiwan, Korea, and even Africa, indicating that the problem was not exclusively with Japan. While many acknowledge the existence of many tariff and nontariff barriers in the Japanese market, Krasner and Okimoto have argued that (with the exception of agriculture) Japan "has rolled back formal tariff barriers and quotas farther than any other country, including the United States" (1989: 129). Others have argued that even if all the restrictions in place in 1985 were removed, the deficit would have been reduced by no more than $10 billion, leaving some $40 billion or more untouched. Moreover, the problem of trade barriers is not a one-way street: it has been calculated that the dollar value of Japanese goods that the U.S. excludes by protectionist measures approaches the value of U.S. imports that the Japanese exclude (Johnson 1988: 134; Bronfenbrenner 1986: 60; *Economist,* June 1989; Christopher 1985).

A second major strand in the conventional wisdom about the Japanese economic threat is that Japanese foreign investment is buying up America. The level of Japan's total foreign investments (in all countries) has grown enormously, from $160 billion in 1980 to $808 billion in 1987. Japan's total foreign investment in the United States has also grown substantially, from $35 billion in 1980 to $194 billion in 1987. This has kept pace with Japan's global policies, but it has not substantially increased Japan's *share* of total foreign assets in the United States, which was 22 percent in 1980, 23 percent in 1985, and holding relatively steady at 24 percent in 1987. The bulk of foreign assets in the U.S. are held by Europeans, with the British and the Dutch being ranked first and second. Equally, while foreigners are buying up U.S. assets, the United States continues to buy foreign assets: between 1980 and 1987, U.S. foreign investments doubled from $607 billion to $1,168 billion (Makin 1988).

It should also be noted that foreign investment comes in two forms. One involves the purchase of U.S. treasury bonds and securities, and the bulk of Japanese investment in the United States (totalling $117 billion— which is only 4 percent of outstanding U.S. securities) is in this form. The other—direct investment in factories and private portfolios—has seen a marked increase, with Japanese holdings rising from $4.2 billion in 1980 to $33.5 billion in 1987. As the most visible form of foreign investment, this is the component that has led to fears of a Japanese buyout of the United States. Two points are worth noting in relation to this. First (and this is an argument that advocates of U.S. investment abroad employ to justify their activities in the host country), the movement of Japanese production offshore will cost Japan an estimated 210,000 jobs by the year 2000, but result in the creation of 824,000 new jobs in the United States. Second, the boundary between "foreign" and "domestic" industry is becoming increasingly blurred. For example, it is estimated that in the early 1990s Japanese manufacturers will make more cars in the United States than they exported there four years earlier. In addition, the proportion of U.S. components in "Japanese" cars manufactured in the United States was expected to increase to just over two-thirds, at the same time as U.S. manufacturers were increasingly importing components from plants in Mexico and other countries. Finally, contrary to the conventional wisdom of a totally closed Japanese economy, U.S. firms have considerable presence in the Japanese market. IBM is Japan's second-largest computer manufacturer; and Coca-Cola makes more money in the Japanese market than it does in the United States. A recent study by the U.S. Chamber of Commerce in Tokyo argues that access to the Japanese market has greatly increased and profitability often exceeds that which companies achieve at home (*New York Times* 1991). Overall, U.S. companies operating in Japan sell over $80 billion in goods and services to local consumers, roughly comparable to what Japanese firms sell in the United States (Makin 1988;

Gill and Law 1988: 197; *Economist* 1987; *Fortune* 1990; *World Press Review* 1990: 26–27; *U.S. News and World Report* 1990). These arguments and statistics are no doubt contestable, but even the admission of their contestability renders problematic the assured way in which some people have come to talk about the Japanese economic threat. If there is a questionable relationship between the "objective" indices of threat and the way in which dangers are articulated around their referents, the way is open to consider how the entailments of (United States) identity are implicated in the inscription of (a Japanese) danger.

INTERPRETING JAPAN

The problematization of Japan as a national security threat in the late 1980s has been made possible by a number of new analyses of United States–Japan economic relations. While assessments of Japanese economic power in earlier years were more often than not centered on the understanding that the Japanese had successfully (perhaps all too successfully) imbibed the norms of the liberal international economic order, the analyses associated with this latest round of threat-perception reject the notion that Japan is playing by the same rules as other developed trading nations. Beginning with Chalmers Johnson (1982), there has developed an interpretation of Japanese economic power that has been dubbed "revisionist" (*Business Week* 1989). Associated with this approach are the writings of Clyde Prestowitz (1988), Karel van Wolferen (1989), James Fallows (1990), and Steven Schlossstein (1989). As academics, former government officials, journalists, and corporate strategists, these writers (among others) have had their distinctive view of Japanese economic power widely disseminated in the United States.[6]

The revisionist interpretation of Japan is predicated on the assumption that Japan is different. These analysts seek to make the case that Japanese society diverges fundamentally from American society in its authoritarian, hierarchical, rigid, and closed ways. This assumption profoundly colors both their assessments of the problems and their prescriptions for solutions.

The previous section outlined how foreign policy and political identity are intertwined through the inscription of danger. In this context, and in order to consider what the recent problematization of Japan as a national security threat says about the United States, I want to examine in more detail the modes of representation employed by one of the revisionist writers: James Fallows. In his *More Like Us*—a book that was widely praised as an example of an original and insightful analysis of "the Japan problem"— the inscription of "Japan" as a danger is an instance of how "America" is written through foreign policy strategies.

Fallows' text is an exemplary case of there being no clear distinction between the "domestic" and the "international." Although the front cover proclaims that this is a work directed at the Foreign Policy problem of the need for America "to work to overcome the Asian challenge," the foreword makes it immediately clear that the focus of the analysis is internal: "This is a book about American values and American culture." These two dimensions are linked in Fallows' concern that in seeking to meet the challenge of Japanese economic power Americans had gone "overboard" by regarding Japan "as a repository of the values Americans had to reclaim." The economic challenge has to be met, he argues, but attempts to improve American economic performance through the emulation of Japanese practices only serve to exacerbate the magnitude of the problem. When these two failings are combined, Fallows declares, a new danger exists: "It is time to acknowledge a cultural danger now" (1990: vii, viii, 4).

The argument is structured around a series of dichotomies. It seeks to "explain American uniqueness largely through contrasts with Asian societies, especially that of Japan." Simply put, "Japan is strong because of its groups; America because of its individuals (1990: 5, 208)." America *allows* people to succeed while Japan *organizes* them to succeed. Japan is closed and orderly; America is open and disorderly (1990: 48). To be sure, notes Fallows, Japan has individualists and America has collectives, but the dominant orientation of each society is along these lines. Confronting the challenge from Japan means, therefore, that Americans should not transform themselves into model Japanese. Rather, the turn must be inward, so that Americans are to be more like "Americans" through the recovery of ethics and values central to their identity:

> If, for some reason, America really tried to make itself like Japan—centrally coordinated, as homogenous as possible, trying to minimize individual differences so society can run as a powerful team—it could never be more than a second-rate version of the real thing. If it tried that, America would also give up the values that not only are crucial to its success but constitute its example to the world. American society is the world's purest expression of the individualist belief (1990: ix–x).[7]

Although its rigid organization and homogeneity prevent Japan from being the new city on the hill for others to emulate, it is "Japan's powerful emphasis on its racial purity and uniqueness that is its most noticeable and exasperating trait" (1990: 28).[8] In contrast, Fallows argues, America is a land of people bound not by "some mystical tribal tie" but by the desire to be in America. Central to this is the assumption that race should not be a point of differentiation. America is unusual because it is the manifestation of the belief "that a society can be built of individuals with no particular historic or racial bond to link them together. This is a noble belief: it makes America better than most other societies" (1990: 2). America might have witnessed "xenophobia" in the 1940s, Fallows concedes, but there can be no doubt that "Japan is today by far the more racially exclusive of the two societies" (1990: 30).[9]

Noting with approval historian James Oliver Robertson's description of the "brave, big-shouldered nineteenth century days," Fallows maintains that "almost every chapter of American history is a saga of people moving from place to place geographically and from level to level socially." The economic success of America's industrialization was derived from the "almost boundless land for pioneers to settle in" that existed after the 1840s and the values that were associated with that movement (1990: 52, 82). While the physical frontier might have been officially closed in the 1890s, the frontier lives on in other dimensions. In chapters 4 and 5 Fallows gives an account of some personal frontier narratives (including that of his own family) in which people have headed West, come from the East, or found work in the South. He concludes, in the story of Vietnamese immigrants, that "the example of the Nguyen family shows that the frontier is still open" (1990:99).[10]

It is at this point that the interpretations of Japan as rigid, closed, and collective, and of America as flexible, open, and individualist combine in Fallows' analysis. For although what made America great was the taming of the frontier, and although there are still many would-be settlers, the contemporary American frontier is replete with interests promoting the "Confucian idea that society should be more orderly" (1990: 131). This "unhealthful, alien" influence has come to America in the guise of meritocracy, which has led to fixed and arbitrary standards that govern labor and the professions (1990: Chap. 7). In this context, the demise of a south Chicago steel mill in the 1980s brought this analysis from Fallows:

> There were powerful, destructive forces at work. The life of the steel communities was dominated by big, unwieldy institutions: the church, the schools, the army, the union, the mill, the Chicago political machine. Despite their many differences, they all taught one lesson: people should know their place. . . . It was a Japanese-style lesson of teamwork, obedience, and conformity (1990: 117–118).

Ridding America of "Confucianism" is thus central to the economic challenge for the future. Although "[a] social hierarchy built largely on academic degrees is fine for Japan" (1990: 175), America has to be "reopened" through a recovery of its past ethics and values, with their emphasis on flexibility, achievement, and mobility (1990: Chap. 10).[11]

Fallows' text is more overtly cultural in its concerns than others in the same genre. But his preoccupation with the (alleged) order, hierarchy, conformity, rigidity, racism, and exclusive nature of Japanese society is a common trait among the revisionist works. Even the work of former trade-negotiator Prestowitz (1988: Chap. 3) contains cultural interpretations nearly identical to those in Fallows. Likewise, a recent analysis produced for the CIA by the Rochester Institute of Technology maintained that, although it had taken care "to avoid harsh stereotypes and stereotyping," it saw the Japanese as "creatures of an ageless, amoral, manipulative and controlling culture" (Cummings 1991: 367). Indeed, many American academic analyses of Japanese culture and society exhibit an ideology of individualism and independence in their arguments (Kondo 1990: 32). The impetus behind this, Kondo argues, is that "relationally defined selves in Japan—selves inextricable from context— . . . mount a radical challenge to our own assumptions about fixed, essentialist identities and provide possibilities for a consideration of cultural difference and a radical critique of 'the whole subject' in contemporary Western culture" (1990: 33). What this demonstrates is not that Fallows and others are correct in their representation of the Japanese as having a social conception of self different from American self-understandings, but that all representations of the self, all representations of the *I,* should be denaturalized. As a consequence, the American *I* needs to be understood as a social construct constituted through various orientations to difference just as the Japanese self is. Indeed, the American *I* is capable of portrayal as autonomous and individuated only through its location in a relationship of difference vis-à-vis the Japanese (among others).

The radical nature of this challenge to identity requires that the challenge be contained at every opportunity. This struggle between challenge and containment occurs in a variety of cultural and political sites, among which the discourse on foreign economic competition is but one.[12] Despite its seemingly benign and apolitical nature, much of the contemporary economic discourse concerning Japan reproduces the themes Fallows has addressed. Most obvious here is the way the imagery of the frontier, upon which Fallows draws heavily, recurs in assessments of the problems and potential remedies for the United States–Japan economic relationship. When observers speak of the need for "market access" to "closed" East Asian economies (an echo of the Open Door policies of the nineteenth century); when they call for the removal of all tariff and nontariff barriers to trade; and when they advocate a policy termed the "Structural Impediments Initiative" to restore a "level playing field" for business; they are invoking a long-held view of the world as an open, economic prairie upon which the only obstacles were those erected by uncivilized and unlawful actors. A rich pool of discursive representations is available for this interpretation.

WRITING THE AMERICAN "SELF": REINVIGORATING THE FRONTIER MYTH

Over the four hundred years from the arrival of Columbus to the official declaration of the U.S. frontier's closure in the 1890s, the *frontier* in

American history was associated with the quest for land by a people possessed with a righteous mission and destiny. But when Secretary of State Elihu Root announced in 1906 that the United States had accumulated a surplus of capital greater than that required for internal development, he gave official imprimatur to a change that had been in the making for some time. The frontier was now associated with the acquisition, maintenance, and security of economic markets for American products (LaFeber 1989: 221). The quest for land to settle was being replaced by the quest for consumers who could purchase. And just as obstacles to the landed frontier were overcome with the full force of the nation, obstacles to the economic frontier were deemed worthy of the same treatment. Indeed, when in the 1850s American businessmen first regarded Japan as an opportunity for economic expansion, they criticized the resistance they encountered on the grounds that "we do not admit the right of a nation of people to exclude themselves and their country from intercourse with the rest of the world." When the Japanese resistance to American pressure did not cease, a North Carolina senator argued that Japan could not be expected to behave like "the civilized portion of mankind." His recommendation was that "you have to deal with barbarians as barbarians" (LaFeber: 127–130).

This link to earlier interpretations and representational practices suggests that the current revisionist assessments of Japan as a national security threat are being driven by the entailments of identity rather than any inherent and unproblematic "reality" of the situation. This can be demonstrated in greater detail by noting how these assessments recall modes of representation prevalent in U.S. accounts of the Japanese during World War II. Secondly, and even more importantly, it can be demonstrated by showing how these representations reproduce judgements about the self and the other in even earlier historical moments when America confronted the alien, foreign, and potentially dangerous "other."

The two most prevalent metaphors used in relation to the Japanese in World War II concerned their "uniqueness" and their "herdlike" behavior. In Frank Capra's film, *Know Your Enemy—Japan*, the overriding theme was that the Japanese were a people devoid of individual identity. Attention was paid to the feudalistic forms of oppressive control that existed behind a parliamentary facade, and the narrative spoke darkly of "an obedient mass with but a single mind" (Dower 1986: 18–23, 30–31, 95–97).[13] This resonated with much earlier assessments of Japanese society. The press coverage surrounding Commander William Perry's mission to Japan in the 1850s "pictured the people as living restlessly under a harsh totalitarian regime which crushed their natural instincts for freedom and individuality" (Neumann 1954: 245).

The nonhuman and subhuman representation of the Japanese as lice, rats, apes, dogs, vipers, and vermin further buttressed the metaphor of the herd; it is replicated in the CIA's *Japan 2000* report by reference to the Japanese as a "lamprey eel, living off the strength of others" (Dower: 81,

83–84; Cummings: 367). This theme was reiterated in all wartime, and much postwar, literature, when reference was made to "the Jap" rather than, as was the case with Germans, "the Nazis." The former is singular and indicts an entire nation through a derogatory abbreviation; the latter is plural and refers only to a particular political movement. Importantly, referring to Germans as Nazis left open the space for the "good German," something that was not possible for the Japanese (Dower: 78–79).

Alternative modes of representation applied to the Japanese in the war years included the ascription of primitive, savage, tribal, and generally uncivilized behavior; the portrayal of them as children and the use of theories concerning childhood traumas and adolescent behavior to analyze them; and the description of them as being emotionally and mentally ill. In the aftermath of the Allied victory, these orientations to otherness were altered, but not in ways that challenged the power relationship between the self and the other. The sentiments of the Japanese as lesser and like children meant that they could be subject to a master and amenable to learning. Primitives could be civilized and the mentally ill could be cured. The victor was now an analyst, healer, and teacher, rather than warrior, but remained confidently superior (Dower: 117, 301–305).

The hierarchy between the American "self" and the Japanese "other" was retained because the other remained homogenous and undifferentiated. The virulent and violent interpretations employed during wartime quickly faded with the U.S. occupation of Japan, indicating that seemingly fixed categories of bigotry potentially can have a soft underside. At the same time, there persisted in the postwar period a particular image of Japan—as made up of paradoxes, alien, insensitive to others, unpredictable, unstable, and with a dubious commitment to democracy (Glazer 1975)—which indicates that "the softer idioms often conceal a hard and potentially devastating edge" (Dower: 312). Nowhere is this more obvious than in the residual racism applied to the Japanese superhuman, who is now dressed in a business suit rather than jungle greens.

For a period during the war, the Japanese were portrayed as superhuman. When the defeat of the British in Singapore and other Japanese successes in the early stages of the Pacific War startled Allied officials, representations of the Japanese as an oversized and powerful man abounded. This change, however, did not represent any basic reassessment of the Japanese. Whether subhuman, nonhuman, inhuman, or superhuman, they were everything but human. This was made clear by the associations that were made with the superhuman designation. As Dower writes, "in times of fear and crisis 'superhuman' qualities too are commonly ascribed to despised outsiders." These take many forms, "including physical prowess, sexual appetite, intuitive genius or 'occult' skills, fanaticism, a special capacity for violence, monopolization of certain forms of knowledge or control, even an alleged capacity for 'evil'" (1986: 116).

The homogenized, undifferentiated view of the Japanese—as "the Jap," herdlike, and endowed with "superhuman" economic prowess—is to be found in contemporary analyses of business practices. The front page of the *New York Times* on November 25, 1990, headlined the story of Matsushita's plans to buy the entertainment conglomerate MCA with the words, "Japanese Expected to Take Over Another Major Hollywood Studio." As one magazine noted:

> In the Eurocentric American mind, Canadians, British, and French may be foreigners, but they are distinguished as individuals. Campeau goes bust, not the Canadians. Maxwell strikes again, not the Brits. But the Japanese have strange names—Mazda, Matsushita, Mitsui, Mitsubishi— and people generalize: "The Japanese bought the factory." That reinforces the illusion that they work in concert to a single end (*Fortune* 1990: 55–56).

But probably the most persistent association with the Japanese that began with the war and pervades contemporary economic discourse is the conviction that the Japanese are "treacherous." The surprise attack on Pearl Harbor in 1941 stood for many as a symbol of deviousness and the willingness to transgress the "normal" bounds of civilized war. Throughout the war, the image of the conniving, scheming, and untrustworthy Japanese was everywhere. In the postwar period, particularly in recent times, the cry of "unfair" trading practices has tapped into this well-established interpretation. The greater the economic success of the Japanese, the greater is the willingness of many competitors to suggest that this success can be attributed only to deviousness (Dower: 36, 313).

Were there no historical precedent for any of these orientations toward otherness, it would be possible to argue that the prejudicial views of the Japanese to be found in contemporary literature were grounded primarily in the experiences of the World War II and the conduct of the Japanese then and since. However, what is most interesting about the modes of representation applied to the Japanese, both in the present and the recent past, is the way they resemble interpretive frames of reference that have been employed in American history and foreign policy studies toward groups other than the Japanese.[14]

This is most obvious in the way American history as recounted by Fallows, and repeated in the lexicon of economic discourse, is the familiar story of the frontier. Fallows' account is of the creative, westward spread of an American people with a mission, drawn to the country by desire rather than tribal tie, and occupying a bountiful and barren landscape ripe for exploitation. It is a powerful and recurring image in American political discourse. When Henry Kissinger calls himself the Lone Ranger of diplomacy, when Vietnam is described by combat troops as "Indian country" (an appellation more recently applied to Iraq), and when cities in space or plans for the Strategic Defense Initiative are tagged as the high frontier, the mythology of the frontier is invoked without explanation as a means of describing the situation (Slotkin 1986: 18–19). The dominant themes of this mythology are those concerned with American history as a full-scale Indian War in which race fights race as part of the rites of modernization and the development of the national state (Slotkin: 32–33). It is now being repeated (as noted above) in the discourse of economic threats from Japan.

The frontier is central to identity because it is not only an open space invitingly beckoning those who seek success, but also the (ever-shifting) boundary between "barbarism" and "civilization" (Williams 1955). The mythology of the frontier achieves, in this sense, more than mere description. It provides also the prescription for action. It mandates that to ensure the survival of "civilization," the forces of "barbarism" have to be constantly repelled, if not overcome. As Slotkin writes: "At the core of the Myth is the belief that economic, moral, and spiritual progress are achieved by the heroic foray of civilized society into the virgin wilderness, and by the conquest and subjugation of wild nature and savage mankind" (1986: 531).

It is, or course, central to the mythology of the frontier that from the time of settlement in North America to the end of the nineteenth century, the constitution and regeneration of the identity of the European "self" has been made possible by the enactment of violence upon the Indian "other."[15] The Indians were scorned and subjugated by the European settlers on a number of grounds, but most prominent was the claim that "they are not industrious, neither have art, science, skill or faculty to use either the land or the commodities of it" (quoted in Kiernan 1980: 34). Central to this interpretation was the Europeans' derision at the communal nature of the Indians' property. In lacking the practice of private ownership, the Indian was thought to lack the capacity for an individuated self and was thus without the basis for civilized society (Rogin 1975: 116–117). As a commissioner for Indian Affairs declared in 1838, "common property and civilization cannot coexist" (quoted in Kiernan 1980: 28). In 1875, the then commissioner for Indian affairs declared that "[a] fundamental difference between Barbarians and a civilized people is the difference between a herd and an individual" (Slotkin 1986: 318). Even reformers who were critical of U.S. policy on Indians, such as Helen Hunt Jackson, did not doubt that the Indians "must be set free from the swaddling bands of tribal collectivism" (quoted in Kiernan 1980: 79). The Indians were thus the "uncivilized herd" long before the Japanese were so regarded.

It was not just Indians who were subject to prejudice on the grounds that communal property and collective action were "foreign." The emergence of some trade unions in the nineteenth century was legally opposed when various judges argued that they were irredeemably alien. The associated rhetoric of class and Indian wars prevalent in the period (when the "reds" on the frontier were aligned with the "reds" in the cities) was intended to demonstrate that any group orientation against the emerging capitalist order was a kind of tribalism, a throwback to a savage past, and a symptom of degeneracy (Slotkin 1986: 316).

What this argument suggests is that a major rationale for the near genocidal violence against the Indians, and the establishment opposition to labor and political movements that embodied collectivism, is now to be observed in the representations of the Japanese as a national security threat. The individual/group dichotomy that is central to Fallows' text (and all others concerned with the inherently different nature of Japanese culture) is replicated in economic discourse when there is talk of private/public distinctions and the contrasts between free enterprise/government intervention. For example, the argument is that America allows individuals to succeed while Japan organizes people; or that the American economy is one of individual entrepreneurship while Japan is a capitalist developmental state in which the corporation and social goals have greater priority.

It is helpful to think of American foreign policy (and Foreign Policy) as being made possible through a discursive economy of identity/difference. The notion of a discursive economy allows us to think of discourse (the representation and constitution of the "real") as a managed space in which some statements and depictions come to have greater value than others. Investments have been made in certain interpretations; dividends can be drawn by those interests that have made the investments; representations are taxed when they confront new and ambiguous circumstances; and participation in the discursive economy is through social relations that embody an unequal distribution of power.

One of the principal virtues of understanding foreign policy as made possible by a discursive economy of identity/difference is that it allows us to appreciate both the continuities and discontinuities witnessed in the confrontation between self and other over time and through space. If we were to talk of "formulaic expressions," "stereotypes," or "archetypes" to describe the continuities between historical moments, we could close ourselves off to the historicity and highly politicized nature of each instance.[16] What we have to try to express is the way in which each confrontation between self and other is both a creative and original act, yet involving the reproduction of dominant dispositions and orientations, so that we are sensitive both to the patterns and the disjunctions. Arguably, the best way to achieve this is to be alert to the indebtedness of each reproduction to a previous production. Therefore, understanding the confrontation between the self and other as taking place in a discursive economy allows us to appreciate the debt that subjectivity owes to otherness.

How can this help us to understand the politics involved in problematizing Japan as an economic threat? The relatively benign nature of *social* or *group* inscribed as a characteristic of the *other* in the revisionist literature should not mislead us into thinking they are without power and importance for the *self*. As the above discussion has sought to demonstrate, the American confrontation with the other has had the individual/group dichotomy as one of its fundamental organizing premises. The historical power of that dichotomy comes from the way in which the concept *individual* was associated with *civilization, progress,* and *private property,* in contradistinction to *barbarism, regression,* and *tribal property.*

The inscription of Japan as rigid, hierarchical, and organized around groups is an instance where the discursive economy of identity/difference draws upon historical themes to suggest the "tribal" nature of Japan, and—as a consequence—its place outside of the "civilized" community of trading nations. But, as in the case of the colonial settlers in America, this inscription of the other has less to do with the demands of accurate ethnography than it does the requirements of identity. For just as the barbarism of the Indian other could be found within, the self of the United States is as subject to the complaints of closed markets, unfair trading practices, and "Confucianism" as are the Japanese.[17]

In an era when the social forces of interdependence and globalization have produced a rift between the loci of economic sovereignty and the national state, there are a range of resistant practices designed to maintain and reproduce the status quo ante. Foreign Policy is one of those practices. As a discourse of power that is global in scope yet national in its legitimation, Foreign Policy is only one of a number of discourses of danger circulating in the discursive economy of a national state at any given time. From weather reports to Central Intelligence Agency net threat assessments, modern life is disciplined by discourses that tell us what to fear.[18] But in the context of the modern national state, Foreign Policy has been granted a privileged position as the discourse to which we should turn for information about the preeminent dangers to our society and ourselves.

The function of the problematization of Japan as an economic threat is therefore one among many practices designed to secure the sovereignty of the United States and contain challenges to the boundaries of American identity. The attempt to draw the line between the nation that promotes the individual versus the nation that promotes the group is the attempt to reinscribe the fictive past of the United States by reproducing the sanitized mythology of the frontier and the values of individualism associated with it. The politics of the "Japanese threat" is that this writing of a boundary establishes divergent spaces, enables different subjectivities, and organizes hierarchies of power between them. The subjectivity of the *United States* accordingly owes a debt to the otherness inscribed in *Japan* through contemporary economic discourse.

INSCRIBING (A GENDERED) WORLD ORDER

In the above discussion of how the Japanese have been represented, there is an absence of gender as a discrete category of difference. This is not to suggest that such references cannot be found: indeed, many historical accounts that regarded Japan as a land of depravity and vice noted the allegedly unique feature of rampant prostitution as evidence (Neumann 1954: 252); rather it is to suggest that gender is insinuated in discourses of international relations concerning Japan in ways that are more important than its most obvious appearance as a category of difference. Most importantly, the "foreign policy" of American dispositions toward the Japanese have, as their effect, the inscription of a world order.

Fallows' text indicated how strategies of otherness and practices of differentiation concerning the Japanese were deeply implicated in the maintenance of the boundaries of American identity. Moreover, as an instance of foreign policy (i.e., the relationship between self and other), these representational practices were brought to bear on areas conventionally understood as being the province of Foreign Policy; namely, the economic relationship of the United States and Japan. But the political and policy implications of this debt of interpretation extend beyond the issue of national legitimation to a concern with the structure of international order. The foreign policy strategies of otherness effectively center a conception of the American self in such a way that the boundaries of the American state and identity are inscribed through the transference of a concern about differences *within* to a concern about differences *between*. In the case of Fallows' text, the differences within (the problems of antiindividualist forces associated with "Confucianism" in American society) are to be contained by a reinvigoration of the myth of the frontier that concomitantly problematizes Japan as an economic threat and proffers a range of policy solutions.

The consequences of this extend, however, beyond the reinscribed boundaries of the American state. Richard Leaver has demonstrated that the biases of the international political economy literature have militated against scenarios in which a Pax Nipponica could replace a declining Pax Americana as the sheet anchor of world order. This has been achieved by a historical rewriting of the concept of hegemony such that international order is said to depend upon a range of factors peculiar to the dominance of the United States in the postwar period. The alleged failure of Japan to meet these "universal" requirements thus makes it ineligible as a candidate for the position of global hegemon (1989: 443ff). Equally, the foreign policy strategies examined here, when combined with the political economy of a superpower, center a particular conception of world order.

The discursive economy of identity/difference gives rise to an American-centric understanding of future world order. Its problematization of Japan as a threat mandates a particular policy response, predicated on the argument that the only alternative to the United States–led liberal international economic order is an (unlikely) authoritarian world order with Japan as hegemon, or anarchy and chaos. The conclusion of Schlossstein is representative of this approach:

America must remain the world's preeminent power as a *primus inter pares* in a more pluralistic age so that the global system can continue to be driven by its values of freedom, liberty, and justice. The alternatives to Pax Americana may either be chaos and instability on the one hand or Pax Japonica on the other, symbolized by a politically more powerful Japan whose controlling values are conformity, loyalty, hierarchy, obedience, and duty—values that resonate in a culturally homogenous nation but command no wider outside audience (1989: xiii).[19]

The discursive economy of identity/difference thus seeks to reinscribe the fragile boundaries of American identity in their multiple locations, whether "inside" or "outside," "domestic" or "international," "local" or "global." The argument that only American leadership can ensure a stable world order is the result of foreign policy strategies writ large as Foreign Policy; strategies that are highly gendered. Specifically, the insinuation of gender in these strategies occurs at two levels.

The representation of the encounter with Japan in terms indebted to the myth of the frontier recalled the masculinity of Machiavellian *virtu* as the problematic for interpretation. Fallows' description of the best of American history resembling the "brave, big-shouldered nineteenth century" needs little explication in this regard (Fallows 1990: 52). Equally, the various representations ascribed to the Japanese—as treacherous, childlike, emotionally disturbed, mentally ill, unstable, fanatical, evil, and endowed with superhuman physical capacities and sexual appetites—reproduces the catalog of conditions long associated with the tropes of *feminine* and *woman*.[20] Moreover, these interpretations extend beyond mere description to provide a prescription for action. For an "other" endowed with such "feminine" features, reason, dialogue, and cooperation are not the favored political modalities. As Commander William Perry declared in a statement concerning the Japanese after his Mexican experience (see note 14): "It is manifest from past experience that arguments of persuasion addressed to these people, unless they be seconded by some imposing manifestation of power, will be utterly unavailing" (quoted in Kiernan: 49). This orientation can be observed in some recent economic analyses. These suggest that negotiations to improve the United States–Japan trade balance are insufficient unless backed by the threat of retaliatory action, a view which, in turn, echoes the Cold War assessments that the Soviets only understood force (Leaver: 443).

The second level in which gender is insinuated into the discourse of international relations concerning Japan pertains to the understanding of international order that centers Pax Americana and marginalizes alternatives. The oft-expressed anxiety that the only alternative to American hegemony in the international system is chaos, instability, and global anarchy is undergirded by a venerable tradition of political thought: those forces that cannot be disciplined and tamed are a threat to "man" and his settled and secure identity; they are to be represented under the sign of "the feminine." The import of this observation extends well beyond the representation of Japan, however. It suggests that the discourse of international relations (IR) as a whole, dependent as it is on the hierarchy of sovereignty/anarchy for its foundational categories and modes of interpretation, is (1) made possible by a gendered discourse of power and (2) deeply implicated in its reproduction.[21] In this context, war—in which some countries "kick ass," expunge the internal doubts that put into doubt the resolve to act decisively, and overcome their sovereign's reputation for "effeminacy"—can be understood as a process of remasculinization.[22]

Few in the practice or study of international relations care to acknowledge the validity of such an interpretation. The influence of gender factors might be noted (under such labels as "extraneous" or "irrational") but only insofar as they influenced others. For example, an English social anthropologist argued in the 1940s that one of the reasons for Japan's aggressiveness in the World War II was its extension of the modalities of male dominance and female passivity to the domain of international relations. Japan found it legitimate to make war on those the Japanese regarded as soft, indecisive, and female. Perceiving the external world sexually, it was maintained, was a perversion restricted to the Japanese. The argument being made here, in contrast, maintains that this quality ascribed to the other is in actuality something that is within the self; it comes to exist as "other" through a process of transference. As argued above, this means that, for the state, identity can be understood as the outcome of exclusionary practices in which resistant elements to a secure identity on the "inside" are linked, through a discourse of "danger" (such as Foreign Policy), with threats identified and located on the "outside."

CONCLUDING REFLECTIONS: THE SUBJECTIVITY DEBT

We are now at a historical juncture where the demise of the Soviet threat as the basis for United States foreign policy has been officially sanctioned; policymakers in Washington are looking forward to a new era in international relations, the outlines of which they can barely discern. What is clear, however, is that the optimistic view in which it was held that the so-called post–Cold War period would be a fundamentally different era in world politics placed too much credence on the essential qualities of a supposedly independently existing "other" as the basis for an assessment of threats. Such a view was possible only because it ignored the debt that subjectivity owes to otherness and the role that the requirements of identity play in giving rise to discourses of danger. What the United States–led war with Iraq in the Gulf demonstrates is that above all else the Cold War was not based exclusively upon an orientation toward the Soviet Union.

The Cold War was a powerful and pervasive historical configuration of the discursive economy of identity/difference operating in multiple sites (Campbell 1992b).

The problematization of Japan as a national security threat is but one manifestation of this discursive economy, although the practices of differentiation and strategies of otherness that have made it possible have mandated a less violent response. Although it is a conflict that has fortunately (at least for the time being, though some would wish otherwise) escaped militarization, it is not a new threat; it has not been recently created. It is one of the many dangers constantly in circulation throughout the discursive economy that rise to prominence and are exacerbated when changes in the political conditions allow it. The major political challenge suggested by this analysis is not simply to address the specifics of each threat (though that is in itself desirable), but to address the process whereby the subjectivity of the United States is continually in hock to strategies of otherness. Practices of differentiation and modes of exclusion are not unique to the United States. But few peoples, groups, or countries have fashioned (or are in a position to fashion) a form of life in which the discursive economy and the political economy have been so closely intertwined and that has so many global ramifications. As a consequence, what this analysis suggests is that what we now need is to bring the "subjectivity debt"—along with the trade deficit, the budget deficit, and consumer debt—to the political agenda.

NOTES

I would like to acknowledge my debt to Kate Manzo, Steve Rosow, and the participants in the 1990–1991 Johns Hopkins Faculty Seminar on Gender for comments, and to Lisa Rood for research assistance.

1. For a sample of the literature that reports on or exhibits a concern for Japanese economic power, see White (1985); Wolferen (1986/1987); Packard (1987/1988); Murphy (1989); Economist (1989); and Fortune (1990).

2. Public opinion polls have indicated a shift in attitudes—from a mixture of opinion toward Japanese business to an outright concern about a new threat. Compare the earlier findings in "A Mix of Admiration" (Time 1987) with the more recent reports in "Rethinking Japan" (Business Week 1989), and "Americans Express Worry on Japan" (New York Times 1990). In the latter report, 58 percent identified Japan as the major threat to the United States, compared with 26 percent who named the Soviet Union.

3. See "Japanese in the New York Region" (New York Times 1990). In an earlier poll, Japanese foreign investment was considered a threat by 67 percent of respondents (an increase from the 45 percent recorded in 1987), compared with only 37 percent who said the same of European foreign investment. See "Americans Express Worry on Japan" (New York Times 1990).

4. For a discussion of the axiological dimension to strategies of "otherness," see Todorov 1984: 185.

5. Indeed, the similitude between the body and the state becomes apparent when we think of how *the body politic* functions as a regulating and normalizing trope for *the political.* On the theme of the body politic, see Kantorowicz (1957); Hale (1971); Le Goff (1989).

6. No matter how pervasive and influential, these assessments are strongly contested by others in the field. See Porter (1990).

7. Schlossstein (1989) makes the nearly identical argument. The economic problems of the United States have to be handled "the American way" (by use of incentives), rather than via the adoption of Japanese techniques. Of such techniques he argues: "While these methods may suit a more homogeneous (and authoritarian) East Asian culture well, they cannot be employed productively in a pluralistic, ethnically diverse, multiracial nation like America" (1989: xii).

8. This ignores the concern for purity in the United States. This can be witnessed in an intolerance for ambiguity at all levels of social life that is expressed in terms of a hierarchical ordering of "self" and "other" through figurations of disease and pollution. For this disposition at the personal and local levels, see Perin (1988). For this disposition at the national and international level, see Ross (1987: 328–348).

9. Schlossstein would endorse this sentiment. He concludes *The End of the American Century* with the statement: "Racism, insularity, arrogance, narrowness, and resentment. The dark side of Japan" (1989: 446). Would it be uncharitable to suggest that the same denunciations could be made of the United States? I think not. Moreover, the views of writers like Fallows and Schlossstein are often marked by an unrelieved lack of reflection about their own society. Consider this example: Schlossstein writes that the Japanese "have absolutely no innate sense of *sharedness* with other cultures. There is little awareness of commonality, no sense of shared fate. Until very recently, foreigners arriving at Tokyo's Narita International Airport were required to queue behind signs marked 'Alien,' as if they were somehow extraterrestrial beings." Yet such practices are still commonplace in America. The U.S. Immigration and Naturalization Service refers to all non-U.S. citizens as "aliens." Those who have successfully obtained permanent resident status are issued with the "green card" (actually, a blue and white plastic form of identification) emblazoned across the top with the words *Resident Alien.* In addition, the State Department and the INS retain a computer file with the names of over 350,000 "aliens" barred from the U.S. on ideological grounds. The National Automated Immigration Lookout System (NAILS) has had over 230,000 of those names added since 1980. There were 4,390 new entries in the first three months of 1990 alone. See *New York Times,* July 10 1990: "After the Cold War" and "Still a Cold War for Aliens." To be sure, "race" is not a specific point of differentiation in these exclusionary policies as practiced by the United States, but there can be little doubt that exclusion by ideology counts as "insularity, arrogance, narrowness, and resentment."

Moreover, the Japanese practice of fingerprinting and documenting the "alien" nature of Japanese-born Koreans derives in part from the continuation of practices established by the United States during the postwar occupation of Japan. See *Nation* 1990. Equally, John Russell (1991: 5) has argued that "Japanese views of blacks have taken as their model distorted images derived from Western ethnocentrism and cultural hegemony."

10. Ironically, the Nguyen family succeeded in large part by being "Japanese" and "un-American." They pooled resources, lived together, and saved communally. As Fallows quotes Nguyen Dong as saying: "We have a tradition of sticking together." When more family arrived to share the same house and save, Dong

remarked: "That is the beauty of the American way, everybody sharing!" Obviously, he did not have the same view of America as Fallows (Fallows: 104).

11. The call to "reopen" the United States of the frontier imagery resonates with the analysis of Alan Bloom (1987) and others that the country has become culturally closed. Indeed, Bloom is approvingly cited by Schlossstein on a number of occasions (1989: 262, 275–276, 328, 330, 342).

12. Occasionally, the cultural and economic sites merge openly in public discourse: witness, for example, the concern expressed when the Sony Corporation bought Columbia Pictures; and when Matsushita purchased the entertainment and publishing conglomerate, MCA. See New York Times December 1990.

13. Dower notes that in a number of instances—particularly those associated with talk of Japanese uniqueness—the claims of Allied propagandists (this involved Australian and British officials as well as Americans) merged with the boasts of the Japanese. Many of the Japanese most cherished symbols were thus exploited for contrary purposes. This coalescence of images does not serve to substantiate the American and Allied arguments, however. As Dower notes with regard to the horror tales of Japanese brutality on the battlefield: "The propagandistic deception lies, not in the false claims of enemy atrocities, but in the pious depiction of such behavior as peculiar to the other side" (1986: 12).

14. An interesting historical analog to this theme is the career of William Perry. Known best for commanding the flotilla of ships that achieved the "opening up" of Japan in 1853, Perry had considerable experience in the use of violence against those whom Americans regarded as threatening outsiders. He fought in an official capacity against the Mexicans in the 1840s, advocating the annexation of the entire country by the United States on the grounds that "they are all villain." Prior to Perry's Mexican service, he was notorious for his "ball-and-power" policy of suppression through naval bombardment during his patrols along the slave coast of Africa. Commander Perry did not limit his animus to those on the outside. He also talked scathingly of the public enthusiasm shown for refugees from the European revolutions of 1848 (like Kossuth of Hungary), whom Perry and other conservatives thought to be propagating "socialism and Red republicanism." Quoted in Kiernan (1980: 18–19).

15. Fallows' one and only mention (and then in a perfunctory manner) of the Indians comes late in his text: "Apart from Native Americans, the African slaves were the only involuntary, nonimmigrant members of this open, mobile society" (1990: 192). For the importance of violence to the self, see Richard Slotkin (1973).

16. In his otherwise superb analysis, John Dower resorts to these rather fixed understandings of what is happening (Dower: 9–10). For a critique of the notion of "archetype," see Slotkin (1986: 27–28).

17. Consider that some two-thirds of Japan's exports to the United States are covered by "Voluntary Export Restraints," and that the dollar value of these Japanese exports subject to quotas since 1982 has trebled. The protestations about a U.S. intrinsic commitment to "free trade" begin to look mythological. See Schlossstein (1989: 40). Fallows, of course, acknowledges the "Confucianism" within, but he does so in an unreflective way, confronting it as a policy problem rather than as part of the foreign policy strategies associated with construction and maintenance of identity.

18. For the idea that weather reports are an example of a modern discourse of "danger" that naturalizes social order, see Ross (1987/1988).

19. This political conclusion is shared by others whose brief is the broader problem of American strategy in an era, if not of decline, then of contested leadership. See, for example, Brzezinski (1988: 694): "Given the fact that the international system cannot operate on the basis of sheer goodwill and spontaneity alone

but needs some center of cooperative initiative, financial control and even political power, it follows that the only alternative to American leadership is global anarchy and international chaos."

20. In addition to the references cited in Note 9, see Herzog (1983) and Gilman (1985).

21. For an analysis of the importance of the hierarchy of sovereign/anarchic to international relations, and that has influenced this argument, see Ashley (1989).

22. See Jeffords (1989). As Wendy Brown observes, "men and states whom Machiavelli calls 'effeminate'—without fortifications, discipline, energy, *virtù*— are the first to fall to the glows of *fortuna* and womankind" (1988: 90).

8

Between Globalism and Nationalism in Post–Cold War German Political Economy

Frank Unger & Bradley S. Klein

> For the hard currency of Deutschmarks even unification can be acquired—and yes, even against the right to self-determination granted without hesitation to other peoples.
>
> —Günter Grass (1990: 122)

The case of German unification represents something of a laboratory for the politics of capitalism's globalizing logic. The spread of market laws, the absorption of seemingly established patterns of everyday life, and the role of the modern state as the bearer and enforcer of new structures of economic production—all can be seen here at play. Talk at one level of "the structural power of capital" and the rearticulation of hegemonic classes (Holman and van der Pijl 1992; Gill 1990, 1992; van der Pijl 1984; Schlupp 1992) thereby becomes embodied and envisaged as contending forces play themselves out as part of a larger geopolitical contest for new political space.

Such is the importance of German unification. It occurred, after all, at the center of four worlds—across the divided city of Berlin; across the two halves of Germany, East and West; across a divided continent that had long shared cultural experiences; and across the global fracture of a great social contest between two mutually incompatible constructs of social movements, ideology, production, distribution, state formation, and world order. Moreover, the politics and finances of German unification bear enormous weight, not only for the project of economic reconstruction in Central (formerly Eastern) Europe but for the whole process of European economic integration. The burdens of financing unification affect the availability of investment funds for Germany's eastern neighbors. And decisions by the German Central Bank on interest rates also shape political economy throughout the Continent. The more cooperation shown by the bank—displaying the last vestiges of German sovereignty—the greater the chances of Paris and London implementing the Maastricht Treaty on economic coordination.

171

Celebratory accounts that trumpet the victory of "the West" over a moribund and politically bankrupt East simply avoid the political dynamics involved in such a process of historical reconstruction. For Germany, and for the world, the demise of the Cold War has not been the end of history but in many ways its beginning. While some may see in a unified Germany evidence of a Fourth Reich on the resurgence, it is also possible to glimpse there the outlines of a search for a different politics of identity and culture in the wake of fundamental transformations in the nature of capitalism. German unification is not merely the exhaustion of one ideology; it is simultaneously the attempt by one state to mediate the disjuncture between its restricted political sovereignty and its more fluid domain of social reproduction. While much of the language of political analysis about it remains mired in nineteenth-century discourses of state power, imperialism, and great power hegemonic striving, the problems confronted by Germany (and not Germany alone) are distinctly contemporary—one is tempted to say postmodern—in scope.

A look at Germany's politics and its emergent civil society, then, suggests much about the dilemmas of European unification, as well as the new prospects for democratic politics and alternative social formations. There are important lessons having to do with the layering-in of cultural identity as regionalist, nationalist, and globalist structures of life compete to fill up the space of the former territorial sovereignty of real, existing East German socialism. Germany represents perhaps the most intractable of these complexes, since the issues there are so bound up with historic concerns about the German question and the legacy of classical nationalism. But it would be wrong to treat the German case entirely on German terms.

For that matter, it would be wrong—or worse yet, a resurgence of Cold War "totalitarian" thought—to presume that the countries formerly treated as part of the East bloc could now be subsumed within the equally totalizing logic of explanation of globalism and modernism. One needs to resist, in other words, the continuation of the Cold War by other means of discursive subterfuge, whereby the same analytical categories of postwar politics are preserved and extended—despite rhetorical exhortations about the end of the Cold War. A whole range of modernist assumptions need to be challenged and reconstructed here: not just East vs. West, socialism vs. capitalism, or us vs. them, but also state over economy, domestic vs. foreign, global vs. local (Walker 1992). Each of these dichotomous representations, crucial to the articulation of politics, identity, and political analysis throughout the modern era, reached their apex in the discursive politics of the Cold War. Today, however, they can no longer (if they ever could) bear the explanatory burden posed by contemporary life.

Across the board of the Atlanticist world, the postwar Keynesian consensus has been displaced by a more domestically polarizing strategy of privatization. This, in turn, is related to fundamental transformations in the structure of employment and production, from the Fordist model of mass assembly in strategically placed core corporations toward more decentralized, flexible modes of accumulation based upon networking, outsourcing, and downsizing (Harvey 1989; Reich 1991). The result is an accelerated dislocation of production from the sites of employment and consumption. On the one hand, this leads to new efficiencies in the labor process. On the other, it creates an intensified international division of labor. In the case of Germany, this restructuring is exacerbated due to the complex internal politics of unification.

GERMAN UNIFICATION

There can be little doubt that life has changed considerably for inhabitants of what used to be called the German Democratic Republic. The much-heralded promise of unification has brought with it a spate of problems associated with some of the harsher dimensions of everyday life in modern capitalist culture. Whole enterprises, heavily subsidized and insulated from economic pressure by the protective hand of Socialist Unity Party (SED) bureaucrats, have been thoroughly submitted to the disciplinary power of the market place. The result, in both East and West, has been massive social dislocation: Depression-era unemployment levels in the East and double-digit unemployment in the West; budget deficits associated with increased social welfare costs; and an alarming string of xenophobic violence directed not only at the recent influx of refugees and asylum applicants, but also at "guest workers" and other long-standing residents of foreign origin, especially Turks.

Prewar property titles to land in the East are now being recognized as valid in German courts. Pricey Western advertising campaigns, for political parties as well as for cola and stereos, are today de rigueur throughout the newly "liberated" territories. Precious historical artifacts that had been under wraps for years are now being bought up by the prestigious London-based auction house, Sotheby's, which has set up shop behind Unter den Linden (Tagliabue 1991). And faculty throughout the East German university system faced wholesale uprooting as various classes of suspect academics—whether as collaborators, ideologues, or those simply deemed behind the times—have been forced to give way to scholars more comfortable with Western modes of inquiry (Bollag 1990).

Despite these dislocations, however, something valuable has been gained in the process. No matter how much harder and less secure everyday existence there has become, even within the first few months of unification, and no matter how much citizens there may deplore some of the excesses of commercialization or their displacement from land returning to prewar property title, a majority of former East Germans clearly enjoy having become elevated to the status of "real Germans." One is tempted to say: of "good, modern Germans." This issue of "pride" or "self-esteem" is brought up by former GDR citizens much more often than any other conceivable notion when the talk is about the fruits of unification. A little observation may illustrate our point: The East German vernacular used to refer to the small coins of the old GDR currency—still valid for a limited time period on the territory of the former GDR after formal currency reform—as "Indians' money." Interpreting this image, the idea suggests itself that the unification apparently implies the upgrading of collective identity, the symbolic admission into the club of the master culture—or, as Jean-Paul Sartre used to call this culture, ironically, the master race. The difference, if we may continue this somewhat tasteless imagery, is that in this case, social mobility has now assumed for the newly arrived the ambiguous status of "white trash."

It goes without saying that these characterizations are to be understood in a figurative sense; yet they do represent a mentality that certainly is conspicuous in the five (formerly East German) northeastern provinces that are now part of the Federal Republic. These traits may tentatively be described in terms of an analogy with well-known mentalities in regions like the southern parts of the United States. Here, the most humble white person was, until relatively recently, a "master," just because of the color of his skin—predominantly in his imagination but, perhaps once a year, for real, as an invited participant in the social life of the plantation.

The analogous nonwhites in the German case are low-status foreigners (like Turks), German people of color, and—most important—East Europeans. They and their cultures with all their alleged "backwardness," their "guttural languages" (even more guttural than German!), their "untidiness," "laziness," and "dishonesty in commercial transaction," combined with their "inefficiency" as workers—all of these associations now well up into average East German minds when asked about their images of Eastern Europeans. Perhaps it is helpful here to recall how what Edward Said (1978) has termed "Orientalism" presented itself to upstanding European diplomats as "the Eastern Question": they took this to mean not events in the far reaches of Arabia and the Gulf, but in the world just on the other side of the Danube. Today these cultural tensions, for half a century relegated to a political netherworld of bloc politics and clumsily proclaimed fraternalism, have returned, this time in a manner that invariably complicates our maps of Europe and the world—and raises compelling questions about the reterritorialization of German (and with it, both European and global) identities. To see this as the resurgence of atavistic nationalism in its nineteenth-century guise is just as mistaken as to presume it to embody the completion of that homogenous cultural project called globalization.

Consider the example of German "nationalism." Was it the driving force behind the process of unification? Who wanted the unity and who did not care? Will Europe have to fear the new united Germany? What histories are being remembered or repressed?

To begin with, the so-called German question has two basic meanings. In the political rhetoric of the old (!) Federal Republic, it meant the continuing separation of German territory into two states. Yet for a great part of the rest of Europe (both East and West) the "German Question" developed with the birth of German unity in 1871; it stood—and continues to stand—for the acute anxiety shared by many Europeans about the control of a particular kind of political behavior that, during the first seventy-five years of German state unity, has somehow managed to initiate two world wars and perpetrated the systematic extermination of six million Jewish people and a like number of other categories of fellow Europeans.

Therefore, many, if not most, Europeans outside of Germany regarded the German question as solved as long as there existed two Germanies. There was the famous remark of Lord Ismay, first secretary-general of the North Atlantic Treaty Organization, who when asked about NATO's purpose said: "To keep the Americans in, to keep the Russians out, and to keep the Germans down." Perhaps more to the point was de Gaulle's wry comment, to the effect that "We French like Germany so much we want to see two of them." Lest this be dismissed as mere rhetoric, remember that the much-vaunted French nuclear Force de Frappe, announced for purposes of securing deterrence in all directions, and thus presumably against both the United States and the Soviet Union, for many years was deployed on the Albion Plain in southeasternmost France and could fly no farther than Munich.

Despite all the Western lip service paid to the rhetoric of reunification, there was a tacit understanding about the continuing existence of two German states, each tied to its respective alliance. Within Germany, of course, the situation was more complex—poised between ambiguous representations of the status of the GDR. The long-awaited acceptance of the East German state by the West German political elites, including the Christian Democrats, did not materialize until recent years. In the mid-1980s, responsible German political discourse shifted its rhetorical emphasis from national reunification to the demand for democratic self-determination of the East German people. In 1988, the progressive wing of the center-right even attempted altogether to remove the explicit reunification goal from the CDU Party platform.

The GDR was an internationally well-regarded state by the mid-1980s. Its leader, Erich Honecker, was an honorable man in the eyes of the international community and this was taken account of by his counterparts in the Federal Republic. In 1987, the conservative Kohl government invited him to a first official state visit to the West German capital. The spirit of mutual acceptance even captured the deadly enemies of the Cold War years, Communists and Social Democrats: on the highest party level, leading theoreticians and functionaries of the SPD and the SED came together in a joint commission and composed a platform calling for a civilized resolution to the dispute between the two great German workers' parties and set out principles for an envisaged long-term cooperation (*Neues Deutschland* 1987). All this had been inspired by the conciliatory behavior of the Honecker government in the early 1980s, when the GDR demonstratively continued its policy of detente and cooperation vis-à-vis the Federal Republic: this at a time when the superpowers were heavily engaged in the rhetorical, military, and economic exercises of the Second Cold War, following the deployment of SS–20 rockets by the USSR and the Western response, leading up to the so-called double-track decision. It was Honecker who explicitly emphasized the distinct responsibility of the Germans for keeping the peace in Europe.

Even the East German refusal to follow the course of Gorbachev's perestroika was not immediately and universally denounced as reactionary stubbornness: it was seen by many West Germans as a further indication of GDR independence from Moscow and of a growing self-confidence. Had not Gorbachev himself repeatedly praised the GDR as a shining example for the socialist countries, referring to the 16 percent productivity advantage the East German state enjoyed over the socialist mother country? Did he not say on more than one occasion that the Soviet people had a lot to learn from the East Germans?

Such was the West German perception of the GDR by the mid- to late 1980s. Surely it did not go unnoticed that there also were certain problems. For example, it was well known that a growing number of young people were determined to leave the country. In fact, the exodus to the West had started in the mid-1980s, when hundreds of thousands of people were allowed to leave the GDR for West Germany or other Western countries. Also, by about 1988, it became a "public secret" that the top political leadership, i.e., the Politburo, was increasingly getting out of tune with the rest of the country, including the most loyal members of their own party. But all this was regarded by the political pundits in West Germany as an internal GDR problem, as sort of the coming-of-age of the GDR, not as the prelude for anything so remote as the unification of Germany.

We could illustrate this with quotations from a host of West German periodicals and so-called quality newspapers. The point we want to make here is this: all of these perceptions obviously turned out to be utterly and dramatically misleading. Less then three years after the greatest diplomatic triumph of the GDR regime, Erich Honecker's state visit to Bonn, his state ceased to exist. This begs explanation.

One point is clear, however. Unification did not emerge as an expression of German nationalism. There was, for example, no burning desire of most West Germans to live in a united political state with all women and men of the same tongue and the same cultural heritage. A nationalism with this practical aim did not exist as a serious political force in the Federal Republic of Germany (Habermas, 1990). The overwhelming majority of West Germans were quite happy with their prosperous republic and longed neither for a unification with the GDR nor with the third major German-speaking country, Austria.

This suggests a rather interesting conclusion: German unification could be achieved—and, from the standpoint of the enforcers, had to be completed in such a breathtakingly short time—not because a growing ir-redentist sentiment in the stronger part of Germany pushed its political leaders from behind, but because the sentiment longing for unification was so feeble *precisely* in the bigger part of the two, the Federal Republic. If there had been a political movement that explicitly and seriously had de-manded German unification as part of a nationalist-expansionist program, then this, without the shadow of a doubt, would have provoked the rise of respective countermovements. Under the threat of serious political strife, brought up by the existence of an organized and argumentatively well-equipped antiunification position, neither Helmut Kohl nor anybody else would have dared to act the way he did. Since such an opposition did not exist, Kohl simply took advantage of the tacit arithmetic of modern demo-cratic politics: the winner is not he who represents the greatest number of voters, but he who offends the smallest number of them. To put it bluntly: in modern democracy, the government can get away with anything, as long as there is no substantial opposition. And since the word *reunification* (as a return to the pre–World War II borders) belonged to the consensualist culture of the West German polity in much the same way as *motherhood* belongs to the American one—i.e., as a rhetorical value that may be taken with a grain of salt in private but must never be questioned publicly—there was virtually no time in West Germany for potentially operational oppo-nents of unification (to the combined borders of the post–World War II FRG and GDR) to gather forces in order to react in a sound political way to this sudden transformation of Sunday speech material into fast action.

EAST GERMAN INITIATIVES

As far as the West German people are concerned, the unification was a process initiated and carried out strictly from above. The GDR, by con-trast, certainly represents a different case: the desire of most of their peo-ple for a unification can hardly be doubted. And here, indeed, the ques-tion about "nationalism does arise: was it nationalism," and if so, which of its many variants was it that incited so many East Germans to display their desires to become citizens of the FRG, as fast as possible and at all costs?

However, it would be a serious misconception to assume that this na-tionalist desire of East Germans to dissociate themselves from their East

European partners and allies was exclusively a mass sentiment, in opposition to a Communist leadership that staunchly tried to save the East European connection and to preserve the integration of the "socialist camp." It is true, the East German leadership did—in order to keep its legitimacy for staying in power—continuously pay lip service to its solidarity with the Socialist countries, including the Soviet Union. In real policy, however, at least a decisive faction of it had long before taken the road of retreating from the perceived East European mess and had turned to the European Economic Community via the German "brother state" instead.

As early as 1983, there were clear indications for an economic "decoupling" from the Soviet Union on the part of the German Democratic Republic. The famous *Milliardenkredit* of 1983, engineered by Franz Josef Straub and Alexander Schalck-Golodkowski, East Germany's commissioner for hard currency acquisition, was perhaps the most telling indication of this new line. Considering the political temperament of the protagonist on the Western side of this deal, it can be safely assumed that the transaction at the time was not arranged without some confidential political conversations preceding it.

According to subsequent statements by Schalck-Golodkowski on German television, the West German political leadership was informed by late 1987 about the East German government's belief that only a confederation with the Federal Republic could save the GDR economy from crippling entanglements in an impending East European economic crisis. Schalck-Golodkowski also indicated that the eventual unification was—in striking ideological contrast to public statements by party functionaries—regarded as "inevitable" by some East German Communist leaders in their confidential conversations among themselves as well as with their leading West German counterparts.

If this is true, then Honecker's above-mentioned conciliatory behavior during the Second Cold War (in the early 1980s) as well as the entire East German "revolution" in the late 1980s appears in a somewhat more complicated light than it is now commonly presented and interpreted by the mostly self-proclaimed pundits of East European affairs. In short, the role of the East German leadership in this process is indisputably much greater than is commonly assumed.

Their denouncement of Gorbachev's perestroika was probably not meant to be an expression of stubborn Socialist-centralist principles; more likely was it tacitly informed and guided by the confidential strategic belief that the GDR's economic future would not reside with COMECON cooperation, but in integration with West Germany and the European Community. What the East German population (and most of the Western media) interpreted as a mulish insistence on "Stalinist" methods and ways of thought may very well simply have amounted to—in the insiders' discourse of East Germany's Communist leaders—an annoyed message to the

Soviet Union and the rest of the East Europeans to leave the GDR alone with their problems of underdevelopment.

What appeared to be an "orthodox" shying away from economic and democratic progress was to some extent a display of nationalist arrogance, nurtured by the notion of German superiority and possibly assured by some vague general promises from leading West German politicians about the future course of economic integration. Alas for them, the East German Communist elite only made a serious miscalculation (or was hopelessly naive) in its obvious confidence that the West German society would not send them packing the day after they guilelessly handed over the keys to their country, but would accept them gladly and thankfully as some kind of "comprador bourgeoisie," in some illusionary confederate system based on a communal "market economy." Elements of this were clearly in effect through the GDR's functional membership in the Common Market—thanks to being snuck in by its Western brethren in the FRG, who were conveniently allowed to use the GDR's economy as part of their own. By expecting this tacit—if not explicit—recognition by West German authorities, the GDR *nomenklatura* displayed a striking ignorance about power mechanics within a capitalist market economy.

THE GERMAN END OF HISTORY

What will it mean to be German in the future? What histories are being remembered or repressed? Will there be a new version of the "German Question," in the European sense, now that Germany is united? First, there will still be two distinctive sorts of Germans for some time to come. The East German social character—which, by the way, does also contain many positive elements—is so different from the West German that it will take at least one generation to "melt" the two into oblivion. Because of the increasingly competitive social climate, there will be popular tendencies toward racism, xenophobia, and chauvinistic nationalism, not just in the provinces of the former GDR. These developments, however, are likely to become compensated by strong leftist and liberal-leftist countermovements designed at least to moderate the more aggressive aspects of post–Cold War German policy. And these counterbalancing movements will likewise extend to that most interesting sphere of German politics, the country's newfound role in foreign policy, especially in terms of overseas military deployments. It is difficult, for instance, to imagine Germany acquiring more than a secondary role as an expeditionary state. Even its dispatch of 1,700 soldiers to Somalia in July 1993, in multilateral cooperation with the United Nations, pushes the envelope of acceptability at home (Whitney 1993).

There are several indications to support this hypothesis, but most convincing to us is the following deliberation: it concerns the psychology of what is sometimes called the West German "left camp." As an electoral force in the old Federal Republic, it consisted of roughly half the population, and all indications from the 1990 federal elections are that it will stay roughly the same. To be sure, the events comprising the unification of Germany were a single process of humiliation for the left—including the SPD. By that we don't mean the result as such, but the manner by which it was hammered home by a conservative government that in constitutional terms carried out something bordering on a postmodern coup d'etat—Bonapartism ushered in not on the back of a white horse but in the form of an attache case. It may be true that the parliamentary opposition wouldn't have known what to do or what to say, anyway, but that is not the point here. They simply were not consulted. Since they have been humiliated and virtually ignored by Helmut Kohl and his handful of experts who worked out the unity treaty in much less time than it normally takes to debate an amendment to local Blue Laws, and since they have no ideological means to combat it, they have virtually no other option for their attempt at regaining dignity and political identity than to concentrate on the foreign policy of the united Germany.

But then, not just the German left will see to it that the united Germany will not grow into a military powerhouse capable of, and eager for, interventions in the vicinity or in more remote parts of the world. Such vigilance seems widespread among the Germans. The United States now faces a Germany that it accuses of not being sufficiently military-minded and of having "wimped out" during the Gulf War.

Most people in Germany, including the conservatives, know that military power did not contribute anything substantial to the phenomenal rise of the Federal Republic to its place as one of the most prestigious nations in the contemporary world, officially acknowledged even before the unification by President Bush as a "partner in leadership." Instead, it was economic strength in combination with unique industrial relations and a social welfare system that, despite its imperfection, still contributed to the creation of one of the most spectacular versions of a capitalist society in the world today. Any German politician or industrialist who would in all seriousness try to propagate the old dreams of a Greater German Empire based on military expansion or outright political domination of neighboring countries would in no time be relegated to the back benches by his peers. If this is so, what does it tell us about the character, about the "historical meaning," of the unification?

There is the Wall Street (or, depending on your political preference, Marxist) school of hardboiled realist economics that says: What the acquisition of the GDR represents for the political and economic elites of the FRG is neither the triumph of the patriotic soul, nor a burning ambition of the political elites to rule over an extended territory, but the cool, calm, and collected striving for new economic opportunities, outlets for capital, leading positions for the hitherto less successful sons and daughters of the upper and middle classes; in short, the conquest of a new frontier. Before this new frontier can fully be utilized, the old structures must be completely destroyed. The West Germans are not only world champions in exporting; they also compete for the title of world record–holder in how fast you can change an economic system. And since the GDR population (perhaps for reasons discussed above) prefer products in fancy Western packings, the complete collapse of its own economy, which according to OECD rankings was tenth on the list of the world's most productive nations in 1989, is all but completed already.

But then this securing of a new frontier for the West German economy and society cannot simply be seen as a matter of economic rationality, or rational economics, if you prefer. It is by no means clear that the acquisition of the new provinces and their incorporation into the West German political economy will be economically and politically advantageous for the West Germans. The long-term costs to the federal treasury—estimated at between $600 billion and $1.2 trillion through 2001 (*Newsweek* 1991; *U.S. News and World Report* 1991)—have forced tax hikes and budget cuts into established social programs, thereby threatening the delicate live-and-let-live consensus between the classes and interests of the former "Modell Deutschland." If we try to look at this from the position of a shrewd captain of industry, Kohl and his government will be seen to have acted more like adventurers than calculating businessmen. So there was obviously something else that contributed decisively to the behavior of the Kohl government.

This missing link may be called the ideology factor. Conventional wisdom maintains that only Communists, and maybe some right-wing lunatics, have something like an ideology. A political proponent of Western capitalist society—or to put it another way, a follower of the concept of "social market economy"—is supposed to be just a pragmatic human being. This is, however, not true. Anyone who has read Francis Fukuyama's seminal essay on "The End of History?" (1989) must come to the conclusion that parts of the political elites in our societies have a very distinctive worldview. Their creed is called "liberalism," and it is explicitly presented by Fukuyama as a tit-for-tat "economic determinism"; i.e., not as an accompanying (superstructural) idea to an economic basis, but as the very mover and shaker of history itself. According to Fukuyama, the acceptance of the idea of a liberal-capitalist society precedes the establishment of those political economies, and not vice versa. Contrary to the Marxists, who believe that the arrival of the Communist stage will mark the "end of history," Fukuyama assures his readers, from his reading of Hegel and Kojeve, that the very liberal-capitalist society of today represents the end of history, because human thinking and human wishes will never come down to a better one. The Marxists, according to Fukuyama, were wrong not in their assumption of an end of history as such, but only in their notion of what this end will look like. Seen from the sober position of a sociologist of knowledge, and judged on the basis of the fact that Fukuyama was by no means universally ridiculed by Western reviewers, this suggests the existence of a comprehensive ideological belief beyond, and independent of, pure economic rationality, which (at least occasionally) guides the thoughts and actions of our Western societies' elites, quite reciprocal with the ideologically motivated parts of the ruling elites in the former Socialist countries.

Fukuyama, it turns out, shares with mainstream and journalistic interpretations of German unification the assumption that we must appraise postwar politics in terms of a binary opposition of socialism vs. capitalism. Yet it may be one of recent history's greatest ironies to have undermined this ideological reading of political economy. The dilemmas of German unification, like those of economic construction in Eastern Europe and of unification throughout the EEC, confirm, on the contrary, the highly politicized, state-saturated nature of social reproduction in modern Western societies.

Perhaps the ideological interpretation of Socialist political economy (as "politicized," unlike the West's) helps to illuminate some of the ruthlessness in the pursuit of the unification. The process was not just accompanied by an ideological offensive; it was a crusade in its own right. Its main purpose was not the abolition of political oppression or the smooth integration of East German compatriots into the West German polity, but no more and no less than the total delegitimization of an economic system that was based on something other than the private ownership of the means of production. To come to our point: the unification of Germany was not primarily the swift creation of a united German national state, it was—and is—first and foremost the ruthless destruction of the German Democratic Republic.

Another aspect may be added here: The society of the GDR started out as an "anti-Fascist democracy"; i.e., it started out on the constituent basis to prevent any further version of fascism on German soil. Its raison d'etre was taken from the Dimitroffian theory of fascism. According to him, German nazism was based on the symbiotic collaboration between private monopolist industries and a terrorist state—the latter saving the former in a structural crisis. Any future relapse to fascism could only be safely prevented by radically changing the social basis of the society; i.e., by abolishing the private ownership of the means of production and the profit motive as an organizing force for industry.

For forty-five years, West German conservatives had to live with the fact that there was always one serious ideological stick that the left could use against them in times of need: to recall German capitalism's Fascist antecedents. There have been conspicuous attempts in the recent past to present German nazism in a new interpretive light: to put it in proportion to the wrongdoings of other European states. Historian Ernst Nolte characterized the Holocaust as an "Asiatic crime," by which he meant that German fascism, with all its weird and murderous aspects, was nothing but the historical response to the attack of the Eastern creed of Stalinism (Nolte 1986; Baldwin 1990). This, of course, was the substance of the already famous *Historikerstreit*. These attempts were made by Nolte and others not because they envisaged a revival of German Fascist expansionism, or because they wanted to belittle the Nazi crimes as such, but in order to attain a new and totally purified legitimacy for the present—the *Modell Bundesrepublik*. What the elites of postwar West Germany long for—maybe legitimately so—is to catch up morally with their British and U.S. counterparts by removing, once and for all, the stigma of the Holocaust from the reformed German capitalism—a stigma that, somehow, the world was always sublimely reminded of by the very existence of the German Democratic Republic.

BETWEEN REGIONALISM AND GLOBALISM

What, then, will be the effects of the German unification for the rest of Europe? In our interpretation, the unification of the two Germanies on the Western model was not primarily motivated by German nationalism, but by anticommunism. Its purpose was not so much the creation of a new political unit, but the destruction of an old one. Anticommunism or antisocialism is the natural, and sometimes strictly enforced, consensus in most Western countries; it is not particularly restricted to Germany. So there should be no reason for good liberal, English-speaking readers—presupposed to sharing the values of Western societies—to be apprehensive of the dynamism displayed by the West German government in its pursuit of the unification. For this seemingly new German nationalism has long since taken the form of what we would like to call the "patriotism of the international marketplace." The spiritual fathers of this unification are neither Bismarck nor the Kaiser nor Hitler, but Adam Smith and Woodrow Wilson.

Those who will primarily suffer from this triumph of liberalism in the heart of Europe will be, paradoxically, the East European countries outside the former GDR, especially Poland, Hungary, and Bulgaria. The Conference on Security and Cooperation in Europe (CSCE), initiated in 1975, took its main impetus in Western Europe, and especially in the Federal Republic, from the idea of keeping the peace between the ideologies, from the idea of change through reapprochement, as it were. Now that the change is there, the Eastern European people will very soon realize that, without their status as pawns and possible dissidents within the Cold War context, their popularity with Western political and economic leaders, not to speak of the Western European people, is quickly going to dwindle away. One need only look at the paltry efforts undertaken by the European Bank for Reconstruction and Development—efforts headed, at least initially, by none other than that visionary of postmodern political economy, Jacques Attali (1991)—to see how dispensable the East has become after the Cold War.

This is a deeply ironic experience for the East Europeans. Precisely on the threshold of their greatest postwar achievement, their incorporation into the cultural and economic realm of the Western European nations, they are confronted with their deepest humiliation: their de facto relegation to second- or third-rate status. They are already having the irritating experience that the long-awaited Western "investments" that they expected to deliver the desired prosperity are simply not showing up. The West sends them shopping centers, but no productive capital to earn the money to buy the goods on sale there. There are "two cheers for capitalism," but no one to foot the bill.

The initial enthusiasm for the politics of the CSCE has more or less vanished, drowned by the ballyhoo about the German unification. The chances for the peaceful and orderly integration of Eastern Europe into the West European community have sunken dramatically. Along with the normal problems of economic reconstruction, and of overcoming fragile state structures, are the more fractious problems of ethnicity and civil conflict—manifested most tragically in the former Yugoslavia. The united Germany, for instance, is already pursuing a policy of bilateral relations toward Eastern Europe. On this basis, most of the East European countries will face the future of "underdeveloped countries" in more distant parts of the world; with all their social contradictions, their anomic violence, and their tendency to produce "superfluous populations" whose more enterprising elements end up as migrants to the prosperous areas of Western Europe. Eastern Europe is envisaged by many as the future Latin America of the Eastern hemisphere, with the EC in the role of the United States.

There is, however, still a chance that this dark picture of the Eastern European future, apocalyptically outlined, for example, by John Mearsheimer, can be avoided (Mearsheimer 1990a, 1990b; Galtung 1990). It might help in this regard to recall that Mearsheimer's analysis has absolutely nothing to do with the internal dynamics of political culture and political economy and everything to do with an image of international relations as guided by a timeless, universal anarchy. It does not take much to realize that such a picture cuts against everything that has taken place on the European continent for forty-five years now. The theory of international anarchy might help us to remember that France is France and Germany is Germany, but it is wholly silent on the complex mechanisms of substate and transnational relations by which formally, legally separated sovereign entities actually manage their day-to-day affairs in realms that are far less mundane—though far more important for everyday life—than the plate-tectonic images of international relations.

The immediate case of a postnationalist Germany takes place in a European-cum-world order freed from the deadening weight of the Cold War and its several reincarnations. This calls for, among other institutional practices, a resuscitation of the CSCE process in the original sense, which had the existence of two different principles of social and economic organization in Europe as its accepted starting point. Now that the Eastern European Communist systems have collapsed, it would be the quintessentially fatal political mistake to draw from this the conclusion that principally all philosophies that advocate any sort of regional economic regulation or ask for the occasional primacy of policy over economics, have failed. It is necessary only to consider the global environmental problems to understand this point. In this sense, a united Germany is the key political arena for this coming strategic struggle.

PART 4
THE CONSTRUCTION OF IDENTITIES: PERIPHERAL CAPITALISM

Inscribing the Nation: Nehru and the Politics of Identity in India

Sankaran Krishna

And this year . . . there was an extra festival on the calendar, a new myth to celebrate, because a nation which had never previously existed was about to win its freedom, catapulting us into a world which, although it had five thousand years of history, although it had invented the game of chess and traded with the Middle Kingdom Egypt, was nevertheless, quite imaginary; into a mythical land, a country which would never exist except by the efforts of a phenomenal collective will—except in a dream we all agreed to dream; it was a mass fantasy shared in varying degrees by Bengali and Punjabi, Madrasi and Jat, and would periodically need the sanctification and renewal which can only be provided by rituals of blood. India, the new myth—a collective fiction in which anything was possible.

—Salman Rushdie (1980: 129–130)

In Western analyses of international relations (IR), the dominant paradigm may be characterized as neorealism. This paradigm discursively articulates a world of sovereign, self-contained entities, called nation-states, that interact, each with the other, primarily via a utilitarian calculus in an overall milieu marked by anarchy. Accordingly, in this Hobbesian domain, the focus of analysis comes to rest on the preservation of national security and the furtherance of national interest at every opportunity. The mainstream discourse effectively marginalizes any analysis of the differential empowerment of social groups and classes arising from this depiction of the world. Equally significant, this discourse of neorealism is a metanarrative that inevitably generates innumerable microscripts for interstate conflicts. State elites, as the heroic defenders of the realm, acquire a degree of autonomy that stands sharply in contrast to the limitations imposed on their activities within the domestic community. The possibility-condition enabling this power over determining relations with the "foreign"—and, inter alia, the domestic(ated)—is the endless reproduction of an antinomy: "anarchy without"/"community within."[1] In a fundamental sense, state power

189

itself inheres in the ability to articulate and maintain distinctions/bound-aries/margins between the domestic and the foreign. The social and essen-tially contestable character of such articulations is displaced by their ob-jective, material density. Thus, in mainstream approaches, a term such as *foreign policy making* is unremarkable. To this understanding, the very categories *foreign* and *domestic* are taken as preexisting, unquestionable, objective givens. Once this is accepted, the domain of international rela-tions becomes the study of actions of state elites motivated purely by a utilitarian calculus. That categories such as foreign and domestic are so-cially articulated, are inherently both inclusive and exclusive; that they si-multaneously valorize some and disempower others—all this is lost as these terms acquire the hegemonic density of *common sense* and enter the everyday discourse of apprehending reality itself.

This discourse of neorealist thought is both modern and Western.[2] Its intimate relationship with capitalism and colonialism is no secret. In the context of the periphery of the modern world-system,[3] the discourse of ne-orealism has a relationship of deep ambivalence with emerging national-ism. On the one hand, the national movements in the periphery were ob-viously reacting to the economic exploitation and cultural and political subjugation inherent in colonialism. Nationalism emerged in the periphery as an oppositional force, with a potentially counterhegemonic historical project. On the other hand, the reigning models of the future in these colo-nial struggles were themselves clearly derivative of the Western experi-ence and its three pillars of Science, Reason, and Capital. How was this ambivalence, indeed this contradiction, finessed in the Third World? What is the historical process by which the "cunning of reason" inveigles colo-nial nationalism? How, ultimately, does the discursive formation called neorealism co-opt and ingest the potential radicalism of peripheral nation-alism? This chapter represents a very preliminary effort at examining this process in the context of a specific peripheral society; namely, India.

CONSTITUTING THE SELF

If a nation is an imagined community, as Anderson (1983) has per-suasively argued, in India the imagination of such a selfhood emerged after the advent of British colonial rule. As in most other peripheral soci-eties, the middle class was the social fragment that was both completely colonized by the West and simultaneously in the vanguard of the struggle to expel the West from (new category) *the nation.* This dual position of the emerging middle class—on the one hand, a class that acquired its identity on the basis of the fluency of its intercourse with the colonizing power; and on the other, a class that was beginning to articulate a new, separate, territorial, cultural, economic, and political essence for itself—underlies the highly ambivalent reception of modernity in the periphery.

The first generation of "nationalist" leaders in India came, almost exclusively, from the English-educated, relatively affluent classes. Although, in political terms, these "moderates," as they came to be called, confined their actions to petitioning the colonial government for very sectarian concessions to the native middle classes, in a broader sense they explicitly recognized that they were in the process of endowing a certain geographical, territorial entity with content, history, culture, and an essence. If, as this process unfolded in the early decades of this century, the historical narrative of this long-standing territorial entity called "India" had to be creatively rewritten; if the central myths and mythologies of this region had to be reinterpreted along the lines of modern nationhood; if past, successful examples of subcontinental conquest were now reinscribed as instances of national unification; if the peasant rebellions of the eighteenth and nineteenth century and the insurrectionary Revolt of 1857 against the British East India Company were now endowed with self-conscious, "patriotic" elements; if past Mughul regimes were now to be re-presented as a dark age in which "India" labored under "alien" rule; if secular political adversaries of these Mughul rulers were now reanointed as nationalist heroes—all these were, in the main, unself-consciously practiced and not perceived as posing a problem in terms of authenticity. They were primarily the uncritical, derivative responses of a dominated people to a "superior" civilization whose success was attributed in large part to its unitary, strong nation-state.

To the more historically self-aware leaders, this eclectic rewriting of history is precisely what imagining a new nation constituted. Thus, a prominent leader of this time (Lala Lajpat Rai) "made it clear that his 'sole object in referring to the past history of India' and in asserting that India was and had always been a 'political unity' was to counter the contemporary imperialist denigration of Indian nationalism as illegitimate and without a foundation in reality" (quote from Bipan Chandra 1986: 214 n. 67). In other words, the real content of the past did not matter; what was crucial was the recovery of an essentialist core, called "India," from this past; a recovery whose content would be critically determined by the contemporary context of colonialism into which it would emerge, which could then be counterpoised against the reality of imperial, alien rule and thus serve as the mythography that legitimized the struggle for independence.

Such an interpretation of history as was occurring at the beginning of the century, even as it began to lay the grounds for the emergence of an entity called India, was sowing the seeds for later fractures (most prominently along religious lines). The "India" that was now being imagined could not be the mere mirror-image of Western nations: that would negate the very basis of the struggle for independence. Rather, as in every other historical context, the discursive practice of nation-writing had to endow the self with a unique, cultural, political, spiritual essence that could energize the society in its struggle against foreign oppression.

Perhaps one of the most significant differences that emerged in the selective appropriation of the neorealism in India was on the spatio-temporal character of the "other." In Western neorealism, the outside, the domain without, was quintessentially the anarchic, dark, noncommunitarian state of nature. What demarcated the within was precisely the presence of authority, of community, of shared values through the contractual commitment to a central power. In a spatial sense, thus, the community stopped "at the water's edge, as it were" (Ashley 1987: 404); and the crucial marker of the outside was anarchy. In a temporal sense, the external was marked by its roots in a past that had been transcended with great difficulty and fortitude—and the price of its maintenance was eternal vigilance. The state of nature that prevailed without was temporally antecedent to the establishment of community within, and simultaneously the possibility-condition that enabled the very maintenance of domestic community.

In the periphery, the outside is defined mainly not by its anarchy, but by hierarchy. The desired futures of the periphery are to be found in the pasts and presents of the developed, the industrialized, and the modern countries. The dominant self-perception of the nationalist elites in India was that of a civilization left behind, one whose historical destiny was ever to play catch-up with the West. Thus, the outside, which was responsible for the long night of colonialism, is also the zone from which historical redemption would arrive—in the form of science, reason, and capital. This imparts a peculiar ambivalence to the characterization of the other in peripheral societies, alternating between seeing it as potentially neocolonialist and yet the yardstick against which to measure and valorize the domestic. Thus, *Third World* is a most appropriate characterization of this zone: it defines itself in terms of its quantitative distance from the modern.

This social articulation of global space, and of India's location within it, served as the foundation for a new basis of state legitimation. It marked the emergence of the developmental state. In terms of this articulation, the newly "independent" state situated itself in a mediatory position between the *domestic,* configured as a violated zone, a precarious, fragile, exploited and fragmented territory; and the *foreign,* correspondingly inscribed as riven with hierarchy, populated by powerful others who until recently had colonized, pillaged, and impoverished the self and yet who, through their superior science and rationality, would remain the wellspring of Indian regeneration. Thus, the historical mandate of the new state was the recovery of the self through the reversal of underdevelopment.

The highly ambivalent nature of this recovery is obvious: the intimate enemy called colonialism (Nandy 1983) was sought to be exorcised by the derivative discourse of modernity (Chatterjee 1986). From the perspective of this chapter, what is interesting is the eclectic translation of the Western community/anarchy antinomy into a peripheral underdeveloped/modern antinomy. It must be emphasized, however, that the result was the same in both societies: the contrast between within and without served as the basis of state legitimation, elevated certain skills and abilities to the level of the nationally indispensable, and put into circulation certain practices that, in the name of national security and development, justified and reinforced the power of these state elites.

WRITING THE NATION

The lyrical bard of nationalism in India was undoubtedly Jawaharlal Nehru. In his *An Autobiography* (1936: reprint 1939), in the *The Discovery of India* (1946: reprint 1989), and in the letters he wrote to friends and contemporaries, one finds a man of both extraordinary literary abilities and, often, of transparent honesty. One of the more interesting aspects of *An Autobiography* is the extent to which Nehru regarded any nationalism that was devoid of an economic program as being spurious, inferior, irrational, passionate, and empty. Repeatedly one finds this criticism of "mere" nationalism devoid of any economic program (1939: 35, 66, 75, 157, 198, 266, 365, 367, 472). Nationalism, to Nehru, was an emotional (and for that reason, limited) reaction to foreign subjection. For it to become the basis of an alternative construction of selfhood, it had to be accompanied by a program of economic and social reconstruction. In terms of the argument in this chapter, the rewriting of the neorealist paradigm in the periphery clearly proceeds with this initial step of endowing nationalism with an economic content.

The nationalist movement in India, however, had been accompanied by the most incisive of critiques of modernity. The pathology of modern, scientific, rationalist civilization, it was argued, was evident in the Europe of the interwar period, specifically in fascism and nazism. The connections between the utilitarian calculus that underlay capitalism on the one hand, and militarism, imperialism, territorial conquest, and colonialism, on the other, were not lost upon Gandhi and Nehru. The reinscription of Western rationality and science into Indian society, as a means of regenerating India, was obviously fraught with contradiction. Gandhi's solution to the problem was crafted in his own terms. He consistently interpreted his struggle as not being one against the British or for political independence but as a struggle against a whole worldview, which today one might characterize as "the modern condition" and which he chose to call "industrial society." Nehru, the modernizer par excellence, finessed the contradiction in a different manner, with implications for the emerging logic of statecraft. Let us take up his ambiguous resolution of the question of science.[4]

Nehru argued, essentially, for an abstraction of Western science and rationality from the context in which they had emerged; viz., post-Enlightenment Western Europe. There could be a secular (and selective) appropriation of the scientific method, of the practice of science, without necessarily con-taminating it with the alienation, the commodification, and the econo-mistic calculus that accompanied it in the West. Nehru, in *An Autobiogra-phy*, reveals his somewhat unsure resolution of this question:

> Most of us were not prepared to reject the achievements of modern civi-lization, although we may have felt some variation to suit Indian condi-tions was possible. . . . It [India] will succumb to this newcomer, for the West brings science and science brings food to the hungry millions. But the West also brings an antidote to this cut-throat civilization—the prin-ciples of socialism [presaging an important argument to be dealt with below–S.K.], of co-operation, and service to the community for the com-mon good. . . . It may be that when India puts on her new garment, as she must, for the old is torn and tattered, she will have it cut in this fashion, so as to make it conform both to present conditions and her old thought (1939: 77, 432).

Aside from this question of "adaptation," Nehru goes on to suggest that there is an essentialist, universalist "core" to science that can be ab-stracted from its "Western-ness." In other words, that the British were merely the carriers of this secular, noncontextual way of thinking that be-longed to humanity at large, and would have come to India anyway. Nehru thus observes:

> In almost every country in the world the educational and material progress has been tremendous during the last century because of science and industrialism. . . . Are we needlessly cantankerous and perverse if we suggest that some such technical progress would have come to us anyhow in this industrial age, and even without British rule? (1939: 434).

In a repetition of the age-old distinction between pure science and dirty politics, Nehru clinches the argument for himself when he notes:

> The industrial age has brought many evils that loom large before us; but we are apt to forget that, taking the world as a whole, and especially the parts that are most industrialized, it has laid down a basis of spiritual progress far easier for larger numbers. This is not at all evident in India or other colonial countries as we have not profited by industrialism. We have only been exploited by it and in many respects made worse, even materially, and more so culturally and spiritually. *The fault is not of in-dustrialism but of foreign domination* . . . this has been our misfortune and we should not allow it to colour our vision of the world today (1939: 520). [The emphasis is mine.]

Thus a critical step in the resolution of the question of science was that, in terms of the deferred logic of selfhood, once independence was achieved science could be made to work for India. Indeed, the new, emerg-ing raison d'etat was to be precisely that: the state as the scientific modernizer of society. The not-accidental result of this was a highly dirigiste (or interventionist) conception of the state itself in its relation to society and to development. The ideological undergirding of the immensely pervasive state that currently characterizes India has to be traced back to this formative period: the state as a scientific, rational, social engineer, remaking society along the trajectory of modernity.

This incipient dirigisme was powerfully supplemented by the other aspect of Nehru's finessing of the ambivalence inherent in an essentially imitative strategy of attaining selfhood; viz., that of socialism. The linearity of the developmental paradigm (and the ignominy of bringing up its rear) was mitigated thus:

> We are trying to catch up today with the Industrial Revolution which came to the western countries long years ago and made great changes in the course of a century or more and which ultimately branched off in two directions, one represented by the very high degree of technological development of the United States and the other by the Soviet Union. Both these patterns are, in fact, branches of the same tree, even though they may look very different. This Industrial Revolution has a long history behind it. We would be wise not to repeat the errors committed in its earlier stages, we would be wise to profit by them (Nehru 1956: 4–5).

In this, as in many other writings, Nehru argued that planned Socialist development offered the way out of the contradictions posed by capitalism and industrialism. It did so by ensuring that accumulation based on individual effort redounded to societal benefit, not by the capricious hand of the market but by the omniscient and visible hand of the state itself. In terms of this finessing of the conundrum of "backward development," India could learn from the "mistakes" of earlier generations of capitalist development and, like the Soviet Union, leapfrog through central planning, and yet, unlike the Soviet Union, avoid the concentration and abuse of power through electoral democracy. Thus, the hierarchy without was appropriated within to justify not only statism, but was done in such a manner as to deflect the charge of slavish imitation. And in a postcolonial society there can be no more damaging charge than one of slavish imitation.

One final point in this regard: the Indian penchant for neologisms in describing the attempted strategies of development (examples: "socialistic pattern of society"; "mixed economy"; an Indian variety of "secularism"; "passive revolution") can be better understood in terms of the constant need to reappropriate and redesign influences from without and from world-time in terms of an indigenous chronometer (call it HMT, if you wish). The numerous neologisms are the signifiers of a society whose elites are deeply imitative and yet uncomfortably aware that such imitation represents the negation of the very basis of their constructed identity.

State planning represented more than just a society's response to the linear needs of catching up in the developmental race. The idea behind the new articulation of *an India* was often highly corporeal: India as a body, a composite of various organs, that needed to be cohered and coordinated. Planning is repeatedly justified exclusively in terms of the exigencies of backward development, and yet its prime proponent in India was very explicit about the necessity of endowing the nation with a corporeal being and identity via the institution of state planning. Thus, Nehru, in inaugurating the First Five Year Plan observed:

> We must remember that it is the first attempt of its kind to bring the whole *picture* of India—agricultural, industrial, social and economic—into one framework of thinking. Even if it is wrong in parts, it is a tremendous achievement. . . . It has made us realise mentally and emotionally that we are a united nation. We tend to go off at a tangent and think along narrow provincial, communal, religious or caste lines. We have no emotional awareness of the unity of our country. Our Plan has challenged us to think in terms of the good of the nation as a whole apart from the separate problems which we have to face in respect of our villages, districts or provinces. Therefore, this mere act of *framing* this plan and of having produced this report is something for which we can congratulate ourselves (Nehru 1956: 7–8). [The emphases are mine.]

Every sentence in this passage is motivated by the desire actually to write a nation, to endow it with a tangible, material density, to inscribe and fixate it as a united, coherent, and corporeal entity that can then be propelled along a certain trajectory of economic and social development. It is also explicit on the status of all alternative self-conceptions as marginalized, inferior, and subversive.

The endowment of the nation with an almost physical quality is most apparent in Nehru's reaction to the Partition of India in 1947:

> All our communications were upset and broken. Telegraphs, telephones, postal services, railway services and almost everything as a matter of fact was disrupted. Our services were broken up. Our army was broken up. Our irrigation systems were broken and so many other things happened. . . . But above all, what was broken up which was of the highest importance was something very vital and that was the body of India. That produced tremendous consequences, not only those that you saw, but those that you could not imagine, in the minds and souls of millions of human beings (Nehru 1950: 247).

To Nehru, as to nearly all others in the quest for independence, it was the absence of this feeling of unity, of being a bounded entity, that accounted for the success of the British conquest of India and its enduring reign. The British reached India riding the crest of a wave of national unity and science, and when India was in the grip of political disintegration following the slow death of the Mughul empire. If this be the original explanation for the decline of India, correspondingly, national unity, science, and planning would be the sources of Indian regeneration.

Thus, the construction and maintenance of domestic community in the periphery acquires an urgency and intensity that both parallels and contrasts the process as found in the West. Unlike the latter, here the consequences of domestic divisions were empirical fact: they resulted in the long night of colonial subjection. The referents of the perils of disunity in the periphery are not primarily theoretical constructs such as the state of nature: they have been seen and felt in real lifetimes as alien rule.

Turning now to the question of the state and violence, the anticolonial struggle in India had been, in the main, nonviolent. This contributed very significantly to the idea that the new nation represented a vastly different force in a world dominated by realpolitik. (The accompanying, horrendous violence of Partition indicated the very limited basis of any such claims.) Yet, Nehru himself, in a closely argued set of passages, revealed the expected role of violence in the future. This understanding was classically realpolitik and frames Indian identity firmly within the parameters of the neorealist worldview:

> Even if we assume that the worst forms of violence will be gradually removed from the State it is impossible to ignore the fact that both government and social life necessitate some coercion. . . . Men so placed in authority must curb and prevent all individual and group tendencies which are inherently selfish and likely to injure society. . . . They will have to exercise coercion . . . till such time when every human being in that State is perfect, wholly unselfish, and devoted to the common good . . . in this imperfect world a national State will have to defend itself against unprovoked attack from outside. . . . The State will also have to pass some laws of a coercive nature, in the sense that they take away some rights and privileges from various classes and groups and restrict liberty of action (Nehru 1936/1939: 542–543).

Such a series of steps justifying internal and external security doctrines is a familiar moment in the construction of a modern state, and Nehru was hardly an exception in this regard. What is interesting, as seen below, is the subtle elevation of Gandhi to a pedestal on this question; and the simultaneous marginalization of his position on such issues. Gandhi, here, serves as the archetypal idealist for the realpolitik of Nehru. And the disarming moves are both subtle and very ancient in their pedigree. The first step is to concede the absolute moral preference for nonviolent social change and peaceful international relations. This is followed by the claim that the world and humanity are far from perfect, necessitating departures from preferred ideals. Then the circle is completed by positing that, while conversion is the preferred means to achieving community within and peace without, it must be underlain by the real possibility of coercion if it is to have any real effect. Thus, Nehru:

> The ideas of non-violent resistance and the non-violent technique of struggle are of great value to India as well as to the rest of the world, and Gandhiji has done a tremendous service in forcing modern thought to consider them. I believe they have a great future before them. It may be that mankind is not sufficiently advanced to adopt them in their entirety. . . . For the present the vision may not materialise sufficiently, but like all great ideas its influence will grow and it will more and more affect our actions. . . . Gandhiji, of course, continues to be a vital force whose non-violence is of a dynamic and aggressive character. . . . With all his greatness and his contradictions and power of moving the masses, he is above the usual standards. One cannot measure him or judge him as we would others. . . . The present conflicts in society can . . . never be resolved except by coercion . . . we must also realise that human nature being what it is, in the mass, it will not always respond to our appeals and persuasions, or act in accordance with high moral principles. Compulsion will often be necessary, in addition to conversion, and the best we can do is to limit this compulsion and use it in such a manner that its evil is lessened (Nehru 1936/1939: 547– 552).

The discursive move enacted in the above extract is transparent: by seemingly conceding the high moral ground to Gandhian idealism, Nehru reserves the low, but practical, pragmatic (unstated: powerful) ground for himself and other practitioners of statecraft. His recognition of the inherent morality of the idealist position further imparts a tragic grandeur to the realpolitician: his is a terrible cross to bear.

THE LOGIC OF DEFERRENCE

Running through this narrative script of Indian nationalism is the notion of redemption that is always over-the-horizon. India would, one day, make her "tryst with destiny," awaken to domestic unity, mature industry, self-sufficient agriculture, and world respect. But, in the meanwhile, sacrifices must be made: the state must be accorded both autonomy and legitimacy; domestic divisions must either be papered over or ruthlessly suppressed.

Underlying this concept of the nation as a process, as something that is ever in-the-making, is what I choose to call a "logic of deferrence." By "deferrence" I mean a process by which outlined tasks are repeatedly postponed. The logic of deferrence essentially secures the legitimacy of state elites, by centering their historical role in the endless pursuit of certain desired futures. It situates them in the precarious and constantly shifting margins of their society, at the dangerous interstices of the domestic and the foreign, attempting to mediate this dialectic in the direction of development.

The logic of deferrence thus undergirds the very legitimacy of the state, by securing for it both time and space. Time in the sense that the journey toward "development" has just begun: it is going to be a long and arduous one. There is much that has to be reversed and many a past wrong that has to be corrected. The state, thus, literally buys time for itself and escapes, for the time being, the adverse judgment of civil society. It secures space in the sense that the task at hand requires the fullest commitment of energy, resources, and attention. As Nehru quite simply put it: "This generation is sentenced to hard labour" (Nehru 1950: 390).

In this logic of deferrence, peripheral societies are not dissimilar to Western societies, although what is deferred in the two zones is not the same. In the West, the endless deferment is on the question of extending domestic community to the global comity of nations. A premature extension of the idea of domestic community beyond the borders quickly draws the charge of irresponsible idealism or utopianism. Thus, within international relations theory, the extension of communitas beyond the borderlines always has a limit that tends to infinity: it is a task that can never be completed. Its completion can only imply the negation of the state itself, and with it the entire hegemonic discourse of state-centric international relations. In other words, the discursive universe of IR theory is built upon the endless reproduction of the inside-outside antinomy. The reiteration of this opposition constitutes the fundamental principle of state legitimacy, coercion, and autonomy. The hegemonic density of neorealism thus arises from the fact that the very practices it entails ensure that its desired futures can never become a reality.

In the periphery of the modern world-system, the endless deferment is on the question of achieving national unity itself. The narrative script of world history, as read in the periphery, has decreed that sovereign, united nation-states succeed; fragmented, dissonant societies fall by the wayside. Thus, economic development, the redressing of social inequality, industrialization, modernization—all these depend on the prior achievement of unified, sovereign nationhood. And yet, by its very logic, the process of inscribing unitary notions of sovereignty in highly diverse and fragmented societies has unleashed a cycle of state repression and societal reaction that is violent and never-ending.

In India, as the jurist Soli Sorabjee (1986) notes, the perils of national insecurity in a newly decolonized state clearly informed the new constitution that was being written at the time of independence. The delicate balance between the state's rights to security and the individual's rights to democratic freedom was resolved clearly in favor of the state. Predictably, once again the justification for doing so arose from the arduous, perilous, and thankless task of constructing and maintaining national unity in very inhospitable domestic and international terrain. In Nehru's time, the temptation to ride roughshod over the rights of individuals and groups in civil society on grounds of national security was often resisted. In the time since, the state has steadily curtailed freedoms and piled coercive measure upon measure on the grounds of the preservation of national security.

This script of neorealist sovereignty is one that would permit endless iterations. In India, as in innumerable other peripheral societies, various ethnic, linguistic, religious, and regional groups are rallying. Their flags, initially, are the symbols under which to renegotiate in an overcentralized context. Rapidly, the powerful symbols of selfhood acquire a logic, a dynamism, and a momentum all their own. The repressive actions of the state can only enhance this feeling of separateness among these various movements. In the context of domestic society, thus, the attempt to construct a united, sovereign nation-state has produced increasingly violent efforts by various groups to break out of the central embrace and embark on their own, parochial visions of selfhood.

It is hardly surprising that this situation makes for a national-insecurity state. The "other" has rapidly proliferated. In colonial times, the British had an exclusive cachet on providing the whetstone for Indian nationalism. Once the foreigner was expelled, the imperatives of nation-building have necessitated the reproduction of numerous threats to nationality from within and from without. In a context such as the Indian subcontinent (that includes other, similarly precarious, dreams—Pakistan, Sri Lanka, Bangladesh, Nepal. . . .) where ethnic, religious, and linguistic affiliations flow uninterrupted across the arbitrary lines drawn by a British cartographer, the modernist discourse of national unity has thus served as the formula for endless suspicion of "neighbors." Thus, each borderline in the subcontinent is the space for armed conflict, for the entry of alien, destabilizing forces, for the inexorable logic of realpolitik to work itself out. National unity is presented as the sine qua non of development; and yet, this unity is chimerical. The very process of cohering multiple identities has released into circulation practices that atomize and differentiate these multiple selves. Thus is the moment of arrival in the periphery deferred endlessly.

CONCLUSION

This chapter has attempted to assess the appropriation of neorealism in a peripheral context. It tried to show how the inherent ambivalences of nationalism in a colonial context were finessed in the writings of Nehru, and how they have since underlain the current national insecurity state in India. Univocal notions of sovereignty dominate the discursive space in India, as in the rest of the world. When all possibilities of progress, hope, and the future are anchored in terms of such exclusivist notions of selfhood, the groundwork for violence is inevitably laid. Perhaps the first step toward alternative discourses of selfhood is to escape the either/or character of concepts such as *the nation-state, domestic, foreign,* and *sovereignty.*

Such alternative discourses are emerging within the political land-scape, in places where mainstream international relations theory is least sensitized to look for them. They can be found in the movement of ordinary people in the state of Kerala to reappropriate and redefine science; in the movements of tribal women in central India to reassert an organic relationship with the land and the trees; in the actions of civil libertarians who argue against the state for a universalist essence captured by the term *human rights;* by activists who champion the cause of those caught at the interstices of nation-states: refugees, migrants, and minorities. The "success" of such movements in the periphery is not to be assessed, in their ability to capture state power. More importantly, they offer the potential of displacing the reigning discourse of state-centric neorealism. They constitute alternative worldviews on apprehending social reality—alternatives to the ones offered by the hypermasculine, technical rationality of mainstream views. They at least begin to question the material reality acquired by such historically constructed categories as foreign and domestic. By problematizing these, such alternative perspectives challenge the normative basis that sanctions the violence of both the state and societal groups. In addition, they offer a way to reconstitute IR: away from the relentless pessimism of its utilitarian calculus and toward a more reflexive, historical, and open-ended discourse.

> The news was broadcast and printed that the country was besieged by the Enemy, and that neither the seas nor the mountains were defence enough. Shantigrama's citizens listened to the sound of gunfire in the night and to the wailing of sirens, they saw the glow of distant fires and spoke in terrified whispers of the enemy within. "My beloved people," the President said in a midnight broadcast, "give me your freedoms, henceforth let them be hidden inside me, because it is to rob you of these that the insidious enemy has penetrated us". . . . The Crisis had come to stay, gently fearsome and familiar like the tiger in the neighbourhood zoo. But soon the President became despondent again, and he lamented to the Ministers who stood around his couch, "We promised the people a Sorrow, we promised them an enemy, and time is running out" (Vijayan 1988: 23).

NOTES

1. This summary description of neorealism owes much to the works of two scholars in critical IR theory, Richard Ashley and R. B. J. Walker. Some of the specific works include Ashley (1983, 1984, 1988); Walker (1987, 1989); and Ashley and Walker (1990a and 1990b).

2. Although political realism and realpolitik are long-standing ideological forces with impressive historical pedigree in both East and West, neorealism (i.e., the concept of the unitary sovereign nation-state, and the attendant model of utility-maximizing, economistic, rational entities interacting in an anarchic milieu that undergirds mainstream international relations) is both relatively recent and Western. This depiction emerges after the Enlightenment, with Science, Reason,

and Capital as its formative pillars. For a discussion of realism and neorealism, see Ashley (1981); for placing the emergence of neorealism alongside the evolution of the "modern," see Walker (1992).

3. By *periphery* I at once mean what the dominant political-economy literature signifies and more. At one level, peripheral societies are locked in relations of dependence and exploitation with core or Western, industrialized powers. At a more fundamental level, however, peripheral societies are characterized by the fact that their very visions of the future have been colonized; and their presents and pasts are evaluated primarily in terms of how well they replicate the putative patterns of Western societies. Thus, they are intimately subject to the tyranny of unseen masters and are truly "people without history" (Wolf 1982).

4. In the sections that follow, my arguments owe a lot to the works of Chatterjee (1986) and Pandey (1988). By focusing on Nehru's writings as the main source of elite constructions of the nation, I am also suggesting that this project was appropriated in very different ways by what one might call the subaltern or nonelite classes. The classic works on the latter appropriation remain the six volumes published by the Subaltern Studies group under Ranajit Guha in India. For a selection, see Ranajit Guha and Gayatri Chakravorty Spivak (1988).

10

Development as a Civilizing Process: State Formation in Mexico

Richard W. Coughlin

In this chapter, I examine the transition from colony to nation in Mexico. In doing so, I attempt to illustrate state formation as a process of embedding non-Western cultures within an expanding sphere of European culture. My first step in formulating this argument is to develop a model of state formation. Here I want to make three basic points. First, I argue that state formation is a means by which societies insert themselves into larger social fields. Second, I view the state as a condition of social life rather than as an agent or governmental apparatus. Third, I use the conception of *lifeworlds* to disclose how the state, as a condition of social life, becomes anchored in society. Here, I examine mediations as communicative practices that meld lifeworlds. In a subsequent section of the chapter, I formulate a conception of development as a civilizing process. This step adds a theory of social change to my model of state formation. At the same time, it establishes a context for my discussion—in the chapter's longest section—of state formation in Mexico.

My discussion of Mexico considers the kinds of mediations that have linked indigenous and mestizo cultures to the dominant, European culture of the ruling elite. The colonizers conceived of these linkages as civilizing processes. Mestizo and indigenous cultures very clearly incorporated themselves into the colonial order. After the cataclysm of the conquest, the indigenous cultures re-created a historical memory of themselves as subjects of the colony. But as they constituted themselves as subjects of the colony, the modes of colonial domination changed. The Spaniards of the eighteenth century (the Bourbons) pursued a more intensive and systematic exploitation of the colony. In the process, they sought to transform the mediations that linked popular cultures to the colonial order. At the same time, the Bourbons set into motion a rupture of these mediations. The rupture of old mediations and the emergence of new ones reinscribed colonized subjects into a new framework of European culture by means of constructing a new form of state. Over time, the latter turned out to be the Mexican nation state.

A MODEL OF STATE FORMATION

State and Society in Global Perspective

Traditionally, international relations (IR) theory has sharply distinguished domestic politics from international politics. This demarcation hinged upon a distinction between power and community. *Community* pertained to domestic politics. Here, agreed upon norms and procedures domesticated the exercise of power within states. This domestication signaled the departure of women and men from the state of nature in which the struggle for power proceeded without limit. The creation of civil societies governed by law transferred this state of nature to the sphere of interstate relations. This transfer was sequential. The struggle for power had to resolve itself domestically before it could assume an international existence. The emergence of an international state system presupposed the creation of domestic social orders.

This understanding of international relations construes states as actors within a system. According to structural realists (Keohane 1986; Ruggie 1983a), states, as actors, form the units of a more encompassing social totality, the international state system. Structural realists derive this totality (or structure) from the association of its constituent units. In the process, however, they close off inquiry into state formation. In their view, state formation antecedes the emergence of their object of study.

Critics of structural realist theory, such as Richard Ashley, have underscored the importance of a dialectical rather than sequential relationship between international and domestic order. Ashley (1980) illustrates how state formation occurs within a milieu of interstate relations. Eric Wolf (1982) makes a similar point. He cites anthropologist Morton Fried's admission that the "tribe . . . is a secondary sociopolitical phenomenon, brought about by the intercession of more complex ordered societies, states in particular." Wolf follows this admission with an even more general point: "I believe that all human societies of which we have record are 'secondary'." This is because "cultural change does not operate upon isolated societies but always upon interconnected systems in which societies are variously linked within wider social fields" (1982: 76).

Wolf's statement raises an important question: How, in fact, do societies link themselves to wider social fields? Ashley finds an answer to this question in the process of state formation. Ashley situates his understanding of state formation within an historical progression of intersocietal relations. This process moves from growth to rivalry, to balance of power dynamics. Within this progression, states form within a framework of intersocietal relations.

In the first phase of Ashley's progression, states emerge in conjunction with intersecting growth processes (1980: 27). Through growth, societies project lateral pressures upon their surrounding environment. This environment includes other societies whose patterns of growth also lead them to exert lateral pressures. These pressures intersect as societies compete for scarce resources. The conflict potential of these intersecting pressures induces state formation. Here, Ashley observes that the emergence and recurrence of rivalries "firehardens" states into societies. Interstate antagonisms strengthen a state's hold over its domestic society. Through rivalry, interstate relations condition societal and state formation. This conditioning assumes a more pervasive form within the context of multilateral relations. Here states "can come to interiorize the regime [of multilateral relations] and its rules within their own unquestioned identities" (Ashley 1980: 38). This interiorization not only affects "high political choices"; they also "rationalize elements of the state itself" (Ashley 1980: 42).

The State as a Condition

What are the limits of the state? States form at the thresholds of domestic and external growth processes. They mediate between the forces of both their domestic society and the external world. Within the context of this liminal space, the state is more than simply a social agent or governmental apparatus. The state comprises a mode through which societies link themselves into their wider field of intersocietal relationships. The state projects this linkage into both domestic and international society. One can conceptualize this linkage between international and domestic society by means of understanding the state as a condition. This understanding draws on different meaning of the term *state*. One can speak of a *state of affairs* or the *state of the union*. These notions refer to conditional states, not legally constituted states.

Conceiving of the state as a condition leads one to include both government and society within an overall conception of the state. Analysts such as Guillermo O'Donnell (1978) have theorized the capitalist state in this manner. O'Donnell observes that the state enforces exchange relations between capitalists and workers. The state intervenes between class subjects in order legally to sanction their interactions. From this perspective, "the dimensions of the state" include aspects of a "social relation" between classes (O'Donnell 1978: 1162).

The "dimensions of the state" extend beyond the immediate enforcement of class relations. The legitimacy of political authority hinges upon how the state represents "the people." The modern conception of sovereignty construes "the people" as the legitimate basis of political authority. This foundation of legitimacy opens spaces of political participation to the governed. It creates possibilities for the democratic construction of a shared future, of what one might call democratic development. Not everyone welcomes the possibilities of democratic development. Conservatives, for instance, attempt to delimit these possibilities by insisting upon the order of the marketplace. This order does not represent a project to be constructed. It exists naturally and manifests "the grim realities of nature"— scarcity and competition (Polanyi 1957: 125).

Lifeworlds and State Formation

Both the enforcement of exchange relations and the opening of spaces of political participation extend and anchor the state as a condition of social life. Ultimately, these mediations anchor themselves within the *lifeworlds* of citizens. As Habermas defines it, this term refers to "the transcendental site where speaker and hearer meet, where they can reciprocally raise claims that their utterances fit the world, and where they can criticize and confirm those validity claims, settle their disagreements and arrive at agreements" (1987: 127). These exchanges bond people together as members of communities. Habermas underscores the binding effect of validity claims in the creation of social identities. "Collectivities maintain their identities only to the extent that the ideas members have of their lifeworld overlap sufficiently and condense into unproblematic background convictions" (1987:136).

When mediations organize these background convictions, they draw social agents into the political community of state. The grounds of their participation in this sphere lie, at least in part, with their own self-understandings. These self-understandings are, of course, channeled and manipulated so as to integrate people within a given form of state. Yet, as Habermas's conception of the lifeworld suggests, this manipulation, whatever form it assumes, always leaves a margin of interpretive autonomy. People use their experience to interpret the state, and ultimately their interpretations ground the state in social life.

The mediations that anchor the state assume different local forms, depending on how they are received and acted upon. As an overall social condition, the state manifests itself unevenly, rather than homogeneously. The state as ruling elites conceive it differs from the state as ordinary people experience and interpret it. These differences illustrate how structural realists reify the state by refusing to acknowledge its pluralistic and unfinished character. With regard to the state, structural realists would "impose a final social unity where none can exist" (Ashley 1980: 28). I argue for a processural alternative to this reified conception of the state. State formation can be seen as a series of ongoing attempts to order social relations. States contain within themselves numerous developmental possibilities—or, to put this point differently, numerous possible states. In my discussion of state formation in Mexico, I focus on conflicting developmental possibilities. In Mexico, elite attempts to order social relationships engendered popular forms of cultural resistance. The point here is that, understood as a condition of social life, the state remains ambiguous and open-ended.

To summarize, I have suggested an understanding of the state as a *condition* of social life. This concept can illuminate the dimensions of state formation. From this perspective, state formation extends well beyond the state as an apparatus or agent. Ultimately, state formation extends into the lifeworlds of social agents where it secures a relatively precarious anchorage in the kinds of validity-claims these agents raise about the world. At the same time that state formation extends into the lifeworlds of social agents, it also links societies into wider social fields. In this regard, state formation has a global focus, even as it manifests itself within the most local contexts.

DEVELOPMENT AS CIVILIZING PROCESS

To explain state formation in the case of Mexico, I will formulate an additional concept: the notion of development as a civilizing process. This perspective arises out of disenchantment with standard theories of development. The standard theories comprised the major positions in the development debate of the 1960s and 1970s: modernization theory and radical approaches to international political economy (IPE). Both modernization theory and IPE understand development in terms of their own theoretical constructs. Modernization theory interprets development in relation to its understandings of "tradition" and "modernity." IPE considers development in terms of the mechanisms that order processes of exchange and production under capitalism. I leave aside both of these positions in favor of a historicist conception of development. This position transfers the concept of development from the paradigms of social scientists to the identities of the people they study.

This move multiplies the possible meanings of development. One can identify this concept of development with the competing, conflicting, and sometimes overlapping projects of historical actors. How does one analyze the projects of social agents? Generally, these projects have a narrative quality about them. They consist of a relevant past, a present predicament, and a desired future. These conceptions of past, present, and future assume a symbolic form. Social agents place themselves in history through language-use. Historical documents provide traces of how social agents formulated their projects. Textual analysis can reconstruct the narrative understandings of social agents.

My focus on development as a civilizing process emerges from this universe of historical projects. I regard "development as a civilizing process" as a genre of such historical projects. I shall argue that these practices form states by creating openings between elite and popular class spheres. This perspective rejects the idea that states emerge by means of domesticating a state of nature. In its place, it considers how civilizing processes suppress popular cultures and create new modes of subjugation that incorporate social agents into societies organized by the state. On the basis of this conception of state formation, I formulate my thesis about the creation of world order. I argue that the subjugation of popular cultures draws upon civilizing processes that are universal in scope. I noted above that state formation links societies into wider social fields. An understanding of "universal" civilizing processes can clarify what, in fact, these linkages consist of.

In this regard, consider Wallerstein's understanding of *universalism* as a transnational ideology of the bourgeoisie: "The concept of a neutral universal culture to which the cadres of the world division of labor would be 'assimilated' . . . serve[d] as one of the pillars of the world system as it historically evolved" (1983: 83). Historically, this "pernicious form of cultural imperialism" (1983: 83) has linked societies into their wider social fields. It has done so by, to use Ashley's (1985) language, "prying open," "disciplining," and "administering" nation-states as fields of practice.

But these fields were not, to mix metaphors, clean slates. Here one can consider another of Wallerstein's notions, *civilizational alternatives* (1984). These alternatives comprise social assets and practices that are rooted in local cultures. These assets do not have to be wholly local or indigenous in character. As Bonfil (1987) notes, they could be (and often are) appropriated from the dominant, "universal" culture. In Mexico, folk-Catholicism provides an example of this sort of appropriation.

One can formulate an ongoing opposition between *civilizational alternatives* and *universalism*. Eric Wolf's definition of culture encompasses both terms of this opposition. Wolf understands culture as "a set of processes that construct, reconstruct and dismantle cultural materials in response to identifiable determinants" (1982: 383). Universalism and civilizational alternatives constitute such processes; both, in other words, "construct, reconstruct and dismantle" cultural materials. These processes occur interactively. In conjunction, they define a process of state formation. In the case of Mexico, an examination of this interactive process can illustrate how this region of the world became inscribed within an expanding arc of European culture.

COLONIAL MEXICO

Conquest and Indigenous Identity

In colonial Mexico, the interactive process described above began with the conquest. The Spanish conquest of Mexico dismantled the

Mesoamerican empires and city-states. In the process, the Spanish disabled the mechanisms that reproduced Mesoamerican culture. These mechanisms included their calendar system, their ideographic writing system, and a set of oral traditions that the calendar and writing systems helped to articulate. The conquest forced indigenous culture back upon local bases of support, dependent upon an oral transmission of knowledge. Local dialects and traditions survived the conquest, but those of city-states and empires perished.

The local traditions, however, underwent profound transformations. The recurrence of epidemics throughout the sixteenth century eliminated huge portions of the indigenous population. Estimates of the population of central Mexico before the conquest range from ten to twenty-five million. By the end of the sixteenth century, this population was reduced to a million. Where the conquest eliminated the administrative and religious centers that organized Mesoamerican societies, the epidemics struck at the grassroots, often wiping out entire communities. Under these conditions, the Spanish undertook the administrative reorganization of the indigenous communities. Their rationale was to render a dispersed indigenous population more tractable to tribute collection, evangelization, and forced labor in mines, workshops, and highways.

Evangelization and administrative reorganization introduced new symbolic orders into the indigenous lifeworld. Under these conditions, the historical memories of indigenous peoples faltered. As Enrique Florescano notes, "the ritual and oral transmission of the past lost their capacity to preserve the authenticity of its traditions." Indeed, "the impossibility to articulate a message with autochthonous indigenous contents opened an irreparable fissure between the pagan past and the colonial present" (Florescano 1987: 161).

These conditions did not, however, completely deculture the indigenous communities. The peoples of central Mexico, for example, continued to speak one version or another of Nahuatl. As Louise Burkhart (1989) has shown, this language provided the filter through which the Indians understood the Spanish, particularly the missionaries. In order better to evangelize the Indians, the missionary orders learned Nahuatl and translated sermons, psalms, and other religious texts into Nahuatl. But, as Burkhart notes, this translation "nahuatized Christianity [and] constituted an implicit patronage of Nahua cultural continuity" (1989: 193).

Christian distinctions between good and evil merged with Nahua categories of order and disorder. For Christians, good and evil categorized ethical conduct before God and determined the individual's ultimate fate; i.e., salvation or damnation. For the Nahua people, moral conduct kept the world in balance. The Nahua concept of *sin* meant "to spoil, to damage, to harm" (Burkhart 1989: 29). The Nahua concept focused on the effect of an action, and not its inherent quality. The effects pertained to the world in which the Nahua lived, not to the Christian's individual quest for salvation.

Burkhart's analysis of evangelization shows how Mesoamerican peoples maintained a capacity to interpret colonization, even when they lacked the capacities to reproduce their old culture. While colonization fragmented indigenous culture, it also provided new cultural materials that these cultures could interpret and appropriate as their own. Indeed, these new materials took the place of the old. Local cultures grafted themselves onto the civilizing processes of the Occident. By interpreting their colonial status, Mesoamericans projected themselves as subjects of the colonial state. Their state, however, was a reinterpreted version of the colonizers' state. Before illustrating this point, I will describe the sort of state that the colonizers attempted to construct.

Colonization as a Civilizing Process

Both the conquerors and the missionaries made claims over the development of the Indians. Both directed these claims to the Spanish throne, but neither would prevail. The New World belonged to the king. Through the royal bureaucracy, the monarch would organize dominion over the New World. The conquerors and missionaries would become the instruments of this dominion rather than its protagonists. The organization of the imperial state occurred through the work of lawyers and administrators. What narratives did these agents follow?

In 1647, Juan de Solorzano published *La Politica Indiana*. This work expounded the legal and philosophical bases of the Spanish empire. Solorzano evoked these bases in a compendium of legal, philosophical, and moral arguments. He drew these arguments from hundreds of different sources: the classical writers of Greece and Rome, the writings of the Church fathers, medieval law, royal decrees of the sixteenth and seventeenth century, and firsthand reports of the conquest and colonization of the New World. Two of Solorzano's modern commentators point out that *La Politica Indiana* was soon "an obligatory book of reference for the judges and the lawyers of the royal courts, for presidents [municipal], viceroys, as well as for the upper clergy, secular [missionary] and regular, and the supreme council of the Indies" (Malagon and Cabdequi 1965: 43).

Solorzano wrote this work for his bureaucratic colleagues. He formulated *La Politica Indiana* out of an intersubjective knowledge base—the opinions of recognized authorities. Solorzano's appeal to established authority left room for interpretation, for these authorities conflicted on certain points. When Solorzano cited royal decrees or classical authors, his readers would not question the truth of these statements. They could, however, raise claims about the contexts in which the claims of these authorities were applied. In this sense, bureaucrats had a certain degree of discretion in the deploying of the civilizing tradition in which they participated. This margin of discretion corresponded to the organization of the imperial bureaucracy. Holders of royal office obtained their commissions from the king. Authority ran from the king to individual officeholder, and not through a vertically ordered bureaucracy (MacLachlan 1988: 38–40). Here a conception of law as wisdom created cohesion between relatively autonomous bureaucrats. This cohesion consisted of an understanding of colonization as a civilizing process.

What did it mean for this bureaucracy to civilize the Indians? It meant bringing them into a society organized by the state. According to Sepulveda, whom Solorzano cites, the Indians "scarcely merit the name men, and need those who, taking their government, support and instruction as their burden, reduce them to a life that is human, civil, sociable and political, so that with this, they become capable of receiving the Faith and the Christian Religion" (1972 reprint: 92). Sepulveda's statement suggests that the imperial bureaucracy pursued a humanizing narrative. The terms "human," "civil," "social," and "political" appear as attributes of a "humanized" existence. A definition of man could not be complete without these attributes. Thus, Solorzano axiomatically affirms that "man is a rational animal," and also "social, political or civil according to the doctrines of Aristotle, Cicero and many others" (1972 reprint: 372).

Solorzano defines *man* normatively. To one degree or another, the Indians lived outside of this norm. Acosta's distinction between sedentary and nonsedentary Indians demonstrates this difference in degree. Sedentary Indians, such as the Mexicans or Peruvians, showed at least a glimpse of "natural reason" in that they were "governed by kings and lived in towns and cities," even if these were "badly ordered and mixed with superstitions and errors" (cited in Solorzano: 94). Nonsedentary Indians had literally nothing human about them: "They are totally wild, wandering naked through the fields like beasts, without face nor form of society, nor human discipline nor control" (Solorzano: 94). Sedentary Indians, however, approached the threshold of humanity in that they lived in societies organized by the state.

Solorzano and the authors he cites refer to rural life as a form of existence that lacks "political form." In the countryside, people live scattered throughout the fields and mountains. Without "political form," they live like animals. In the name of humanity, princes and kings have the right to impose this form (Solorzano: 372–373). Evidently, the threshold between the human and subhuman was not unique to the Spaniards' encounter with the inhabitants of the New World. This threshold always existed at the limits of societies organized by the state.

In this sense, the Roman Empire provided a model for the Spanish Empire. According to Solorzano, authorities like Saint Augustine "praised the Romans with grand eulogies, and said that their empire was just . . . because it tamed with just wars very barbarous nations, and reduced them, and taught them to live in natural law and in political form" (1972 reprint:

93). In undertaking to civilize the Indians, the Spaniards enacted a well-established civilizing process. Like the Romans, the Spaniards would also bring barbarous peoples within natural law. For both the Spaniards and the Romans, the extension of empire humanized the barbarous peoples that live at the margins of civilization.

Barbarous peoples had few options in front of this civilizing process. Solorzano cites the edicts of the Roman emperors Adrian and Nero to the Ethiopians, whom they were colonizing. The edicts ordered the Ethiopians to cease their wandering and to populate cities. If they refused, the Ethiopians could be killed or enslaved, depending on the whims of whomever pursued them. If, in other words, the Ethiopians refused the social state that the Romans sought to impose upon them, they lost any claim to human status (Solorzano: 372). The Indians of the New World confronted a similar dilemma. Like the Ethiopians, the Indians could not refuse membership in the Spaniards' universal conception of human existence without, at the same time, renouncing their humanity. Solorzano mentions the example of Indians in Chile who, for years, resisted the encroachments of the Spaniards. Their intransigence induced the Spanish to declare a "just war." Soldiers who captured Indians could enslave them. This was punishment for indigenous resistance that "disfigured and degraded the face of man . . . which is also understood as the image of the Divine" (Solorzano: 139).

Outside the limits of civilization, the Spanish placed the Indians within the category of "barbarous peoples." Within the limits of civilization, they classified the Indians as "miserable peoples" whom, according to Solorzano, "we pity for their state, quality and works" (1972 reprint: 419). Here the Indians fit into the same slot as the rustics of the Old World. Solorzano's deliberations on their "miserable" status extended an already existing juridical regime to a new subject people. This regime conferred to the Indians the status of perpetual minors. Hence, their disputes would be resolved through summary judgments rather than through the formal application of law. Like rustics, Indians would be held incompetent to uphold contractual agreements, or to make statements under oath (Solorzano: 418–429).

By the middle of the seventeenth century, this seems to have been the only permissible understanding of the Indians. Solorzano's work emerged within a tightly controlled sphere of letters. Like all writings of his time, Solorzano's book required the approval of the royal censor. Florescano underscores the significance of this approval by noting that "parallel to the destruction of the power of the conquerors, encomenderos and friars, and the creation of a political apparatus run from the metropolis, the Crown imposed rigid control over historical and literary production" (1987: 133). Among the principal casualties of this censorship were the inquiries of the sixteenth-century missionaries into the culture of the Mesoamericans. The decree that banned Sahagun's writings in 1577 prohibited any writing by any person in any language "over the superstitions and the way of life that these Indians had" (cited in Florescano: 136). This suppression shut down the possibility of developing an understanding of the Mesoamericans that was not articulated from a purely Occidental point of view.

Representations of Civilization

Colonization followed a pattern of incorporating Mesoamericans within a tributary state. The imperial state incorporated the Indians within the system of indigenous towns and villages that the Spanish had created in the sixteenth century. These communities separated the Indians from the Spanish and mestizo populations. They were sites where the Spanish "civilized" the Indians. Through the staging of representations, the Spanish sought control over the "public spheres" of the Indian towns and villages. Their purpose was to create identification between the Indians and themselves within the symbolic order of the colony. One can regard these representations as attempts to anchor the colonial state within the lifeworlds of the colonized.

Religious processions and services comprised one of the important forms that this anchorage assumed. Robert Ricard (1966) notes the "pomp and magnificence" of both religious services and processions during the sixteenth century. Processions "were held on almost all Sundays and feast days, accompanied . . . by singing and playing, and also . . . a complete theatrical setting. The way was covered with flowers and boughs and decorated with arches" (1966: 180). These processions were meant to express an Occidental rather than indigenous conception of religion. Joseph Francis Brooks (1977) notes how both the crown and the church proscribed the public dances and celebrations of the Indians. He goes on to interpret this proscription as a "fear felt by the [church] hierarchy of movement and initiative by parishioners" (1977: 82).

In Europe, the Counter Reformation church authorities of the sixteenth and seventeenth centuries replaced popular feasts with religious spectacles. The purpose was to suppress the practices of popular cultures and to implant, in their place, communicative strategies that were elaborated and deployed by the clergy. This was true of both Europe and Mexico. The ecclesiastic organization of processions in Europe separated the "sacred" from the secular world by means of diminishing or excluding the active role of the people. In processions, for example,

> we can imagine these crowds gathered along the route of the cortege, immobile except for occasional groups of women and children that attempted to follow along after. Before them passed the splendor and pomp of the Tridentine Church: it was a grandiose spectacle, with brilliantly

colored vestments, the gold of the reliquaries, canopies, and candles, with church bells ringing out, at times even covering the music and chanting. The secular world was on one side, and sacred on the other (Muchembled 1985: 174).

This separation sought to position popular cultures as spectators rather than producers of the sacred. The clergy of the New World pursued a similar end. In 1622, the Franciscan missionary Juan de Torquemada described how the missionary church staged spectacular masses that "conserved" Indians in the faith (1622/1971). According to Torquemada, these spectacles appealed to the ritualistic inclinations of the Indians: "Indeed who is there who knows the Indians that does not see that by their nature they are very inclined towards rights and ceremonies. . . . Who does not see and know that it is very necessary to always keep them occupied and busy in the service of their [Christian] idols?" (Torquemada: 172) By means of music, voices, candles, bells, incense, and sacred garments, the mass would reach a crescendo in the celebration of the holy eucharist. At this point, the church would appear "as an abbreviated heaven on earth" (Torquemada: 173).

Torquemada's mass played upon a Nahua conception of power in order to direct it toward colonial ends. Nahua power, as Serge Gruzinski observes, manifested itself sensually: "There exists . . . a physical presence of power, a visual, perceptible, palpable, olfactory dimension" (1989: 19). Florescano notes how these sensual aspects of power emerged in the context of ritual. In these situations, "the representation of the past implied more the use of visual, acoustic, scenic and ritual media than the written word" (1987: 79). For the Nahua (and other Mesoamerican peoples), power assumed the form of a living presence. Rituals manifested this living presence. Torquemada, on the other hand, theorized ritual as a purposive mode of acting on others.

The object of ritual was to move people by appealing to their responsive behaviors. Seventeenth-century Europeans recognized these responsive behaviors as a way to subjugate others. These responsive behaviors corresponded to the human passions (lust, avarice, sloth, and so forth). According to religious moralists, these passions emanated from man's sinful nature. With Machiavelli, these passions began to assume a useful aspect. Like the Christian moralists who preceded him, Machiavelli recognized that men are wretched creatures: "They are ungrateful, fickle, liars, and deceivers, they shun danger and are greedy for profit" (1961 reprint: 93). Their very wretchedness, however, could be a source of strength to the prince. Human passions pertained to the effective truth of things (1963 reprint: 90–91). According to Machiavelli, princes (and anyone else interested in power) must master this domain of effective truths.

In the seventeenth century, European intellectuals developed this conviction into a widespread philosophy of power. The philosopher Spinoza opposed those who "prefer to detest and scoff at human affects and actions" (cited in Hirschman 1977: 14). Human passions were far too important to pass up. A seventeenth-century Jesuit, Senault, maintained that "those who want to remove the passions from the soul render it useless and without power." Senault advocated the converse position; namely, that "there is no passion in our soul that cannot be usefully manipulated" (cited in Maravall 1986: 76).

The creation of graphic spectacles concerned not only religious celebrations. The crown also projected its power through the staging of spectacles. In Spain, these assumed the form of royal fiestas that commemorated marriages, births, deaths, victories, and other noteworthy accomplishments of royal personages. Such fiestas were deliberately public in character. They consisted of plays, fireworks, bullfights, and mock battles. The monarchy staged these spectacles in order to win the adherence of the urban masses. Antonio Maravall notes that "it was not the spectator's diversion that counted so much as the people's wonder in the face of the 'magnificence' of the rich and powerful" (1986: 243).

Torquemada was no stranger to this kind of rhetoric. Masses employed communicative strategies similar to those seen in royal fiestas. Thus, Torquemada accounted for the effect of magnificence in terms of a distinction between common things and novelties.

> Common things . . . are not estimated nor revered, nor valued, but those things that with some degree of excellence . . . are admired as particular things that leave the ordinary and common things behind . . . [thus] . . . by custom and universal use . . . kings and princes of the world go adorned with most precious forms of dress, and they have advantage in the grandeur and amplitude of their royal houses and palaces and in the beauty and curiosity of their buildings. For these things in this excess and majesty cause reverence and admiration (1971 reprint: 175–176).

Displays of excess and majesty assumed violent as well as festive forms. Michel Foucault (1979: 3–69), for example, has analyzed "the spectacle of the scaffold" in seventeenth-century France as a public ritual. In the ritual, the sovereign displayed his power over the body of the condemned through corporal punishments such as mutilation, flogging, branding, or burning. The body of the condemned provided an object over which royal power publicly manifested itself. Foucault emphasizes that these spectacles did not simply comprise residues of a barbaric past; rather, they formed part of a carefully organized mechanism of power that emerged with the absolutist state.

In Mexico, too, public rituals conveyed the exercise of royal power. Chronicles from a peasant rebellion (1660–1662) in the province of Oaxaca show how the Spanish authorities deployed a number of different spectacles in their attempts to pacify the Indians. During the first phases of the uprising, Bishop Alonso of Oaxaca visited the rebellious villages. In his own testimony, Alonso took special note of how he presented himself before the Indians. "I entered this village . . . [of Nejaba] and because I know with what motion God works in the hardest of hearts, I disposed to enter in pontifical style, in order to attract the people with this novelty" (Garcia 1974: 328–329). Aside from wearing his pontifical regalia, Alonso employed other authoritative signs. He conducted "reverent ceremonies," using the "coat of arms" and other "royal insignias." Upon seeing these signs, the Indians turned over their arms and manifested a renewed royalty to the crown. According to Alonso, the Indians "with so many acts of Vassalage prostrated themselves . . . offering in high voices that they would give their lives for Our Lord the King to whom, with clamors, their humble and faithful hearts repeated new obediences" (1974: 329).

Just as Torquemada sought to conserve the Indians in the church's faith, so Bishop Alonso sought to conserve them in obedience to the king. These examples suggest the narrative understandings of the colonizers—constantly to reengender the subjugation of the colonized. Through spectacles, rituals, and representations, these understandings conveyed the civilizing process of the colony.

To return to the peasant revolt in Oaxaca, the pacifying efforts of Bishop Alonso failed. After the bishop, a detachment of soldiers and a judge from Mexico City arrived in the province. They rounded up the ringleaders of the revolt and condemned some to whippings and others to execution. They inflicted these punishments in the plazas of the insurgent villages. The Spaniards jailed numerous other Indians. After the executions and the whippings, they granted the remaining captives clemency. The point of both the punishment and the clemency was to achieve the effect of renewing the subjugation of the Indians to the crown. As one Spaniard noted, "it follows that after the tempest comes serenity, after the storm, the rainbow, so that the horror that punishment induces in their hearts is mitigated by pardon and attenuated by grace" (Garcia 1974: 291).

The Spanish commemorated their royal pardon with solemn rituals. The judge ordered all the Indian governors of the region to attend this act of clemency on pain of ten years' incarceration (1974: 292). The day before the pardon, the scaffold was removed from the plaza. In its place the Spaniards erected a stage, consisting of eight different levels, adorned with carpets, curtains, flowers, gold and silver embroidery, and a portrait of the king. From the top of this stage, the pardon was read. Then, as the infantry fired their guns, the prisoners were released from jail and everybody in the village celebrated a *Te Deum* mass, giving thanks to the king. The next day, the Spaniards dismissed the Indians, instructing them to commemorate the day of their pardon every year:

> On the day of Saint Theresa, they have to celebrate . . . with solemn evening prayers and devotions the night before, and on that day, a sung

mass, giving thanks, and for the health and fortune of the Monarch, in memory of the mercy that the natives of this province receive from the liberal hand of the monarch (Garcia 1974: 294).

In both Mexico and Europe, spectacles had their theoretical and practical underpinning in the quest to control human passions. Antonio Maravall identifies this quest with baroque culture, which he defines as "a complex of cultural media of a very diverse sort that are assembled and articulated to work adequately with human beings . . . so as to succeed in directing them and keeping them integrated with the social system" (1986: 58). These cultural media included the church, the theatre, and the monarchy.

These institutions produced spectacles that congregated people and acted upon their responsive behaviors. In doing so, they also mediated class spheres. These mediations emerged in the place of rituals that originated within popular cultures. This was the case with both the popular cultures of Counter Reformation Europe and the village societies of colonial Mexico. In both instances, the identity-producing effects of popular rituals shifted (in part) to the spectacles organized by elite cultures.

One can characterize the identity-producing effects of rituals in terms of Durkheim's understanding of religious representations. These he considers as "collective representations which express collective reality; the rites are a manner of acting which take rise in the midst of the assembled group and which are destined to excite, maintain or re-create certain mental states in these groups" (cited in Habermas 1987: 53). Durkheim's understanding of religious representations suggests an important aspect of the shift from rituals to spectacles. With this shift, popular cultures came to exercise less control over "collective representations which express collective reality." As elite spectacles constructed collective realities, the mediations of the state penetrated into the lifeworlds of popular cultures.

Popular Interpretations of the Colony

Popular cultures interpreted the mediations of elite cultures in terms of their own background understandings of the world. From 1625 to 1629, Ruiz de Alacron collected materials for a treatise on the idolatrous practices of Indians. In the preface to the treatise he noted that "a tradition of their false gods is hardly found among their stories" (1629/1984: 39). Alacron referred, of course, to the traditions formulated by the empires and city-states of Mesoamerica. Roughly one hundred years after the conquest, the "great traditions" of the Mesoamerican civilizations had been forgotten. But the "little traditions" of village societies continued to exist, as Alacron's detailed inquiry demonstrates.

These "little traditions" did not exist in isolation. An important aspect of their development consisted in how they attached themselves to the new "great traditions" of the Occident. This cultural rapprochement occurred by means of indigenous cultures interpreting the symbolic orders of religion and royal power. These interpretations rendered the colonial state problematic. Local cultures appropriated the civilizing ethos of the colonizers and turned it into the vehicle of their own desires.

Burkhart's (1989) conception of a "nahuatized" Christianity shows how language differences transformed the meaning of Christianity by fitting it into the categories of the Nahua universe. Another instance of this displacement of meaning can be found in one of the great myths of Mexican nationality, the myth of the Virgin of Guadalupe. Outside Mexico City, there existed an important shrine of the Nahua people—the shrine of Tonantzin, a fertility goddess. After the conquest, Indians continued to make pilgrimages to the shrine, but now Tonantzin had become the Virgin Mary of Guadalupe. In the seventeenth century, European settlers made a legend out of the practices and oral traditions of the Indians. According to legend, the Virgin appeared in 1531 to Indian peasant Juan Diego. She instructed him to inform the bishop of Mexico of her appearance. For the Creoles, the appearance of the Virgin signaled the incorporation of Mexico into the Christian world. Until the time of the conquest, Mexico had been a land of idolaters. The appearance of the Virgin to an Indian (and a commoner, no less!) washed away the sins of this indigenous idolatry. This event even conveyed to Mexico the signs of a superior spiritual status.

In its Nahuatl version, the legend conveys quite a different message. The legend unfolds within Nahua conceptions of space and time. The place where the Virgin appears is described by five attributes. The five attributes, according to Miguel Concha Malo, evoke a figure of Nahua cosmology, the fifth direction "where the paths of God and man crossed, where the cosmic and the social were superseded by means of a work divine and human" (1986: 112). The time of the encounter was dawn. In Nahua mythology, dawn signifies a time of creation of humanity and the world. Prior to the conquest, the Nahuas believed they existed at the center of creation. They organized their ritual practices around renewing and restoring the energies of this creation. The conquest, of course, relegated them to the periphery of the Occident. But with the appearance of the Virgin, the Nahua, in the figure of Juan Diego, reappear at the center of world, and at a moment of creation. From this position, Juan Diego describes himself in the most striking terms: "I am diminished man (a man without historical place), a man without protection, I am a stairway of tablets (a man who is tread upon), I am excrement (a man who is repugnant), I am hoja (a dead man, torn from the tree of life)" (Concha Malo 1986: 112).

Compare this with how Juan Diego appears in the Spanish version of the legend. Here is part of the dialogue between Juan and the Virgin that appeared in Miguel Sanchez's 1648 version of the legend: "Juan my son [said the Virgin] where do you go . . . and he, thankful and obligated by the tenderness of her words, responded to her. Senora, I follow the doctrine and obedience of the religious fathers who have instructed us" (cited in Florescano 1987: 189). Here Juan appeared as an exemplary neophyte, not as the victim of the conquest.

Consider another difference between the two legends. In the Spanish version, the Virgin refers to Juan as "Juanito, Juan Dieguito," thus using diminutives that suggest maternal tenderness. In the Nahuatl version, the Virgin refers to Juan as "Iuantzin, Iuan Diegotzin." In Nahuatl, *tzin* conveys respect and reverence. The Spanish diminutive and the Nahuatl *tzin* suggest distinct interpretations of the Virgin's first words to Juan: in the Spanish version, "Juan Diego, my son"; in the Nahuatl version, "Juan, you who have dignity and is worthy of all respect" (Concha Malo 1986: 114). In addition, the Nahuatl version changes another aspect of Juan's identity: in the Spanish version, the Virgin refers to Juan as "the smallest of my children" (Juan thus appearing as both worthy of respect and, at the same time, of diminished stature); Concha Malo, on the other hand, interprets the Virgin's interpellation of Juan as: "Juan, to you, who is dignified and worthy of all respect, they have reduced you, they have diminished you" (Concha Malo 1986: 117).

Finally, consider the scene of the Virgin's apparition as a whole: Juan, worthy but diminished, appears before the Virgin at the center of the world and at a moment of creation. This scene suggests a rebirth of the Nahua people. But this rebirth could not return them to the origins of their world. Rather, it occurs within the context of a colonized world. Nothing marks this better than the figure of the Virgin herself. She was, after all, a foreigner. But in the Nahuatl version of the legend, she has gone native. Within this context, the rebirth of the Nahua people exemplifies the re-creation of indigenous identity within the symbolic order of the colony.

Throughout the colonial period, and indeed into the national period as well, the re-creation of indigenous identity occurred constantly and assumed diverse forms. Below, I give a brief overview of these different processes.

James Lockhart (1982) has analyzed a series of documents known as the "primordial titles." These documents were written by village scribes in the late seventeenth century and the early eighteenth century. They recount the histories of their communities. Thematically, they focus on the struggle of these communities against outside powers. Lockhart notes that "nowhere in the texts is any derivative of the Spanish word 'indio' used, nor is anyone called by any other term that could be translated as 'Indian'" (1982: 383). The source of the indigenous identity rested with the corporate identity of the village. This identity openly incorporated itself within the colonial state. The documents recalled the acts by which the Spanish constituted the community as an entity of the colonial state. They upheld the legitimacy of these acts with references to the king, the viceroy, the archbishop, or some other famous personage. They often mistook the identity of these individuals. Yet the role of these references is clear: to ground the village's claim to its surrounding lands in an appeal to higher authority (Lockhart: 389).

The primordial titles conveyed the village's claims through a kind of pre-Hispanic mode of communication known as "the speech of the elders." The elders constitute the narrative voice of the titles. Through these documents, the elders speak to the generations that succeed them. And while the elders exalted Spanish authorities such as the king, the archbishop, or the viceroy, they also admonished their descendants not to associate with the Spanish: not to eat with them, nor become their compadres, nor, above all, permit them to see the primordial titles. Like the Aztecs before them, the Spanish threatened the community. Indeed, the presence of the Spanish probably explains why these documents were written at all. In the seventeenth century, the Spanish began to settle the countryside. They often occupied lands that indigenous communities claimed as their own, and attempted to acquire indigenous workers for their estates, often through the mechanism of debt peonage. In response to these pressures, the primordial titles fixed in writing what had previously been an oral tradition. The presence of the Spanish led indigenous communities to more rigorously affirm their identity.

In 1799, Abad y Quiepo (1963 reprint), the bishop of Michoacan, observed that 80 percent of the priests in Mexico depended on their parishioners for revenues. Local customs dictated what priests could do as religious authorities. These customs took shape within community religious organizations (cofradias) rather than through the institutions of the church. For this purpose, the cofradias held village lands, and used the revenues from them to finance communal celebrations. These celebrations assembled the community around the observance of local rituals; in particular, around burial ceremonials and commemorations of the community's local saint. In this sense, the cofradias were a centrifugal force that pushed folk-Catholicism away from elite conceptions of religion.

The clergy, on the other hand, acted in a centripetal manner by attempting to pull the local traditions into the universal traditions of the church. This was an interactive tension. On the one hand, as Serge Gruzinski notes, the church introduced Marian cults (such as the Virgin of Guadalupe, the Virgin of Ocotlan) in order to regulate local devotions (1989: 97). On the other hand, local cults created their own Virgins and affirmed their authenticity while rejecting the authority of the church.

Throughout the colonial period, numerous local ruptures with the civilizing traditions of the church can be discerned. Victoria Reifler Bricker (1981) notes the recurrence of indigenous virgin cults in Chiapas, from 1708 to 1712. The virgins appear with the claim that they descended from heaven in order to help the Indians. The clergy acted to suppress these indigenous cults. These suppressions created even deeper antagonisms between the Indians and the Spanish. As Bricker notes, "the Spanish became 'Jews' in the minds of the Indians because they had persecuted the Virgin, the mother of Jesus" (1981: 62).

Gruzinski (1989) examines the creation of a succession of indigenous virgin cults in the highlands of Central Mexico. A description of the image (in this case, a statue) of one such Virgin reads: "the image seemed not to be a true image of Our Lady because of the monstrous nude breasts it sported and the face, which was more male than female" (quoted in Gruzinski 1989: 126). Gruzinski observes that this Virgin comprised a composite, drawn from both the virgins of the Roman Catholic tradition and fertility figures of the various indigenous traditions. The Indians used a syncretic discourse in order to compose their own conceptions of the sacred. As creators of the sacred, the Indians negated the authority of the church. Thus they could posit themselves as the makers of their own history.

FROM COLONY TO NATION

The history that religious dissidents claimed depended on the nature of colonization as a civilizing process. In the eighteenth century, colonization changed significantly as a civilizing process. The ceremonies, processions, and festivals that represented colonization diminished in importance. In the seventeenth century, these phenomena helped to anchor the colonial state within the lifeworlds of the colonized. In the eighteenth century, the colonizers began to suppress the participation of the popular classes within these public spectacles. As Gruzinski (1985) notes, this suppression did not attack indigenous cultures, but rather "colonial indigenous cultures elaborated by the Indians after the shock of the conquest" (1985: 192).

In Mexico City, this wave of cultural suppression consisted of eliminating the public spaces in which the popular classes had customarily projected their identities. These spaces included Corpus Christi ceremonies. The day of the Corpus commemorated the unity of the Roman Catholic faithful by including all believers, no matter what their social station, in the celebration. In these ceremonies, companies of Indians, mulattos, and Negroes danced in the procession, and carried a huge dragon that symbolized, among other things, sin defeated by grace. In 1790, the viceroy excluded these groups, along with "badly dressed Indians," prisoners, and madmen (Viquiera 1987: 159). The celebration of numerous other festivities came under the close scrutiny of the authorities, who deemed that in dances men and women should not mix, that intoxicating beverages should be proscribed, and that fiestas should end early, before evening prayers. (Viquiera 1987: 155).

These kinds of proscriptions dismantled the mechanisms through which the colonial order represented itself. The imagined community of the colony fragmented into increasingly differentiated class spheres. In place of public religious festivals, the popular classes celebrated religious processions and social gatherings within their homes and neighborhoods.

As old forms of imagined community deteriorated, new ones emerged. Primary schools multiplied throughout Mexico (Gruzinski 1985: 185–186). Their emergence coincided with an attack on cofradias. In 1793, the viceroy of Mexico (Revillagigedo) decreed that the royal bureaucracy, not the clergy, would control the funds of the cofradias (Brooks 1978: 198). Bourbon administrators had long criticized the cofradias for their "useless expenditures" and their disorderly ceremonies. Now the policy of 1793 would channel cofradia resources toward a "useful" end: paying the salary of schoolteachers "so that the Indians might learn Christian doctrine and to read and write the Spanish language" (Brooks: 198). Colonial authorities would repress indigenous colonial culture (the cofradias) in order to construct new mediations (Christian doctrine, literacy, and Spanish) that would anchor a new form of state.

Literacy comprised an especially important mediation, in that it formed a new medium of imagined community. The old processions, festivals, and ceremonies congregated colonial subjects as spectators. The print media would now begin to congregate national subjects as readers (Anderson 1983). Texts, rather than spectacles, would serve as the vehicles of imagined community in independent Mexico.

Throughout the colonial period, the royal bureaucracy had absorbed lettered culture, leaving little room for its development outside of the church or the crown. With the defeat of the Spanish, however, the practices of literacy would disentangle themselves from these bureaucratic commitments. After independence, no one would petition the king and his officials, nor expect decrees from them. The royal bureaucracy, as a vast medium of literary production and consumption, would vanish. Independence would transfer control over lettered culture to new institutions, such as the print media.

This transfer occurred in conjunction with the Creole struggle for independence. By joining the ranks of the insurgency, Creoles went from occupying subaltern positions within the colonial order, which denied them privileges, to claiming new positions outside of this order. By stepping outside the colonial order, the insurgent Creoles also relocated themselves within the cultural sphere of the Occident. They began to identify Iberian culture as a backward and superseded phase of European culture.

This transformation implied a renunciation of the past. For the insurgents, nothing in the past could be useful to them in their construction of the future society. Consequently, their future society consisted solely of proposals. Luis Villoro observes that for the liberals "society no longer falls under the category of having but of making; this term is regarded as a conscious activity directed toward a chosen end." Moreover, construction of the new society "is not given to spontaneous or irrational forces; it will be the fruit of a will illuminated by reason" (1967: 162–163).

The print media communicated and represented this social will. It constituted the space in which educated and politically active Creoles began to imagine Mexico as a national society. Within the print media of the 1820s, 1830s, and 1840s, the Creole intelligentsia formulated the mediations that would anchor the nation-state into the lifeworlds of Mexicans. But this new round of state formation is a story that I shall have to tell in another place.

SUMMARY AND CONCLUSIONS

My analysis of state formation in Mexico has examined a progression of communicative practices. The spectacles of the colonial period displaced rituals that originated within indigenous cultures. At the outset of the independence period, the circulation of texts displaced the staging of spectacles. This transition from spectacles to texts illustrates how lettered elites relocated Mexico within the cultural sphere of the Occident. Within both the colony and the nation-state, intellectuals remained the contemporaries of the Western civilization. They followed the changing narratives of Occidental culture in order to "civilize" regions that were peripheral to this culture.

To conclude, I would suggest that the global expansion of Occidental culture proceeded, at least in part, through the emergence of state-forming processes at the peripheries of the West. This has been an interactive process in which local cultures have continually reformulated their identities in response to the civilizing processes of state formation. These responses are extremely important to consider. They can disclose how the state, as a condition of social life, anchors itself within the lifeworlds of popular cultures. In turn, this anchorage can disclose developmental possibilities for the creation of new forms of world order.

NOTE

The author would like to thank M. J. Peterson, Naeem Inayatullah, and Stephen Rosow for comments on earlier drafts of this chapter.

References

Abad y Quiepo, Don Manuel (1799/1963) "Estado Moral y Politica en que se Hallaba la Poblacion del Virreinato de Nueva Espana" in J.M.L. Mora, *Obras Sueltas.* Mexico: Porrua.

Agnew, John (1984) "Devaluing Place: 'People Prosperity' versus 'Place Prosperity' and Regional Planning" *Society and Space* 2:35–45.

———— (1989) "The Devaluation of Place in Social Science" 9–29 in John Agnew and James Duncan, eds., *The Power of Place: Bringing Together Geographical and Sociological Imaginations.* Boston: Unwin and Hyman.

———— (1992a) "Representing Space: Space, Scale, and Culture in the Social Sciences" in J. S. Duncan and D. Ley, eds., *Representing Culture.* London: Routledge.

———— (1992b) "The United States and American Hegemony" in P. J. Taylor, ed., *The Political Geography of the Twentieth Century.* London: Belhaven Press.

Alacron, Hernando Ruiz de (1629/1984) *Treatise on the Heathen Superstitions and Customs That Today Live Among the Indians Native to This New Spain, 1629,* J. Richard Anders and Ross Hassig, eds. and trans. Norman: University of Oklahoma Press.

Alvarez, Sonia E. (1989) "Women's Movements and Gender Politics in the Brazilian Transition" 18–71 in Jane S. Jaquette, ed., *The Women's Movement in Latin America.* Boston: Unwin and Hyman.

———— (1990) *Engendering Democracy in Brazil.* Princeton: Princeton University Press.

Anderson, Benedict (1983) *Imagined Communities: Reflections on the Origins and Spread of Nationalism.* London: Verso.

Anderson, Perry (1974) *Lineages of the Absolutist State.* London: New Left Books.

Andrews, Kenneth R. (1984) *Trade, Plunder and Settlement: Maritime Enterprise and the Genesis of the British Empire, 1480–1630.* Cambridge: Cambridge University Press.

Arblaster, Anthony (1984) *The Rise and Decline of Western Liberalism.* New York: Basil Blackwell.

Ashley, Richard K. (1980) *The Political Economy of War and Peace.* New York: Nicolas Publishing Company.

———— (1981) "Political Realism and Human Interests" *International Studies Quarterly* 25: 204–236.

———— (1983) "Three Modes of Economism" *International Studies Quarterly* 27: 463–496.

225

—— (1984) "The Poverty of Neorealism" *International Organization* 38: 225–286.

—— (1985) "The Power of Power Politics: Towards a Critical Social Theory of International Politics." Manuscript.

—— (1987) "The Geopolitics of Geopolitical Space: Toward a Critical Social Theory of International Politics" *Alternatives* 12: 403–434.

—— (1988) "Untying the Sovereign State: A Double Reading of the Anarchy Problematique" *Millennium* 17: 227–262.

—— (1989) "Living on Border Lines: Man, Poststructuralism, and War" 163–187 in J. Der Derian and M. Shapiro, eds., *International/Intertextual Relations: Postmodern Readings of World Politics*. Lexington, Mass.: Lexington Books.

Ashley, Richard and R.B.J. Walker (1990a) "Speaking the Language of Exile: Dissident Thought in International Studies" *International Studies Quarterly* 34: 259–268.

—— (1990b) "Reading Dissidence/Writing the Discipline: Crisis and the Question of Sovereignty in International Studies" *International Studies Quarterly* 34: 367–416.

Attali, Jacques (1991) *Millennium: Winners and Losers in the Coming World Order*. New York: Random House.

Augelli, Enrico, and Craig Murphy (1988) *America's Quest for Supremacy and the Third World*. London: Pinter Publishers.

St. Augustine (1972) *Concerning the City of God Against the Pagans,* edited by David Knowles. Harmondsworth: Penguin.

Axelrod, Robert (1981) "The Emergence of Cooperation Among Egoists" *American Political Science Review,* 25: 306–318.

Axelrod, Robert, and Robert Keohane (1985) "Achieving Cooperation Under Anarchy" *World Politics* 38: 226–254.

Baldwin, P. ed. (1990) *Reworking the Past: Hitler, the Holocaust and the Historians' Debate.* Boston: Beacon Press.

Ball, Terence (1989) *Transforming Political Discourse: Political Theory and Critical Conceptual History.* Oxford: Basil Blackwell.

Ball, Terence, James Farr, and Russell Hanson, eds. (1989) *Political Innovation and Conceptual Change.* Cambridge: Cambridge University Press.

Barrios de Chungara, Domitila with Moema Viezzer (1978) *Let Me Speak!* New York: Monthly Review Press.

Behar, Ruth (1990) "Rage and Redemption: Reading the Life Story of a Mexican Marketing Woman" *Feminist Studies* 16: 223–258.

Benedict, Richard E. et al. (1991) *Greenhouse Warming: Negotiating a Global Regime.* Washington, D.C.: World Resources Institute.

Benjamin, Medea, ed. and trans. (1989) *Don't Be Afraid Gringo.* New York: Harper and Row.

Berman, Marshall (1982) *All That Is Solid Melts into Air: The Experience of Modernity.* New York: Simon and Schuster.

Bernstein, Richard J. (1978) *The Restructuring of Social and Political Theory.* Philadelphia: University of Pennsylvania Press.

Berryman, Philip (1987) *Liberation Theology.* New York: Pantheon Books.

Beverley, J. and M. Zimmerman (1990) *Literature and Politics in the Central American Revolutions.* Austin: University of Texas Press.

Bitar, Sergio (1988) "Neo-conservatism versus Neo-structuralism in Latin America" *CEPAL Review* 34: 45–62.

Blomström, Magnus, and Björn Hettne (1984) *Development Theory in Transition.* London: Zed Books.

Bloom, Alan (1987) *The Closing of the American Mind.* New York: Simon and Schuster.

Bodin, Jean (1969) *Method for the Easy Comprehension of History.* Beatrice Reynolds, trans. New York: Columbia University Press.

Bollag, B. (1990) "In Both East and West, Reunification Will Bring Big Challenges to German Higher Education" *The Chronicle of Higher Education,* October 3, 1990.

Bonfil, Guillermo (1987) "Los Pueblos Indios y las Culturas Politicas" 89–125 in Garcia Canclini, ed. *Culturas Politicas en America Latina.* Mexico: Grijalbo.

Booth, David (1985) "Marxism and Development Sociology: Interpreting the Impasse" *World Development* 13: 761–787.

Braudel, Fernand (1984) *Civilization and Capitalism 15th–18th Century.* Volume 3: "The Perspective of the World." New York: Harper and Row.

Bricker, Reifler Victoria (1981) *The Indian Christ, The Indian King.* Austin: University of Texas Press.

Bronfenbrenner, Martin (1986) "Japan-Bashing: A View From Over There" *Challenge* 28: 58–61.

Brooks, Joseph Francis (1978) *Parish and Cofradia in Eighteenth-Century Mexico.* History dissertation. Princeton University. Michigan: University Microfilms International.

Brown, Wendy (1988) *Manhood and Politics: A Feminist Reading in Political Theory.* Totowa, N.J.: Rowman and Littlefield.

——— (1991) "Feminist Hesitations, Postmodern Exposures," *Differences* 3: 63–84.

Brzezinski, Zbigniew (1988) "America's New Geostrategy" *Foreign Affairs* 66, 680–699.

Burch, Kurt (1992) "A Critique of the Premises of World System Theory." Manuscript.

Burgos-Debray, Elisabeth, ed. (1984) *I . . . Rigoberta Menchu.* New York: Verso.

Burkhart, Louise (1989) *The Slippery Earth: Nahua-Christian Moral Dialogue in Sixteenth-Century Mexico.* Tucson: University of Arizona Press.

Business Week. August 7, 1989 "Rethinking Japan."

Butler, Judith (1990) *Gender Trouble: Feminism and the Subversion of Identity.* New York: Routledge.

Caldeira, Teresa Pires de Rio (1990) "Women, Daily Life and Politics" 47–78 in Elizabeth Jelin, ed. *Women and Social Change in Latin America.* London: Zed Books.

Campbell, David (1992a) *Writing Security: United States Foreign Policy and the Politics of Identity.* Minneapolis: University of Minnesota Press.

——— (1992b) "Cold Wars: Securing Identity, Interpreting Danger" in Frederick M. Dolan and Thomas L. Dumm, eds. *Rhetorical Republic: Representing American Politics.* Amherst: University of Massachusetts Press.

Caporaso, James (1993) "International Relations Theory and Multilateralism: The Search for Foundations," 51–90 in J.G. Ruggie, ed. *Multilateralism Matters: The Theory and Praxis of an Institutional Form.* New York: Columbia University Press.

Caporaso, James A., et al. (1987) "The Comparative Study of Foreign Policy: Perspectives on the Future" *International Studies Notes* 13.

Carr, Edward H. (1939) *The 20 Years' Crisis, 1919–1939: An Introduction to the Study of International Relations.* London: Macmillan.

Chandra, Bipan (1986) "Nationalist Historians' Interpretations of the Indian National Movement" in Sabyasachi Bhattacharya and Romila Thapar, eds. *Situating Indian History.* Delhi: Oxford University Press.

Chase-Dunn, Christopher (1981) "Interstate System and Capitalist World-Economy: One Logic or Two?" *International Studies Quarterly* 25: 19–42.

Chatterjee, Partha (1986) *Nationalist Thought and the Colonial World: A Derivative Discourse.* Delhi: Oxford University Press.

Choucri, Nazli, and North, Robert (1975) *Nations in Conflict: National Growth and International Violence.* San Francisco: W. H. Freeman.

Christopher, Robert C. (1985) "Let's Give Pearl Harbor a Break" *Newsweek,* October 14.

Chuchryk, Patricia M. (1989) "Feminist Anti-Authoritarian Politics: The Role of Women's Organizations in the Chilean Transition to Democracy" 149–184 in Jane S. Jaquette, ed. *The Women's Movement in Latin America.* Boston: Unwin Hyman.

Cipolla, Carlo M. (1980) *Before the Industrial Revolution: European Society and Economy, 1000–1700* 2d edition. New York: W.W. Norton.

Clifford, James (1986) "Introduction: Partial Truths" 1–26 in James Clifford and George Marcus, eds. *Writing Culture.* Berkeley: University of California Press.

Clifford, James, and George Marcus, eds. (1986) *Writing Culture.* Berkeley: University of California Press.

Clough, Shepard B. (1959) *The Economic Development of Western Civilization.* New York: McGraw-Hill.

Collingwood, R.G. (1933) *Essay on Philosophical Method.* Oxford: Clarendon.

Collins, Stephen (1989) *From Divine Cosmos to Sovereign State: An Intellectual History of Consciousness and the Idea of Order in Renaissance England.* Oxford: Oxford University Press.

Concha Malo, Miguel (1986) "El Mito de Guadalupe y el Nacionalismo Mexicano desde las Classes Populares" 107–123 in *Hacia el Nuevo Milenio* vol 1. Mexico: Universidad Nacional Autonoma.

Connolly, William (1988) *Political Theory and Modernity.* Oxford: Basil Blackwell.

Conybeare, J.A.C. (1984) "Public Goods, Prisoners' Dilemmas, and the International Political Economy" *International Studies Quarterly* 28: 5–22.

Coughlin, Richard (1990) "Development as a Civilizing Process: State Formation in Mexico." Paper presented at the meetings of the Northeast International Studies Association.

Cox, Robert W. (1981) "Social Forces, States, and World Orders: Beyond International Relations Theory" *Millennium* 10:126–155.

——— (1983) "Gramsci, Hegemony and International Relations: An Essay in Method" *Millennium* 12: 162–175.

——— (1987) *Production, Power, and World Order.* New York: Columbia University Press.

Cummings, Bruce (1991) "CIA's *Japan 2000* Caper" *Nation,* September 30.

Dalby, Simon (1991) *Rethinking Security: Ambiguities in Policy and Theory.* International Studies, Simon Fraser University, Burnaby, B.C., Canada.

de Vries, Jan (1976) *The Economy of Europe in an Age of Crisis, 1600–1750.* Cambridge: Cambridge University Press.

Debus, Allen G. (1978) *Man and Nature in the Renaissance.* Cambridge: Cambridge University Press.

Dower, John W. (1986) *War Without Mercy: Race and Power in the Pacific War.* New York: Pantheon.

Doyle, Michael (1990) "Thucydidean Realism" *Review of International Studies* 16: 223–237.

Dunn, John (1979) *Western Political Theory in the Face of the Future.* Cambridge: Cambridge University Press.

Eckstein, Susan, ed. (1989) *Power and Popular Protest.* Berkeley: University of California Press.

Economist, May 2, 1987 "Why America Needs Japan as Much as Japan Needs America."

———— June, 10, 1989 "Dialogue of the Deaf."

———— August 19, 1989 "And Never the Twain Shall Meet."

Ekelund, Robert B., Jr., and Robert D. Tollison (1981) *Mercantilism as a Rent-Seeking Society.* College Station, Tex.: Texas A & M University Press.

Elshtain, Jean (1987) *Women and War.* New York: Basic Books.

Enloe, Cynthia (1989) *Bananas, Beaches and Bases: Making Feminist Sense of International Relations.* London: Pandora.

Fallows, James (1990) *More Like Us: Making America Great Again.* Boston: Houghton Mifflin.

Febvre, Lucien (1977) *Life in Renaissance France.* Marian Rothstein, ed. and trans. Cambridge: Harvard University Press.

Ferguson, Kathy (1993) *The Man Question: Visions of Subjectivity in Feminist Theory.* Berkeley: University of California Press.

Flax, Jane (1990) *Thinking Fragments: Psychoanalysis, Feminism, and Postmodernism.* Berkeley: University of California Press.

Florescano, Enrique (1987) *Memoria Mexicana.* Mexico: Editorial de Joaquin Mortiz.

Fortune, February 26, 1990 "Fear and Loathing of Japan."

Foucault, Michel (1972) *The Archeology of Knowledge.* Sheridan Smith, trans. New York: Pantheon Books.

———— (1979) *Discipline and Punish: The Birth of the Prison.* Alan Sheridan, trans. New York: Vintage Books.

Foweraker, Joe (1990) "Popular Movements and Political Change in Mexico" 3–22 in Joe Foweraker and Ann L. Craig, eds. *Popular Movements and Political Change in Mexico.* Boulder: Lynne Rienner Publishers.

Foweraker, Joe, and Ann L. Craig, eds. (1990) *Popular Movements and Political Change in Mexico.* Boulder: Lynne Rienner Publishers.

Foxley, Alejandro (1987) "Latin American Experiments in Neo-Conservative Economics" 244–260 in James L. Dietz and James H. Street, eds., *Latin America's Economic Development.* Boulder: Lynne Rienner Publishers.

Freire, Paulo (1970) *Pedagogy of the Oppressed.* New York: Continuum.

Frug, G. E. (1980) "The City as a Legal Concept" *Harvard Law Review* 93: 1059–1154.

Fukayama, Francis (1989) "The End of History?" *The National Interest* 16: 3–18.

Galtung, Johan (1990) "Die Deutschen werden die Amerikaner aus Europa werfen: Interview mit dem norwegen Friedensforscher Johan Galtung" *Die Tagezeitung,* December 12.

Garcia, Genaro (1974) *Documentos Ineditos o muy Raros para la Historica de Mexico.* Mexico: Editorial Porrua.

Garst, Daniel (1989) "Thucydides and Neorealism" *International Studies Quarterly* 33: 3–27.

George, Jim, and David Campbell (1990) "Patterns of Dissent and the Celebration of Difference: Critical Social Theory and International Relations" *International Studies Quarterly* 34: 269–293.

Gibson, Charles (1965) *The Aztecs Under Spanish Rule.* Stanford: Stanford University Press.

Giddens, Anthony (1984) *The Constitution of Society.* Berkeley: University of California Press.

Gill, Stephen (1986a) "Hegemony, Consensus and Trilateralism" *Review of International Studies* 12: 205–221.

———— (1986b) "American Hegemony: Its Limits and Prospects in the Reagan Era" *Millennium* 15: 311–336.

———— (1990) *American Hegemony and the Trilateral Commission.* Cambridge: Cambridge University Press.

———— (1992) "The Emerging World Order and European Change: The Political Economy of European Union" 157–196 in Ralph Miliband and Leo Panitch, eds. *The Socialist Register 1992.* London: Merlin Press.

Gill, Stephen, and David Law (1988) *The Global Political Economy.* Baltimore: Johns Hopkins University Press.

Gilligan, Carol (1982) *In a Different Voice: Psychological Theory and Women's Development.* Cambridge, Mass.: Harvard University Press.

Gilman, Sander L. (1985) *Difference and Pathology: Stereotypes of Sexuality, Race, and Madness.* Ithaca: Cornell University Press.

Gilpin, Robert (1975) *U.S. Power and the Multinational Corporation.* New York: Basic Books.

———— (1977) "Economic Interdependence and National Security in Historical Perspective" 19–66 in Klaus Knorr and Frank Trager, eds. *Economic Issues and National Security.* Lawrence: Allen Press.

———— (1981) *War and Change in World Politics.* Cambridge: Cambridge University Press.

———— (1987) *The Political Economy of International Relations.* Princeton: Princeton University Press.

Glazer, Nathan (1975) "From Ruth Benedict to Herman Kahn: The Postwar Japanese Image in the American Mind" 138–168 in Akira Iriye, ed. *Mutual Images: Essays in American-Japanese Relations.* Cambridge: Harvard University Press.

Gonzalbo, Pilar (1985) *El Humanismo y la Educacion en la Nueva Espana.* Mexico: Secretaria de Educacion Publica (SEP).

Gould, Carol (1978) *Marx's Social Ontology.* Cambridge: MIT Press.

Gramsci, Antonio (1971) *Selections from the Prison Notebooks.* New York: International Publishers.

Grass, Günter (1990) "Writing After Auschwitz" 94–123 in *Two States—One Nation?* K. Winston and A.S. Wensinger, trans. San Diego: Harcourt Brace Jovanovich.

Grieco, Joseph (1990) *Cooperation Among Nations: Europe, America, and Non-Tariff Barriers to Trade.* Ithaca: Cornell University Press.

Gruzinski, Serge (1985) "La 'Segunda Aculturacion': el Estado Ilustrado y la Religiosidad Indigena en la Nueva Espana" *Estudios de Historia Novohispana* 8: 175–201.

———— (1989) *Man-Gods in the Mexican Highlands: Indian Power and Colonial Society, 1520–1800* Eileen Corrigan, trans. Stanford: Stanford University Press.

Guha, Ranajit, and Gayatri Chakravorty Spivak, eds. (1988) *Selected Subaltern Studies.* New York: Oxford University Press.

Gupta, A., and Ferguson, J. (1992) "Beyond 'Culture': Space, Identity, and the Politics of Difference" *Cultural Anthropology* 7: xx–xx.

Habermas, Jürgen (1971) *Knowledge and Human Interests.* Jeremy J. Shapiro, trans. Boston: Beacon Press.

———— (1987) *The Theory of Communicative Action* Vol. 2 Thomas McCarthy, trans. Boston: Beacon Press.

———— (1990) "Der DM-Nationalismus" *Die Zeit,* March 30.

Hale, David George (1971) *The Body Politic: A Political Metaphor in Renaissance English Literature*. The Hague: Mouton.

Hamilton, John Maxwell, with Nancy Morrison (1990) *Entangling Alliances*. Washington, D.C.: Seven Locks Press.

Hannay, David (1926) *The Great Chartered Companies*. London: Williams and Norgate.

Harding, Sandra (1986) *The Science Question in Feminism*. Ithaca: Cornell University Press.

Hartsock, Nancy (1983) *Money, Sex, and Power: Toward a Feminist Historical Materialism*. New York: Longman.

Harvey, David (1989) *The Condition of Postmodernity*. Oxford: Basil Blackwell.

Heckscher, Eli (1934) *Mercantilism* in 2 volumes. London: George Allen and Unwin.

Hellman, Judith Adler (1990) "Latin American Social Movements and the Question of Autonomy" *LASA Forum* 21: 7–12.

Hermann, Charles F. et al. (1987) *New Directions in the Study of Foreign Policy*. Boston: Allen and Unwin.

Herzog, Kristin (1983) *Women, Ethnics, and Exotics: Images of Power in Mid-Nineteenth-Century American Fiction*. Knoxville: University of Tennessee Press.

Hilton, Rodney, ed. (1976) *The Transition from Feudalism to Capitalism*. London: New Left Books.

Hintze, Otto (1975) "Economics and Politics in the Age of Modern Capitalism" 422–452 in Felix Gilbert, ed. *The Historical Essays of Otto Hintze*. Oxford: Oxford University Press.

Hirschman, Albert O. (1977) *The Passions and the Interests: Political Arguments for Capitalism Before Its Triumph*. Princeton: Princeton University Press.

Hirschmann, Nancy (1989) "Freedom, Recognition, and Obligation: A Feminist Approach to Political Theory" *American Political Science Review* 83: 1227–1244.

Hobbes, Thomas (1981) *Leviathan* C.B. Macpherson, ed. New York: Penguin.

Hobsbawm, Eric J. (1990) *Nations and Nationalism Since 1780: Programme, Myth, Reality*. Cambridge: Cambridge University Press.

Hoffmann, Stanley (1977) "An American Social Science: International Relations" *Daedalus* 106: 41–60.

Holman, O., and K. van der Pijl (1992) *Restructuring the Ruling Class and European Unification* Working Paper no. 28. Amsterdam: University of Amsterdam Department of International Relations and Public International Law.

Holsti, K. J. (1985) *The Dividing Discipline: Hegemony and Diversity in International Theory*. Boston: Allen and Unwin.

Hopmann, Terrence (1976) "Identifying, Formulating, and Solving Puzzles in International Relations Research" 192–197 in James Rosenau, ed. *In Search of Global Patterns*. New York: Free Press.

Horkheimer, Max (1972) *Critical Theory: Selected Essays*. New York: Seabury Press.

Howat, G.M.D. (1974) *Stuart and Cromwellian Foreign Policy*. New York: St. Martin's Press.

Hume, David (1970) *Writings on Economics,* edited by Eugene Rotwein. Madison: University of Wisconsin.

Inayatullah, Naeem (1988) *Labor and Division of Labor: Conceptual Ambiguities in Political Economy*. Doctoral dissertation, University of Denver, Graduate School of International Studies.

——— (1991a) "Conflict and Cooperation in Thomas Hobbes and Adam Smith: Political and Economic Constructions of the 'State of Nature'." Working paper, Syracuse University.

——— (1991b) "Self, Other, and the Social Construction of Global Political Economy." Working paper, Syracuse University.

Inayatullah, Naeem, and David P. Levine (1990) "Politics and Economics in Contemporary International Relations Theory." Paper prepared for presentation at the annual meeting of the International Studies Association, Washington, D.C., April 1990.

Israel, Jonathan (1975) *Race, Class and Politics in Colonial Mexico, 1610–1670.* Oxford: Oxford University Press.

Jaquette, Jane S., ed. (1989). *The Women's Movement in Latin America.* Boston: Unwin and Hyman.

Jara, R., and H. Vidal, eds. (1986) *Testimonio y Literatura.* Minneapolis: Institute for the Study of Ideologies and Literature.

Jeffords, Susan (1989) *The Remasculinization of America: Gender and the Vietnam War.* Bloomington: Indiana University Press.

Jervis, Robert (1978) "Cooperation Under the Security Dilemma" *World Politics* 30: 167–214.

Johnson, Chalmers (1982) *MITI and the Japanese Miracle.* Stanford: Stanford University Press.

Johnson, Sheila (1988) *The Japanese Through American Eyes.* Stanford: Stanford University Press.

Jones, Kathleen (1993) *Compassionate Authority: Democracy and the Representation of Women.* New York: Routledge.

Julius, DeAnne (1990) *Global Companies and Public Policy: The Growing Challenge of Foreign Direct Investment.* New York: Council on Foreign Relations.

Kantorowicz, Ernst H. (1957) *The King's Two Bodies: A Study in Medieval Political Theology.* Princeton: Princeton University Press.

Kay, Cristobal (1989) *Latin American Theories of Development and Underdevelopment.* London: Routledge.

Kenyon, John P. (1978) *Stuart England.* New York: Penguin Books.

Keohane, Robert (1980) "The Theory of Hegemonic Stability and Changes in International Economic Regimes, 1967–77" 131–162 in O. Holsti, R. Siverson, and A. George, eds. *Change in the International System.* Boulder: Westview.

——— (1982) "Hegemonic Leadership and U.S. Foreign Economic Policy in the 'Long Decade' of the 1950s" 49–76 in William Avery and David Rapkin, eds. *America in a Changing World Political Economy.* New York: Longman.

——— (1984) *After Hegemony.* Princeton: Princeton University Press.

——— (1986) "Theory of World Politics: Structural Realism and Beyond" 158–203 in R. Keohane, ed. *Neorealism and Its Critics.* New York: Columbia University Press.

——— (1989) *International Institutions and State Power: Essays in International Relations Theory.* Boulder: Westview.

———, ed. (1986) *Neorealism and Its Critics.* New York: Columbia University Press.

Keohane, Robert, and Joseph S. Nye (1977) *Power and Interdependence.* Boston: Little, Brown.

——— (1987) *"Power and Interdependence* Revisited" *International Organization* 41: 725–753.

Kern, Stephen (1983) *The Culture of Time and Space, 1880–1918.* Cambridge, Mass.: Harvard University Press.

Kiernan, V. G. (1980) *America: The New Imperialism. From White Settlement to World Hegemony.* London: Zed Books.

Kindleberger, Charles P. (1973) *The World in Depression.* Berkeley: University of California Press.

—— (1981) "Dominance and Leadership in the International Economy" *International Studies Quarterly* 25: 242–254.

Kondo, Dorinne K. (1990) *Crafting Selves: Power, Gender, and Discourses of Identity in a Japanese Working Place.* Chicago: University of Chicago Press.

Krasner, Stephen (1976) "State Power and the Structure of International Trade" *World Politics* 28: 317–347.

—— (1978) "U.S. Commercial and Monetary Policy: Unraveling the Paradox of External Strength and Internal Weakness" 51–87 in Peter Katzenstein, ed. *Between Power and Plenty.* Madison: University of Wisconsin Press.

—— (1982) "Structural Causes and Regime Consequences: Regimes as Intervening Variables" *International Organization* 36: 185–206.

Krasner, Stephen D., and Daniel I. Okimoto (1989) "Japan's Evolving Trade Posture" 117–144 in Akira Iriye and Warren I. Cohen, eds. *The United States and Japan in the Postwar World.* Lexington: University Press of Kentucky.

Kratochwil, Friedrich (1993) "Norms Versus Numbers: Multilateralism and the Rationalist and Reflexivist Approaches to Institutions—a Unilateral Plea for Communicative Rationality" 443–474 in J.G. Ruggie, ed. *Multilateralism Matters: The Theory and Praxis of an Institutional Form.* New York: Columbia University Press.

Kratochwil, Friedrich, and John Gerard Ruggie (1986) "International Organization: A State of the Art on the Art of the State" *International Organization* 40: 753–776.

Kriedte, Peter (1983) *Peasants, Landlords and Merchant Capitalists: Europe and the World Economy, 1500–1800* V.R. Berghahn, trans. Cambridge: Cambridge University Press.

Lafaye, Jacques (1976) *Quetzalcoatl and Guadalupe* Benjamin Keen, trans. Chicago: University of Chicago Press.

LaFeber, Walter (1989) *The American Age: United States Foreign Policy at Home and Abroad Since 1750.* New York: W. W. Norton.

Lakatos, Imre (1970) "Falsification and the Methodology of Scientific Research Programmes" 91–196 in *Criticism and the Growth of Knowledge* Imre Lakatos and A. Musgrave, eds. Cambridge: Cambridge University Press.

Le Goff, Jacques (1989) "Head or Heart? The Political Use of Body Metaphors in the Middle Ages" 12–26 in Michael Feher, with Ramona Naddaf and Nadia Tazi, eds. *Zone 5: Fragments for a History of the Human Body, Part Three.* New York: Urzone.

Leach, Edmund (1961) *Rethinking Anthropology.* London: Athlone Press.

Leaver, Richard (1989) "Restructuring in the Global Economy: From Pax Americana to Pax Nipponica?" *Alternatives* 14: 429–462.

Lefebvre, Henri (1991) *The Production of Space.* Oxford: Blackwell.

Levine, David P. (1977) *Economic Studies.* London: Routledge and Kegan Paul.

—— (1978) *Economic Theory Vol. 1* London: Routledge and Kegan Paul.

—— (1981) *Economic Theory Vol. 2* London: Routledge and Kegan Paul.

—— (1988) *Needs, Rights and the Market.* Boulder: Lynne Rienner Publishers.

Lloyd, Genevieve (1986) "Selfhood, War and Masculinity" 63–76 in Carole Pateman and Elizabeth Gross, eds. *Feminist Challenges: Social and Political Theory.* Boston: Northeastern University Press.

Lockhart, James (1982) "Views of Corporate Self in Some Valley of Mexico Towns: Late Seventeenth and Eighteenth Centuries" in George Collier,

Renato Rosaldo, and John Wirth, eds. *The Inca and Aztec States, 1400–1800.* New York: Academic Press.

Lugones, Maria (1990) "Playfulness, World-Travelling, and Loving Perception" 390–402 in Gloria Anzaldua, ed. *Making Face, Making Soul—Haciendo Caras: Creative and Critical Perspectives by Women of Color.* San Francisco: Aunt Lute.

Lukes, Steven (1973) *Individualism.* Oxford: Basil Blackwell.

——— (1977) *Essays in Social Theory.* New York: Columbia University Press.

Lyotard, Jean-Francois (1986) *The Postmodern Condition: A Report on Knowledge.* Manchester: Manchester University Press.

Machiavelli, Niccolo (1961) *The Prince*, George Bull, trans. New York: Penguin Books.

MacIntyre, Alasdair (1981) *After Virtue: A Study in Moral Theory.* Notre Dame: University of Notre Dame Press.

MacLachlan, Colin (1988) *Spain's Empire in the New World: The Role of Ideas in Institutional and Social Change.* Berkeley: University of California Press.

Makin, John H. (1988) "Japan's Investment in America: Is It a Threat?" *Challenge* 31: 8–16.

Malagon, Javier, and Cabdequi, Jose Maria. (1965) *Solorzano y la Politica Indiana.* Buenos Aires, Mexico: Fondo de Cultura Economica.

Mann, Michael (1984) "The Autonomous Power of the State: Its Origins, Mechanisms and Results" *European Journal of Sociology* 25:185–213.

——— (1988) *States, War and Capitalism.* New York: Basil Blackwell.

Maravall, Antonio (1986) *Culture of the Baroque: Analysis of a Historical Structure* Terry Cochran, trans. Minneapolis: University of Minnesota Press.

Marchand, Marianne H. (1991) "Latin American Women Are Speaking on Development: Are We Listening Yet?" Presented at the Fifth International Meeting of the Association of Women in Development, Washington, D.C., November 20–24, 1991.

——— (1992) "Perspectives on Latin America: Theories of Development as Political Struggles" Ph. D. dissertation. Tempe, Ariz.: Arizona State University.

Marx, Karl (1844/1964) *Economic and Philosophic Manuscripts of 1844* Dirk J. Struik, ed., Martin Milligan, trans. New York: International Publishers.

——— (1975) *Early Writings.* New York: Vintage Books.

——— (1977) *Capital*, Vol. I. New York: Vintage Books.

Marx, Karl, and F. Engels (1970) *The German Ideology* C.J. Arthur, ed. New York: International Publishers.

Massey, Doreen (1984) *Spatial Divisions of Labour: Social Structures and the Geography of Production.* London: Methuen.

Mastanduno, Michael (1991) "Do Relative Gains Matter? America's Response to Japan's Industrial Policy" *International Security* 16:73–113.

Mazzolani, Lidia S. (1970) *The Idea of the City in Roman Thought: From Walled City to Spiritual Commonwealth.* Bloomington: Indiana University Press.

McGowan, Patrick J., and Howard B. Shapiro (1973) *The Comparative Study of Foreign Policy: A Survey.* Beverly Hills: Sage Publications.

McKeown, Timothy (1983) "Hegemonic Stability Theory and 19th-Century Tariff Levels in Europe" *International Organization* 37: 73–92.

McNeill, William H. (1982) *The Pursuit of Power: Technology, Armed Force, and Society since AD 1000.* Chicago: University of Chicago Press.

Mearsheimer, John (1990a) "Back to the Future: Instability in Europe After the Cold War" *International Security* 15: 5–56.

——— (1990b) "Why We Will Soon Miss the Cold War" *Atlantic Monthly* August 1990: 35–50.

Meek, Ronald L. (1965) "The Rise and Fall of the Concept of the Economic Machine" inaugural lecture delivered at the University of Leicester, November 12, 1964. Leicester: Leicester University Press.

Meinecke, Friedrich (1962) *Machiavellism* Douglas Scott, trans., New Haven: Yale University Press.

Meller, Patricio, ed. (1991) *The Latin American Development Debate*. Boulder: Westview.

Mendes, Chico (1989) *Fight for the Forest: Chico Mendes in His Own Words*. London: Latin America Bureau.

Merchant, Carolyn (1980) *The Death of Nature: Women, Ecology and the Scientific Revolution*. New York: Harper and Row.

Milliken, Jennifer L. (1990) "Sovereignty and Subjectivity in the Early Nineteenth Century." Unpublished paper, Department of Political Science, University of Minnesota.

Milner, Helen (1991) "The assumption of anarchy in international relations theory: a critique" *Review of International Studies* 17: 67–85.

Modelski, George (1978) "The Long Cycle of Global Politics and the Nation-State" *Comparative Studies in Society and History* 20: 214–235.

——— (1987) *Long Cycles in World Politics*. Seattle: University of Washington Press.

Molyneux, Maxine (1985). "Mobilization Without Emancipation? Women's Interests, the State, and Revolution in Nicaragua" *Feminist Studies* 11: 227–254.

Montaigne, Miguel de (1958) *The Complete Essays of Montaigne*. Donald M. Frame, trans. Stanford: Stanford University Press.

Montesquieu, Baron de (1951) "Essai sur les causes qui peuvent affecter les esprits et les caractères" 39–68 in *Oeuvre Complètes II*. Gallimard: Pléiade.

Morgenthau, Hans J. (1946) *Scientific Man vs. Power Politics*. Chicago: University of Chicago Press.

Muchembled, Robert (1985) *Popular Culture and Elite Culture in France, 1400–1750*. Lydia Cochrane, trans. Baton Rouge: Louisiana State University Press.

Murphy, R. Taggart (1989) "Power Without Purpose: The Crisis of Japan's Global Financial Dominance" *Harvard Business Review* 67: 71–83.

Nandy, Ashis. (1983) *The Intimate Enemy: Loss and Recovery of Self Under Colonialism*. Delhi: Oxford University Press.

——— (1987) *Traditions, Tyranny, and Utopias*. Delhi: Oxford University Press.

Narayan, Uma (1989) "The Project of Feminist Epistemology: Perspectives from a Nonwestern Feminist," 256–269 in Alison Jaggar and Susan Bordo, eds. *Gender/Body/Knowledge: Feminist Reconstructions of Being and Knowing*. New Brunswick, N.J.: Rutgers University Press.

Nation, June 25, 1990 "Testing Japan's Anti-Korean Laws."

Navarro, Marysa (1989) "The Personal Is Political: Las Madres de Plaza De Mayo" 241–258 in Susan Eckstein, ed. *Power and Popular Protest*. Berkeley: University of California Press.

Neff, Stephen C. (1990) *Friends but No Allies: Economic Liberalism and the Law of Nations*. New York: Columbia University Press.

Nehru, Jawaharlal (1936/1939) *An Autobiography*. London: John Lane, 1939. Reprinted from 1936 edition.

——— (1950) *Independence and After: A Collection of Speeches 1946–1949*. New York: John Day Company.

————— (1956) *Speeches on Science and Planning*. Government of India.

————— (1946/1989) *The Discovery of India*. Delhi: Oxford University Press. Reprinted 1989 from 1946 edition.

Neues Deutschland, August 28, 1987 "Der Streit der ideologien und die gemeinsame Sicherheit."

Neumann, William L. (1954) "Religion, Morality and Freedom: The Ideological Background of the Perry Expedition" *Pacific Historical Review* 23: 247–257.

Newsweek, April 1, 1991 "Why Don't They Share?"

New York Times, July 10, 1990 "After the Cold War."

—————, July 10, 1990 "Americans Express Worry on Japan, As Feelings in Tokyo Seem to Soften."

—————, July 10, 1990 "Still a Cold War for Aliens."

—————, July 11, 1990"U.S. Ads Increasingly Attack the Japanese and Their Culture."

—————, July 18, 1990 "After the Cold War, the Land of the Rising Threat."

—————, July 20, 1990 "Japanese in the New York Region Begin to Feel the Sting of Prejudice."

—————, December 2, 1990 "The Deal for MCA: Why the Anxiety Over Japan's Latest Find in America."

—————, June 12, 1991 "U.S. Companies in Japan Say Things Aren't So Bad."

Nolte, E. (1986) "Vergangenheit, die night vergehen will" *Frankfurter Algemeine Zeitung,* 6 June.

Northrup, Terrell (1989) "The Dynamic of Identity in Personal and Social Conflict," 55–82 in Louis Kriesberg, Terrell Northrup, and Stuart Thorson, eds. *Intractable Conflicts and Their Transformation*. Syracuse: Syracuse University Press.

Nye, Joseph (1990) *Bound to Lead: The Changing Nature of American Power*. New York: Basic Books.

O'Donnell, Guillermo (1978) "Apuntes para una Teoria del Estado" in *Revista Mexicana de la Sociologia* 40: 1157–1199.

Ollman, Bertell (1976) *Alienation: Marx's Conception of Man in Capitalist Society* 2d edition. Cambridge: Cambridge University Press.

Onuf, Nicholas G. (1991) "The Constitutional Experience" (tentative title). Manuscript, with Peter Onuf.

Packard, George R. (1987/1988) "The Coming U.S.—Japan Crisis," *Foreign Affairs* 66: 348–367.

Padden, R. C. (1967) *The Hummingbird and the Hawk*. Columbus: Ohio State University Press.

Pandey, Gyanendra (1988) "Congress and the Nation, 1917–1947" 121–133 in Richard Sisson and Stanley Wolpert, eds. *Congress and Indian Nationalism: The Pre-Independence Phase*. Berkeley: University of California Press.

Parry, J. H. (1940) *The Spanish Theory of Empire in the Sixteenth Century*. Cambridge: Cambridge University Press.

————— (revised 1981) *The Age of Reconnaissance: Discovery, Exploration and Settlement, 1450 to 1650,* revised edition. Berkeley: University of California Press.

Patai, Daphne (1988) "Constructing a Self: A Brazilian Life Story" *Feminist Studies* 14: 143–166.

Perin, Constance (1988) *Belonging in America: Reading Between the Lines*. Madison: University of Wisconsin Press.

Plato (1974) *The Republic*. G. M. A. Grube, trans. Indianapolis: Hackett Publishing Company.

Pocock, J. G. A. (1957) *The Ancient Constitution and the Feudal Law*. Cambridge: Cambridge University Press.

—— (1975) *The Machiavellian Moment: Florentine Political Thought and the Atlantic Republican Tradition.* Princeton: Princeton University Press.

—— (1985) *Virtue, Commerce, and History.* Cambridge: Cambridge University Press.

Poggi, Gianfranco (1978) *The Development of the Modern State.* Stanford: Stanford University Press.

Polanyi, Karl (1957) *The Great Transformation: The Political and Economic Origins of Our Times.* Boston: Beacon Press.

Porter, Michael D. (1990) "Japan Isn't Playing by Different Rules" *New York Times* July 22.

Poulantzas, Nicos (1980) *State, Power, Socialism.* London: Verso.

Prestowitz, Clyde (1988) *Trading Places: How We Allowed Japan to Take the Lead.* New York: Basic Books.

Randall, Vicky, and Robin Theobald (1985) *Political Change and Underdevelopment.* Durham: Duke University Press.

Rapaczynski, Andrzej (1986) *Nature and Politics: Liberalism in the Philosophies of Hobbes, Locke, and Rousseau.* Ithaca: Cornell University Press.

Reeve, Andrew (1986) *Property.* Atlantic Highlands; N.J.: Humanities Press.

Reich, Robert (1991) *The Work of Nations.* New York: Alfred A. Knopf.

Ricard, Robert (1966) *The Spiritual Conquest of Mexico.* Lesley Byrd Simpson, trans. Berkeley: University of California Press.

Ricoeur, Paul (1981a) *Hermeneutics and the Human Sciences.* Cambridge: Cambridge University Press.

—— (1981b) "Narrative Time" 165–186 in William Mitchell, ed. *On Narrative.* Chicago: University of Chicago Press.

Riley, Denise (1988) *"Am I That Name?" Feminism and the Category of "Women" in History.* Minneapolis: University of Minnesota Press.

Rogin, Michael Paul (1975) *Fathers and Children: Andrew Jackson and the Subjugation of the American Indian.* New York: Alfred A. Knopf.

Rosenau, James N. (1968) *The Scientific Study of Foreign Policy.* New York: Free Press.

—— (1976) "The Restless Quest" 1–9 in J. Rosenau, ed. *In Search of Global Patterns.* New York: Free Press.

——, ed. (1976) *In Search of Global Patterns.* New York: Free Press.

Rosenberg, Justin (1990) "What's the Matter with Realism?" *Review of International Studies* 16: 285–303.

Rosow, Stephen J. (1990) "The Forms of Internationalization: Representation of Western Culture on a Global Scale" *Alternatives* 15: 287–301.

Ross, Andrew (1987) "Containing Culture in the Cold War" *Cultural Studies* 1.

—— (1987/1988) "The Work of Nature in the Age of Electronic Emission" *Social Text* 18: 116–128.

Rousseau, Jean-Jacques (1978) *On the Social Contract,* edited by Roger D. Masters and translated by Judith R. Masters. New York: St. Martin's Press.

—— (1983) *On the Social Contract and Discourses.* Indianapolis: Hackett Publishers.

Ruggie, John G. (1983a) "Continuity and Transformation in the World Polity: Toward a Neorealist Synthesis" *World Politics* 35: 261–285.

—— (1983b) "International Regimes, Transactions and Change: Embedded Liberalism in the Postwar Economic Order" 195–231 in S. D. Krasner, ed. *International Regimes.* Ithaca: Cornell University Press.

—— (1993), ed. *Multilateralism Matters: The Theory and Praxis of an Institutional Form.* New York: Columbia University Press.

Rupert, Mark (1990) "Producing Hegemony: State/Society Relations and the Politics of Productivity in the United States" *International Studies Quarterly* 34: 427–456.

——— (1993) "Alienation, Capitalism and the Interstate System: Toward a Marxian/Gramscian Critique of IPE" 67–92 in Stephen Gill, ed. *Gramsci, Historical Matrialism and International Relations*. Cambridge: Cambridge University Press.

Rushdie, Salman (1980) *Midnight's Children*. New York: Avon Books.

Russell, John (1991) "Race and Reflexivity: The Black Other in Contemporary Japanese Mass Culture" *Cultural Anthropology* 6: 3–25.

Ryan, Alan (1987) *Property*. Minneapolis: University of Minnesota Press.

Sack, Robert D. (1980) *Conceptions of Space in Social Thought: A Geographic Perspective*. Minneapolis: University of Minnesota Press.

Safa, Helen I. (1990) "Women's Social Movements in Latin America" *Gender and Society* 4: 354–369.

Sahlins, Marshall (1972) *Stone Age Economics*. New York: Aldine Atherton.

——— (1976a) *The Use and Abuse of Biology*. Ann Arbor: University of Michigan Press.

——— (1976b) *Culture and Practical Reason*. Chicago: University of Chicago Press.

Said, Edward (1978) *Orientalism*. New York: Random House.

——— (1979) "Zionism from the Standpoint of Its Victims" *Social Text* 1: 7–58.

Sayer, Derek (1987) *The Violence of Abstraction: The Analytic Foundations of Historical Materialism*. Oxford: Basil Blackwell.

Schlossstein, Steven (1989) *The End of the American Century*. New York: Congdon and Weed.

Schlumbohm, Jurgen (1981) "Excursus: The Political and Institutional Framework of Proto-Industrialization" 126–134 in P. Kriedte, et al. eds. *Industrialization Before Industrialization* Beate Schempp, trans. New York: Cambridge University Press.

Schlupp, F. (1992) "World-Market Strategy and World-Power Politics: German Europeanization and Globalization Projects in the 1990s" 307–345 in William D. Graf, ed. *The Internationalization of the German Political Economy*. New York: St. Martin's Press.

Schmink, Marianne (1981) "Women in Brazilian *Abertura* Politics" *Signs* 7: 115–134.

Schumpeter, Joseph A. (1954) *History of Economic Analysis*. Oxford: Oxford University Press.

Scott, William Robert (1912/1968) *The Constitution and Finance of English, Scottish, and Irish Joint-Stock Companies to 1720* in 3 volumes. Gloucester, Mass.: Peter Smith.

Shapiro, Ian (1986) *The Evolution of Rights in Liberal Theory*. Cambridge: Cambridge University Press.

Showalter, Elaine (1985) *The Female Malady: Women, Madness, and English Culture 1830–1980*. New York: Pantheon.

Slotkin, Richard (1973) *Regeneration Through Violence: The Mythology of the American Frontier, 1600–1860*. Middletown: Wesleyan University Press.

——— (1986) *The Fatal Environment: The Myth of the Frontier in the Age of Industrialization, 1800–1890*. Middletown: Wesleyan University Press.

Smith, Adam (1976) *An Inquiry Into the Nature and Causes of the Wealth of Nations* Edwin Cannan, ed. Chicago: University of Chicago Press.

Smith, Anthony D. (1979) *Nationalism in the Twentieth Century.* Oxford: Martin Robertson.

Smith, Dorothy (1990) *The Conceptual Practices of Power: A Feminist Sociology of Knowledge.* Boston: Northeastern University Press.

Smith, Neil (1984) *Uneven Development: Nature, Capital, and the Production of Space.* Oxford: Basil Blackwell.

Smith, Steve (1985) "Foreign Policy Analysis" 45–55 in Steve Smith, ed. *International Relations: British and American Perspectives.* Oxford: Basil Blackwell.

Snidal, Duncan (1985) "The Limits of Hegemonic Stability Theory" *International Organization* 39: 579–614.

Soja, Edward W. (1989) *Postmodern Geographies: The Reassertion of Space in Critical Social Theory.* London: Verso.

Solorzano y Pereya, Juan de. (1947/1972) *La Politica Indiana* in *Biblioteca de Autores Espanoles* Vol. 252. Madrid.

Sorabjee, Soli (1986) "The State and Human Rights" *Seminar* 32: 18–21.

Southern, R.W. (1962) *Western Views of Islam in the Middle Ages.* Cambridge: Harvard University Press.

Spero, Joan (1977) *The Politics of International Economic Relations.* New York: Columbia University Press.

Stace, W.T. (1955) *The Philosophy of Hegel.* London: Dover.

Staniland, Martin (1985) *What Is Political Economy?* New Haven: Yale University Press.

Stavrianos, Leften S. (1981) *Global Rift.* New York: Morrow.

Stein, Arthur (1984) "The Hegemon's Dilemma: Great Britain, the United States and the International Economic Order" *International Organization* 38: 355–386.

Stevens, Evelyn P. (1973) "Marianismo: The Other Face of Machismo in Latin America" 89–101 in Ann Pescatello, ed. *Female and Male in Latin America.* Pittsburgh: University of Pittsburgh Press.

Strayer, Joseph R. (1970) *On the Medieval Origins of the Modern State.* Princeton: Princeton University Press.

Suganami, Hidemi (1989) *The Domestic Analogy and World Order Proposals.* Cambridge: Cambridge University Press.

Sylvan, David (1981) "The Newest Mercantilism" *International Organization* 35: 375–393.

Sylvester, Christine (1991a) "'Urban Women Cooperators,' 'Progress', and 'African Feminism' in Zimbabwe" *Differences* 13: 39–62.

——— (1991b) *Zimbabwe: The Terrain of Contradictory Development.* Boulder: Westview.

——— (1992) "Feminist and Realists Look at Autonomy and Obligation in International Relations," 259–306 in V. Spike Peterson, ed. *Gendered States: Feminist (Re)Visions of International Relations Theory.* Boulder: Lynne Rienner Publishers.

——— (1993a) ed. "Feminists Write International Relations" special issue of *Alternatives* 18.

——— (1993b) "Homeless in International Relations? 'Women's' Place in Canonical Texts and in Feminist Reimaginations" in Adam Lerner and Marjorie Martin, eds. *Reimagining the Nation.* London: Open University Press.

——— (1994) *Feminist Theory and International Relations Theory in a Postmodern Era.* Cambridge: Cambridge University Press.

Tagliabue, J. (1991) "Auction Business Is in Good Health in Germany" *New York Times*, March 12.

Tamayo, Jaime (1990) "Neoliberalism Encounters *Neocardenismo*" 121–136 in Joe Foweraker and Ann L. Craig, eds. *Popular Movements and Political Change in Mexico.* Boulder: Lynne Rienner Publishers.

Thompson, William R. (1988) *On Global War: Historical-Structural Approaches to World Politics.* Columbia: University of South Carolina Press.

Tickner, Ann (1992) *Gender in International Relations: Feminist Perspectives on Achieving Global Security.* New York: Columbia University Press.

Tillyard, E. M. W. (1943) *The Elizabethan World Picture.* London: Chatto and Windus.

Time, April 13, 1987 "A Mix of Admiration, Envy and Anger."

Todorov, Tzvetan (1984) *The Conquest of America.* New York: Harper and Row.

——— (1987) *La Conquista de America.* Flora Button Burla, trans. Mexico: Siglo Veinteuno.

Toffler, Alvin (1990) *Powershift: Knowledge, Wealth, and Violence at the Edge of the 21st Century.* New York: Bantam Books.

Tooze, Roger (1988) "The Unwritten Preface: 'International Political Economy' and Epistemology' *Millennium.* 17: 285–293.

Torquemada, Juan de, (1622/1971) "Razones Informativas" in *Codice Mendieta: Documentos Franciscanos Siglos XVI y XVII* Vol. II. Guadalajara, Mexico: E. Avina Levy.

Tronto, Joan (1987) "Beyond Gender Differences to a Theory of Care" *Signs* 12: 644–663.

U. S. News and World Report, April 9, 1990 "Thank You, Japan."

———, April 1, 1991 "The Cost of German Unity."

van der Pijl, K. (1984) *The Making of an Atlantic Ruling Class.* London: Verso.

Vasquez, John A. (1983) *The Power of Power Politics.* New Brunswick: Rutgers University Press.

Vijayan, O.V. (1988) *The Saga of Dharmapuri.* New Delhi: Penguin.

Villoro, Luis (1967) *El Proceso Ideologico de la Independencia.* Mexico: Universidad Nacional Autonoma de Mexico.

Viquiera Alban, Juan Pedro (1987) *Relajados o Reprimidos: Diversiones Publicas y Vida Social en la Ciudad de Mexico durante el Siglo de las Luces.* Mexico: Fondo de Cultura Economica.

Walker, R. B. J. (1984) "The Territorial State and the Theme of Gulliver" *International Journal* 39: 529–552.

——— (1987) "Realism, Change and International Political Theory" *International Studies Quarterly* 31: 65–86.

——— (1988) *One World, Many Worlds.* Boulder: Lynne Rienner Publishers.

——— (1989) "History and Structure in the Theory of International Relations" *Millennium* 18: 163–183.

——— (1990) "Security, Sovereignty, and the Challenge of World Politics" *Alternatives* 15: 3–27.

——— (1992) *Inside/Outside: International Relations as Political Theory.* Cambridge: Cambridge University Press.

Wallerstein, Immanuel (1974a) "The Rise and Future Demise of the World Capitalist System: Concepts for Comparative Analysis" *Comparative Studies in Society and History* 16: 387–415.

——— (1974b) *The Modern World System I.* New York: Academic Press.

——— (1980) *The Modern World System II.* New York: Academic Press.

——— (1983) *Historical Capitalism.* London: Verso.

——— (1984) *The Politics of the World Economy.* Cambridge: Cambridge University Press.

Walton, John (1989) "Debt, Protest, and the State in Latin America" 299–328 in Susan Eckstein, ed. *Power and Popular Protest*. Berkeley: University of California Press.

Waltz, Kenneth (1959) *Man, the State and War*. New York: Columbia University Press.

——— (1979) *Theory of International Politics*. Reading: Addison-Wesley.

——— (1986) "Reflections on Theory of International Politics: A Response to My Critics" 322–345 in Robert Keohane, ed. *Neorealism and Its Critics*. New York: Columbia University Press.

Walzer, Michael (1984) "Liberalism and the Art of Separation" *Political Theory* 12: 315–330.

Watson, Lawrence C., and Maria-Barbara Watson-Franke (1985) *Interpreting Life Histories: An Anthropological Inquiry*. New Brunswick: Rutgers University Press.

Wendt, Alexander E. (1987) "The Agent-Structure Problem in International Relations Theory" *International Organization* 41: 335–370.

White, Theodore (1988) "The Danger from Japan" *New York Times Magazine*. July 28.

Whitney, C. (1993) "German Soldiers Head for Somalia" *New York Times*, July 23.

Williams, Raymond (1977) *Marxism and Literature*. Oxford: Oxford University Press.

——— (1981) *The Sociology of Culture*. New York: Schocken Press.

Williams, William Appelman (1955) "The Frontier Thesis and American Foreign Policy" *Pacific Historical Review* 24: 379–395.

Wilson, Charles (1977) "The British Isles" 115–154 in C. Wilson and G. Parker, eds. *An Introduction to the Sources of European Economic History 1500–1800*. Ithaca: Cornell University Press.

Wolf, Eric R. (1982) *Europe and the People Without History*. Berkeley: University of California Press.

Wolferen, Karel G. van (1986/1987) "The Japan Problem" *Foreign Affairs*. 65: 288–303.

Wolferen, Karel van (1989) *The Enigma of Japanese Power*. London: Macmillan.

Wolin, Sheldon (1960) *Politics and Vision: Continuity and Innovation in Western Political Thought*. Boston: Little, Brown.

——— (1989) *The Presence of the Past: Essays on the State and the Constitution*. Baltimore: Johns Hopkins University Press.

World Press Review 37 (1990): "More Friend than Foe": 26–27.

Xenos, Nicholas (1989) *Scarcity and Modernity*. London: Routledge.

Young, Oran (1988) *International Cooperation: Building Regimes for Natural Resources and the Environment*. Ithaca: Cornell University Press.

Zermeño, Sergio (1990) "Crisis, Neoliberalism, and Disorder" 160–182 in Joe Foweraker and Ann L. Craig, eds. *Popular Movements and Political Change in Mexico*. Boulder: Lynne Rienner Publishers.

The Contributors

John A. Agnew teaches geography and geopolitics at Syracuse University.

Kurt Burch teaches international political economy at the University of Delaware.

David Campbell teaches U.S. foreign policy and international political theory at Johns Hopkins University.

Richard W. Coughlin teaches comparative politics and international relations at Drury College.

Naeem Inayatullah teaches international political economy, politics of the Third World, and international relations theory at Syracuse University.

Bradley S. Klein teaches U.S. foreign policy, international relations, and political theory at Trinity College.

Sankaran Krishna teaches international relations and Indian politics at the University of Hawaii at Manoa.

Marianne H. Marchand teaches Latin American politics and international political economy at the University of Amsterdam.

Stephen J. Rosow teaches political theory and international studies at the State University of New York at Oswego.

Mark Rupert teaches international politics and political economy at Syracuse University.

Christine Sylvester teaches African politics, international politics, and feminist theory at Northern Arizona University.

Frank Unger teaches German politics, American culture, and political economy at Humbolt University, Germany.

Index

Abstract individualism, 72–73, 76–79, 94

Agent-structure relations, 41–43, 48

Alliances, social movements, 132

Alvarado, Elvia, 140–141

Alvarez, Sonia, 133–134

Anarchy without/community within dichotomy, 189, 192

Anticommunism, German unification, 182–183

Aristotle, 56

Ashley, Richard, 42, 204–205

Augustine, Saint, 28, 211

Authority, religious-dynastic, 98

Authorship, testimonies, 139

Autonomy, neoliberal institutionalism, 112; neorealism, 110; relational vs. reactive, 113, 115; social movements, 131–132

Bacon, Francis, 24

Balance of power, interstate relations, 90

Barrios, Domitila, 140–141

Bitar, Sergio, 130

Bodin, Jean, 22–27

Boundary crossing, 1, 3

Braudel, Fernand, 17

Burkhart, Louise, 209–210, 218

Caldeira, Teresa Pires de Rio, 134–135

Capitalism, agents, 52; development, 95; expansion, 50; fascist antecedents, 182–183; German nationalism, 183; internationalization, 7–8, 10; relation to state system, 47–48;

social relations, 80. *See also* Global capitalism

Carr, E.H., 95

Censorship, 212

Chase-Dunn, Christopher, 40

Christian base-communities, 133

Civil society, 92; formation, 64–65; Hobbes, Thomas, 63

Civilization, representations, 213

Civilizational alternatives/universalism dichotomy, 208

Civilizing processes, colonization, 210, 212–213, 221; development, 207–208; Roman Catholic church, 220

Cold War, demise, 93, 172

Cold War dichotomies, 172

Colonial order, transition to nation-state, 222

Colonization, civilizing process, 210, 212–213, 221

Commerce, promotion by the state, 51

Commercial society, 27–28; expansion, 32; theories, 34

Competitiveness, acceleration, 104

Concientización, 133

Conquest, indigenous identity, 208

Constitutive principles, concept, 41

Construction of identities, 1, 10–11. *See also* Identity

Cooperation, feminist theories, 114–117; impact on states, 109; incentives, 91; IR theories, 110–113; relational forms, 114; transnational, 7; views of women cooperators, 122

245

Cooperatives, gendered views, 121. *See also* Producer cooperatives; Women's cooperatives
Core/periphery relation, 73–74
Corporations, development, 48
Cox, Robert, 95–96
Critical modernism, 41
Critical theory, 3, 39, 56
Cultural identity, layering-in, 172
Culture, 81–83

Dependency theory, 127; decline, 129
Desire vs. need, 28–30
Development, 129; concept, 128, 207
Development policies, women's resistance, 142
Development theories, capitalist, 129; critique, 207; current debates, 130; neoconservative economics, 127
Dialectical political economy, 79–83
Dichotomies, Cold War, 172; IR theory, 199–200
Differentiation, 150, 166
Discourse of danger, state identity, 149–150; U.S./Japan, 147–148
Division of labor, Gilpin, Robert, 71; origins, 69; Smith, Adam, 65–67
Domestic/international dichotomy, 205
Domestic/national polarity, 94–97, 102
Domestic politics, relation to international politics, 204
Durkheim, Emil, 93

East Europeans, status, 174, 183–184
Eastern Europe, integration into Western Europe, 184
Economic integration, Europe, 171
Economic strength, FRG, 180; Japan, 147
Economic survival, women's roles, 133–134
Economics, division of labor, 70; Gilpin, Robert, 76–77
Economics/politics, reciprocal relation, 71–72, 74
Economism, 74; logical, 76; variable, 77
Enlightenment, 34–35, 41
European social life, transition 16th-18th centuries, 18–22
Evangelization, indigenous communities, 209

Fallows, James, 153–155
Federal Republic of Germany. *See* FRG
Female identity, concept, 135–136. *See also* Gender identity
Feminine movements, 134, 137; definition, 136
Feminist movements, 134; definition, 136
Feminist theories, 114. *See also* Standpoint feminism; Postmodern feminism
Feudalism, decline, 18–19
Florescano, Enrique, 212
Folk Catholicism, Mexico, 220–221
Foreign investment, United States, 152
Foreign policy, concept, 56; Germany, 179; identity/difference dichotomy, 161; relation to political identity, 150; state-centric, 148
Foreigners, status in Germany, 174
Fragmentation, 105; colonial order, 222; relation to globalization, 104; spatial representation, 103
FRG, economic strength, 180
Frontier imagery, United States, 155–157, 159–160, 162
Fukuyama, Francis, 129–130, 181–182

Gandhi, nonviolence, 197
GDR, delegitimation, 182; international perception, 175–176; relation to Soviet Union, 178; unification initiatives, 177–179; West German perception, 175–176
GDR citizens (former), self-esteem, 174
Gender cooperation, IR theories, 114; multilateralism, 124
Gender identity, 124, 149. *See also* Female identity
Gender relations, changes, 8–9; IR theories, 114
Gendered practices, resistance, 132, 137; social movements, 142
German Democratic Republic. *See* GDR
German unification, European perceptions, 175; GDR initiatives, 177–179; ideology factor, 181–182; impact on Europe, 183; importance, 171; nationalism, 174, 176–177;

realist view, 180–181; social dislocation, 173
Giddens, Anthony, 42–43
Gilpin, Robert, 2, 70–74, 77–78
Global capitalism, global order, 38;
politics, 171; property, 46; property
rights, 44, 46, 49; relation to state
system, 37, 39–40, 57; women's
roles, 110. *See also* Capitalism
Global economy, cultural effects, 10;
representation in 18th century
Europe, 17; U.S. hegemony, 96
Global order, 40; organizing structures,
38–39; schema, 24
Globalism, Europe, 184–185
Globalization, 105; capitalism, 171; relation to fragmentation, 104; spatial
representation, 103. *See also* Internationalization
Government, legitimation, 178
Gramscian theory, 10

Habermas, Jürgen, 206
Harvey, David, 9–10
Hegel, Georg W.F., 93, 98
Hegemonic states, 71–72, 74; emer-
gence, 73
Hellman, Judith Adler, 131–132
Hobbes, Thomas, 1, 27, 30, 62–65, 73,
77–78, 90, 94
Human existence, attributes, 211
Human/subhuman dichotomy, 211
Hume, David, 17, 30–32

Idealism, 91–93; and neorealism,
197–198; territorial state, 89
Identity, construction, 10–11; forma-
tion, 80; gendered, 149; German uni-
fication, 172; social construction,
149, 156
Identity/difference dichotomy,
148–149, 161–165
Identity-shifting, 117, 123
Ideology, German unification, 181,
184
Independence movement, Creoles,
222–223
India, constituting selfhood, 190–191
Indians (Mesoamerican). *See* Meso-
american Indians
Indians (North American), European/
U.S. representations, 160

Indigenous identity, re-creation,
219–220
Indigenous lifeworlds, transformation,
209–210, 213
Indigenous virgin cults, Mexico,
220–221
Individual/group dichotomy, 161–162
Individual rights, 52, 98; vs. states'
rights, 199
Individual will, 26–27
Inside/outside dichotomy, women, 120,
122–123
Instrumental utilitarianism, 55; prop-
erty, 45
Interdependence, 8
International anarchy theory, 184–185
International competition, growth, 49
International division of labor, 24;
changes, 8–9; intensification, 173
International donor agencies, views of
women's cooperators, 120–121, 123;
women's cooperatives, 117–119
International political economy, devel-
opment of field, 6–11; identity-
inducing, 5
International political economy theory,
critique, 207
International politics, relation to do-
mestic politics, 204
Internationalization, 2, 6; capitalism,
7–8, 10. *See also* Globalization
Interstate relations, anarchic, 74; state
formation, 204–205; structure, 90
Interstate system, anarchic, 71–72

Japan, economic strength, 147; revisionist interpretation, 153–155
Japanese people, U.S. representations,
157–159
Joint-stock companies, 48–51
Jurisprudential tradition, 52; property,
45

Keohane, Robert, 91, 111–112
Knowledge, cooperative production,
120; as power, 24; production, 127
Kratochwil, Friedrich, 109, 114

Leaver, Richard, 163
Legitimation, basis, 205; government,
178
Liberal-capitalist worldview, 181

Liberalism, 7, 27, 38, 52–55, 94, 96, 181; property, 45
Liberation theology, 133
Life histories, concept, 138–139
Lifeworlds, concept, 203, 206
Literacy, Mexico, 222
Locke, John, 31, 100
Lockhart, James, 219–220
Logic of deferrence, 198, 200; Third World and the West, 199
Logical economism, 76
Luxury, concept, 31; social construction, 28
Luxury consumption, 32–33

Machiavelli, Niccolo, 20, 90, 150–151, 214
Madres de Plaza de Mayo, 134, 136
Mann, Michael, 92–93
Maravall, Antonio, 215, 217
Marian cults, Mexico, 220–221
Marianismo, 137
Market economy, operation, 74; preconditions, 73
Market society, expansion, 19
Marx, Karl, 79–80
Marxian theory, 2, 7, 38
Masculine/feminine dichotomy, 151
Mearsheimer, John, 184
Menchu, Rigoberta, 140–141
Mercantilism, 48, 94–95
Mesoamerican Indians, resistance, 212, 215–216, 220; view of Spanish civilization, 217–218
Methodological nationalism, social sciences, 93–94
Mexico, Spanish conquest, 208–209
Middle class (India), dual position, 190
Missionaries (Mexico), civilizing role, 210; evangelization, 209
Modern world, social differentiation, 53–55
Modernism, position of theorist, 41
Modernity, ambivalence, 192
Modernization, 32
Modernization theory, challenges, 128; critique, 207; resistance, 131; resurgence, 129–130
Molyneux, Maxine, 136
Montaigne, Miguel de, 27
Moral/civic tradition, property, 45

Morgenthau, Hans J., 39
Multilateralism, cooperation, 112–113; gender cooperation, 114, 124
Multinational corporations, 8; U.S. firms, 96–97
Mythology, Mexico, 218–219

Nahuatized Christianity, 209, 218
Nation-writing, India, 191, 194
National identity, corporeal imagery, 196; formation, 223; social construction, 190–191, 194
Nationalism, German unification, 174, 176–177; leadership, 191; Third World, 190
Nationhood, alternative discourses, 200–201; concept, 198; strategies, 195
Natural determinism, 18, 20, 24, 34
Natural ontology, Hobbes, Thomas, 63–65
Natural poverty, Smith, Adam, 66
Nature, concept, 18, 20–23, 26–27, 30; Marx, Karl, 79
Nature/society, abstract opposition, 77–78; internal relation, 64, 79–80
Nature/society dichotomy, 69; Hobbes, Thomas, 63; neorealism, 61–62
Need vs. desire, 28–30
Nehru, Jawaharlal, socialist development, 195; state planning, 196; use of violence, 197–198; on Western science, 193–194
Neoconservative economic policies, 127
Neoliberal institutionalism, cooperation, 111–112; gender cooperation, 114
Neorealism, 38, 92, 94–95; abstract individualism, 78; cooperation, 110–111; critique, 2, 4, 8, 61, 189; economics, 70; gender cooperation, 114; and idealism, 197–198; othering, 192, 200; politics, 70; Third World nationalism, 190
Neostructuralism, 130
Nonstate actors, emergence, 1
Nye, Joseph, 67

O'Donnell, Guillermo, 205
Ontology, international relations theory, 4

Other, relation to self, 81–82
Othering, concept, 99–100; of East Europeans, 174; identity maintenance, 163; of India, 192, 200; of Iraq, 165; of Japan, 147–148, 153–156, 161; of Mesoamerican Indians, 211–213; of North American Indians, 160–161; process, 150; of the Soviet Union, 165; of women's cooperatives, 120–121
Overseas military intervention, German role, 179–180

Paracelsians, concept of history, 23; view of nature, 22
Part/whole relation, culture, 81–82
Particularity, culture, 81–82
Partition of India and Pakistan, 196
Peripheral underdeveloped/modern dichotomy, 192
Plato, 28
Polis, 89
Political authority, legitimation, 205
Political elites, worldview, 181
Political identity, 105; concept, 99; construction, 1; definition, 104
Political movements. See Social movements
Political repression, women's resistance, 134
Political spaces, mapping, 4
Politics, Gilpin, Robert, 76–77; state of nature, 70
Politics/economics, reciprocal relation, 71–72, 74
Popular culture, appropriation of Spanish civilization, 218; suppression, 213, 221
Popular movements. See Social movements
Positivism, 6, 8
Postmodern feminism, 115–117; cooperation, 124
Postmodernism, ontological assumptions, 41
Postpositivism, 41
Poststructuralism, 102
Power, gendered discourse, 150–151, 165
Primary schools, Mexico, 222
Primordial titles, indigenous identity, 219–220

Privatization, 172
Producer cooperatives, 119–120. See also Women's cooperatives
Property, concept, 37, 43–44, 46; constitutive principle/definition, 55; political theory, 53; real vs. mobile, 37, 46–47, 53; state system/global capitalism dichotomy, 44
Property rights, concept, 37, 43, 55
Public/private spheres, changes, 8–9; women, 134–137
Public spectacles, identity-producing effects, 217; role in colonization, 215–216; suppression, 221
Public sphere, development, 19–21; women's participation, 132–133

Realism, 38, 92, 95; critique, 4; German unification, 180; International Relations theory, 1; territorial state, 89–90. See also Structural realism
Reciprocity, interstate relations, 112
Regime theory, 9
Regimes, concept, 91; relation to states, 109
Regulation school, 9
Reimagining Indian history, colonialism, 191
Religious spectacles, role in colonization, 213–214
Resistance, 131; Creoles, 222; development theories, 132; forms, 128; gendered practices, 132, 135, 137, 142; Mesoamerican Indians, 212, 215–216, 219–220; neoconservative economics, 127; use of testimonies, 141, 144
Roman Catholic church, civilizing process, 220; Latin America, 133
Roman Empire, model for Spanish Empire, 211
Rousseau, Jean-Jacques, 30
Ruggie, John, 109–110, 112–113

Safa, Helen Icken, 133–134
Said, Edward, 174
Savage nations/civilized nations dichotomy, 68
Savages, Smith, Adam, 66, 68
Scale, concept, 87
Security, concept, 97; relation to sovereignty, 99–101

Smith, Adam, 65–69, 77–78, 94
Social contract theory, 18–19, 26–27, 29–30, 33–34
Social dislocation, German unification, 173
Social identity, Germany, 179
Social movements, gendered practices, 142; Latin America, 128, 131; sources of power, 132; women, 134–136
Social ontology, Hobbes, Thomas, 64–65
Social sciences, methodological nationalism, 93–94
Socialism, India, 195
Society, concept, 92; Marx, Karl, 79; organic whole, 53
Solorzano, Juan de, 210–212
Sovereignty, 4–5, 25–27; concept, 56, 205; property rights, 44, 47–48, 55; relation to security, 99–101; relational concept, 113; territorial state, 97–98, 101–102; unitary concept, 199–200
Space, concept, 87–88
Spanish conquest, impact, 209
Specialization and exchange, Smith, Adam, 67–68
Standpoint feminism, 114–116
State, concept, 88–89, 91; institutional-legal infrastructure, 49–50; as social condition, 205–207
State-centrism, International Relations theory, 105
State development, 19, 25
State formation, historical issue, 56; India, 189; model, 203–206, 208; process, 100; property rights, 47
State identity, construction, 149–150
State legitimation, basis, 199; process, 192
State of nature, ambiguity, 64; Hobbes, Thomas, 62–63; Smith, Adam, 65–66
State system, global order, 38; property, 44, 46; property rights, 44, 46, 49; relation to capitalism, 47–48; relation to global capitalism, 37, 39–40, 57
Statecraft, agents, 51; relation to economic activity, 50–51
Statehood, violence, 197

States' rights vs. individual rights, 199
Structural realism, critique, 204, 206
Structuration theory, 56
Subhuman existence, attributes, 211
Surplus, Smith, Adam, 66–67

Territorial state, 91; concept, 89; IR theory, 88; mercantilist view, 94; relation to society, 92–93; sovereignty, 97
Testimonies, author-intentionality, 140; concept, 138–139; tools of resistance, 141–142
Third World, modernity, 192
Threat perception, U.S./Japan, 151, 153, 162, 166
Thucydides, 1, 90
Torquemada, Juan de, 214–215
Trade, expansion, 19–21, 31–32; global system, 34; U.S./Japan, 95, 151
Trade deficit (United States), 96–97
Trade unions, U.S. representations, 160
Transnational cooperation, political dynamic, 7
Transnational regimes, 5–6
Tzvetan, Todorov, 18

Underdevelopment, 128–129
Universal history, 22–27, 30; social construction, 33
Universality, culture, 81–82
U.S. hegemony, global economy, 96, 106
U.S./Japan dichotomy, 154–155
U.S./Japan relations, 147–148, 151; gendered inscription, 164–165

Variable economism, 77
Virgin of Guadelupe, myth, 218–219

Walker, R.B.J., 129
Wallerstein, Immanuel, 208
Waltz, Kenneth, 2, 90–91, 110–111, 114
Walzer, Michael, 53
Weber, Max, 1
Wolf, Eric, 204
Women, public sphere, 132; social movements, 134–136
Women cooperators, on cooperation, 122; dual position, 120; relations with donor agencies, 121

Women's cooperatives, international donor agencies, 117–119; as marginalized insiders, 122–123. *See also* Producer cooperatives

Women's movements, Latin America, 132

Women's roles, changes, 21; economic survival, 133–134

World economy theory, Hume, David, 30–34

World order, gendered inscription, 162–163; historical structures, 95–96

World-systems theory, 2–3, 38, 40, 88

About the Book

As contemporary capitalism integrates the planet to an unprecedented extent, the international political economy defines and constitutes new forces, practices, and movements. Not only are power centers shifting away from Cold War poles, but also the spatial and temporal frames of social life, both domestic and international, are reorganizing. Addressing these transformations, the authors of this book reach beyond mainstream, economistic approaches to explore the social, political, philosophical, and cultural dimensions of the shift from a nation-state-based to a global economy.

The book neither presents nor endorses any particular critical perspective, but brings together scholars who engage in multiple boundary crossings—traversing disciplines, social identities, histories. The result is a dialogue among participants who, while they may disagree on specific issues, share a commitment to the need for a critical theory of international political economy.

Other Books in the Series

The State in Transition
     Joe Camilleri, editor

Politics Without Principle:
Sovereignty, Ethics, and the Narratives of the Gulf War
     David Campbell

Discourses of Global Politics:
A Critical (Re)Introduction to International Relations
     Jim George

A Question of Values:
Johan Galtung's Peace Research
     Peter Lawler

Transcending the State-Global Divide
     Ronen P. Palan and Barry Gills, editors